WITHDRAWN

SINGER
Sewing Step·by·Step

CY DeCOSSE
INCORPORATED
MINNETONKA, MINNESOTA USA

SINGER

Sewing Step·by·Step

Contents

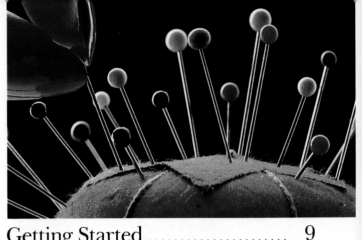

Copyright © 1990
Cy DeCosse Incorporated
5900 Green Oak Drive
Minnetonka, Minnesota 55343
United States of America
All rights reserved
Printed in U.S.A.

Singer Sewing Step-By-Step draws pages
from the individual titles of the Singer
Sewing Reference Library. Individual
titles are available from the publisher
and in book stores and fabric stores:
*Sewing Essentials, Sewing for the Home,
Clothing Care & Repair, Sewing for Style,
Sewing Specialty Fabrics, Sewing Activewear,
The Perfect Fit, Timesaving Sewing, More
Sewing for the Home, Sewing Update,
Tailoring, Sewing for Children, Sewing with
an Overlock, 101 Sewing Secrets, Sewing
Pants That Fit, Quilting by Machine*

Library of Congress
Cataloging-in-Publication Data

Singer sewing step-by-step.
p. cm.
Includes index.
ISBN 0-86573-257-4
1. Machine sewing. 2. Sewing
machines. I. Cy DeCosse
Incorporated.
TT713.S56 1990
646.2' 044 — dc20
90-39717
CIP

Published in the U.S.A. in 1990
and distributed in the U.S. by:
Cy DeCosse Incorporated
5900 Green Oak Drive
Minnetonka, MN 55343

CY DECOSSE INCORPORATED
Chairman: Cy DeCosse
President: James B. Maus
Executive Vice President: William B. Jones

Created by: The Editors of Cy DeCosse
Incorporated, in cooperation with the
Singer Education Department. Singer
is a trademark of The Singer Company
and is used under license.
Color Separations: ScanTrans
Printing: R. R. Donnelley & Sons (0990)

91 92 93 94 / 5 4 3 2

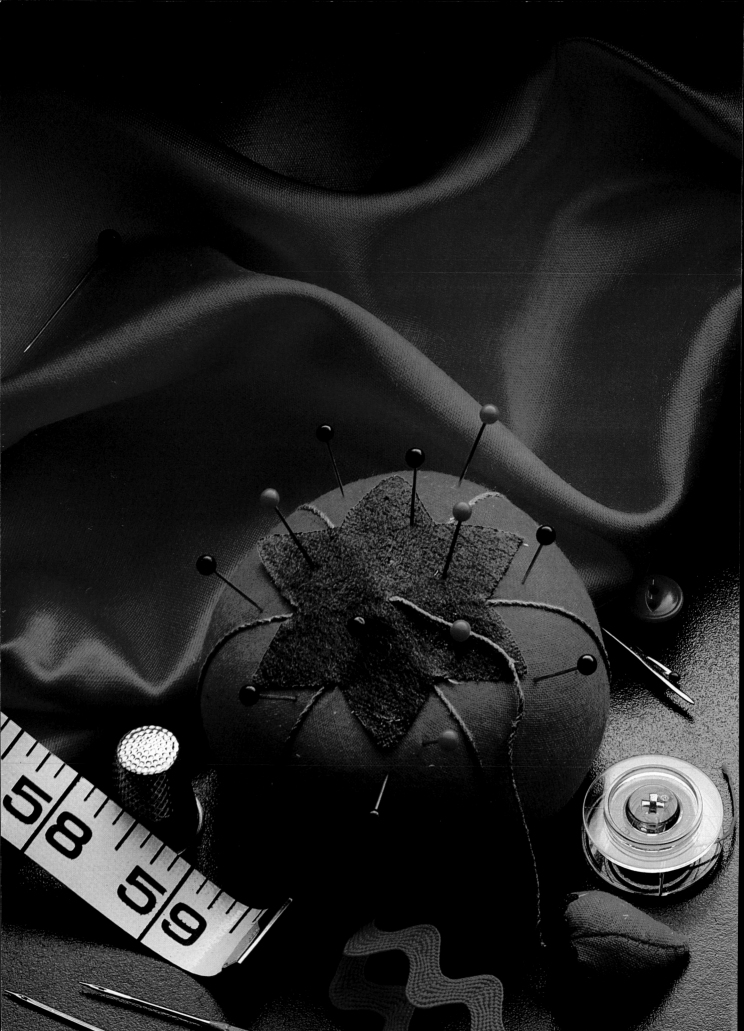

How to Use This Book

Like any other art or craft, sewing begins with basic techniques. *Singer Sewing Step-by-Step* gives you the essential information you need for sewing garments and for sewing for the home. In addition to basic techniques, specialty sewing topics, such as tailoring, sewing activewear, and sewing for children, are also included.

Getting Started

This section gives you information on the sewing machine and the overlock machine. We show you how to get the perfect stitch and tell you about special features and accessories for both machines. We also tell you about the equipment and notions you will need for all of your sewing, plus some timesaving equipment that will make your sewing easier.

Also covered in the first section is the pattern. You will learn how to take your measurements and select the correct size. A comprehensive guide to fabric selection is included as well as cutting and sewing tips. There is also information on how to choose and test interfacing.

Sewing Techniques

The first part of this section features the basic techniques you will use for nearly everything you sew: garments and home decorating projects. The basic sewing techniques include fitting, seams, darts, gathering, sleeves, collars, waistbands, cuffs, and closures. Each is given an overview, followed by a step-by-step description of how to achieve the best results. Often several methods are presented with guidance as to when and where to use each one.

The remainder of this section concentrates on specific sewing techniques for tailored garments, children's clothing, and activewear. "Tailoring" introduces you to using fusible interfacing for timesaving and professional results. "Sewing for Children" includes projects for infants, fun ideas for adding durability and grow room, as well as appliqués. A special section on heirloom sewing gives you the skills to make beautiful heirloom gifts.

Home Decorating Projects

We start with the basics of fabric and color selection and other tips on planning a project. Instructions for many of the projects include alternate sewing methods and suggest timesaving techniques.

The Home Decorating section is divided into four project categories: windows, pillows, tables, and beds. For windows, we give instructions for standard favorites, such as pinch-pleated draperies, and many others. Pillows range from simple knife-edge styles to ones with flanged edges. For tables, learn how to make a ruffled tablecloth and many variations of placemats and napkins. Make a comforter cover for your bed, and add pillow shams and a dust ruffle to match.

Each category includes an overview and how to take measurements for the projects. For easy reference, fabric and notions required to complete a project are included in a box labeled YOU WILL NEED. The step-by-step instructions are complete: you do not have to purchase additional patterns. The photographs show you how each project should look each step of the way.

Step-by-Step Guidance

The photos add depth and dimension to the instructions, giving you a close-up look at each step. In some cases, the stitches are shown in heavier thread or a contrasting color to make them more visible. Some marking lines have also been exaggerated to show a crucial matching point.

If you are learning to sew or getting back to sewing, you may want to practice your skills on an easy project before starting a larger one. Try sewing simple placemats and napkins to practice a new edge finish. When you sew a first garment, choose a simple style that is easy to fit, with few details.

Whether you are a new sewer, an experienced sewer, or a returning sewer, this book is designed to be a help and an inspiration. Use it as your step-by-step guide to the satisfaction and fun of successful sewing.

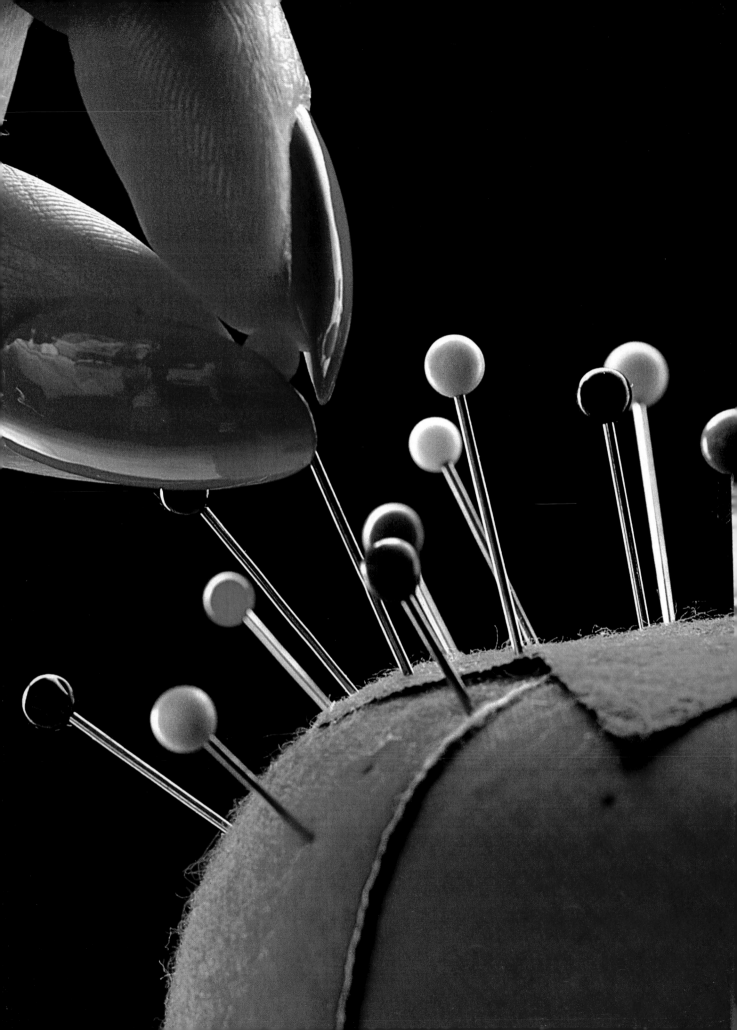

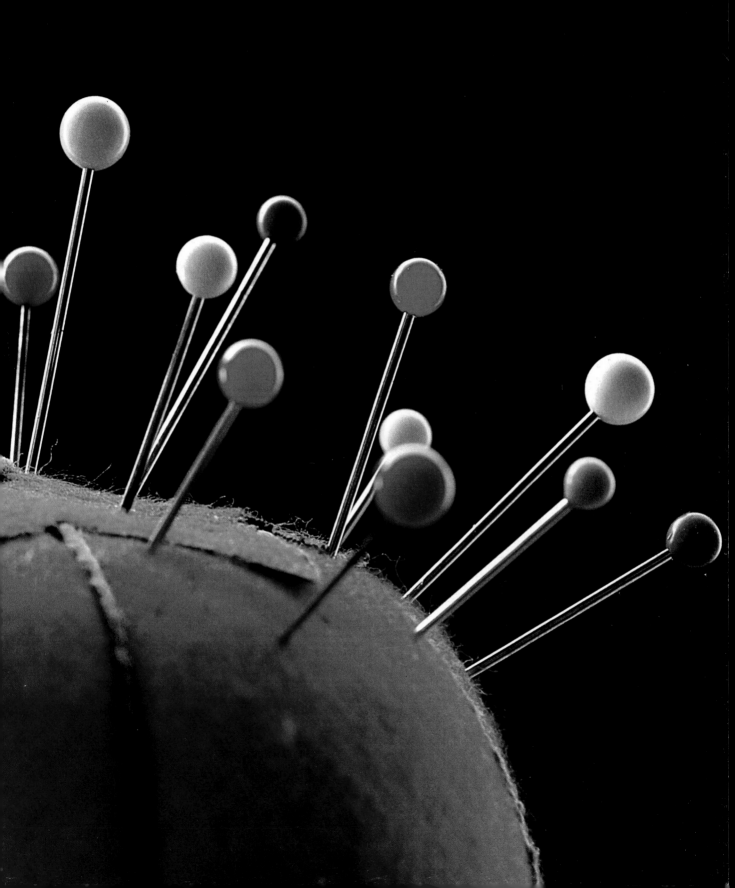

Getting Started

The Sewing Machine

A sewing machine is your most important piece of sewing equipment, so select one with care. A sturdy, well-built machine will give you many years of sewing enjoyment.

If you are buying a new machine, there are a variety of models available to fit any budget or sewing need. Types range from a basic zigzag with one or two built-in stitches, to the electronic machine that uses advanced computer technology to control and select the stitching.

Available features include built-in buttonholer, color-coded stitch selection, instant reverse, snap-on presser foot, free arm for stitching small round areas (such as pants legs), built-in bobbin winder, automatic tension and pressure adjustment, and automatic stitch length adjustment. Each feature usually adds to the cost of the machine, so look for a machine to match your sewing projects. Buy a machine that satisfies your sewing needs, but don't pay for features you will rarely use. Also consider the amount and difficulty of the sewing you do, and the number of people you sew for. Talk to fabric store personnel and friends who sew. Ask for demonstrations, and try out and compare several models. Look for quality workmanship and ease of operation as well as stitching options.

The machine's cabinetry is another factor to consider. Portable machines offer the flexibility of moving to various work surfaces. Machines built into cabinets are designed to be the right height for sewing. They also help you stay organized by providing a convenient place to store sewing equipment and keep it handy.

Although sewing machines vary in capabilities and accessories, each has the same basic parts and controls. The equipment you will need for your machine is described on pages 14 and 15.

The principal parts of the sewing machine (opposite) are shown on a free-arm portable, but its basic parts are representative of all machines. Check your manual for specific location of these parts on your machine.

Machine Essentials

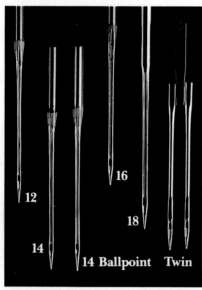

Needles are available in four basic types: *general-purpose* for a wide range of fabrics, in sizes 9/65 (finest) to 18/110; *ballpoint* for knits and stretch fabrics (size 9/65 to 16/100); *twin needle* for decorative stitching; and *wedge-point* (not shown) for leather and vinyl. Change the needle after sewing two to three garments or after hitting a pin. Damaged fabric is often caused by a bent, blunt or burred needle.

Thread for machine sewing comes in three weights: *extra fine* for lightweight fabrics and machine embroidery, *all-purpose* for general-purpose sewing, and *topstitching and buttonhole twist* for decorative and accent stitching. Thread should match the weight of the fabric and the size of the needle. For perfect tension, use the same size and type thread in the bobbin as you use in the needle.

Bobbins may be built-in or removable for winding. Bobbins with a built-in case are wound in the case. Removable bobbins have a removable bobbin case with a tension adjustment screw. They may be wound on the top or side of the machine. Start with an empty bobbin so the thread will wind evenly. Do not wind it too full or the bobbin thread will break.

Principal Parts of the Sewing Machine

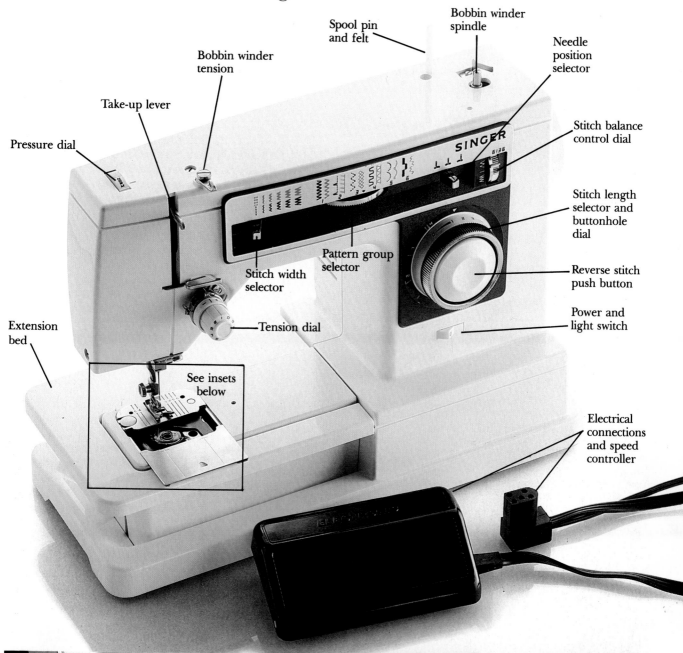

Spool pin and felt

Bobbin winder spindle

Needle position selector

Bobbin winder tension

Take-up lever

Pressure dial

Stitch balance control dial

Stitch length selector and buttonhole dial

Pattern group selector

Reverse stitch push button

Stitch width selector

Tension dial

Power and light switch

Extension bed

See insets below

Electrical connections and speed controller

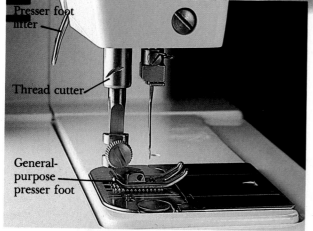

Presser foot lifter

Thread cutter

General-purpose presser foot

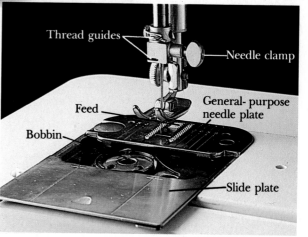

Thread guides

Needle clamp

Feed

General-purpose needle plate

Bobbin

Slide plate

Creating the Perfect Stitch

Perfect machine stitching is easy to achieve if you thread the machine properly and make the right adjustments in the stitch length, tension and pressure. These adjustments depend on your fabric and the kind of stitch desired. Consult your machine manual for threading procedures and location of controls.

The *stitch length regulator* is on either an inch scale from 0 to 20, a metric scale from 0 to 4, or a numerical scale from 0 to 9. For normal stitching, set the regulator at 10 to 12 stitches per inch, or at the number 3 for metric scale machines. On the numerical scale, higher numbers form a longer stitch; if a shorter stitch is desired, dial a lower number. An average stitch length is at number 5.

A perfect stitch depends on the delicate balance of pressure on the fabric, action of the feed, and tension on the stitch formation. In the ideal stitch, both top and bobbin thread are drawn equally into the fabric, and the link is formed midway between fabric layers.

The *stitch tension control* determines the amount of pressure on the threads as they pass through the machine. Too much pressure results in too little thread fed into the stitch. This causes the fabric to pucker. Too little pressure produces too much thread and a weak, loose stitch.

Adjust the *pressure regulator* for light pressure on lightweight fabrics, more pressure on heavy fabrics. Correct pressure ensures even feeding of the fabric layers during stitching. Some machines automatically adjust tension and pressure to the fabric.

Always check tension and pressure on a scrap of fabric before starting to sew. When experimenting with pressure and tension, thread the machine with different colors for top and bobbin thread to make the stitch links easier to see.

Straight Stitch Tension and Pressure

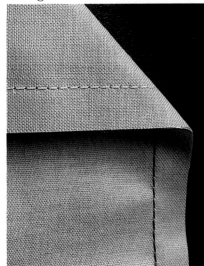

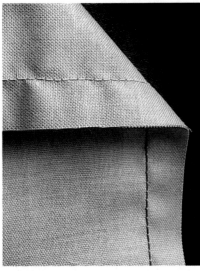

Correct tension and pressure makes stitches that are linked midway between the fabric layers. The stitches look even in length and tension on both sides. Fabric layers are fed evenly through the feed and fabric is not marred.

Too tight tension results in stitch links that are near the top layer of fabric. Fabric is puckered, and stitches are easily broken. Turn tension dial to a lower number. If pressure is too heavy, the bottom layer gathers up and may be damaged. Stitches may be uneven in length and tension. Dial pressure regulator to a lower number.

Too loose tension results in stitch links that are toward the bottom fabric layer. Seam is weak. Correct the problem by turning tension dial to a higher number. Too light pressure causes skipped and uneven stitches, and may pull fabric into the feed. Dial pressure regulator to a higher number.

Zigzag Stitch Tension and Pressure

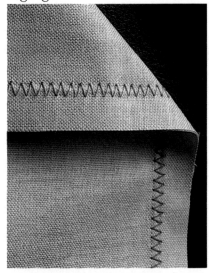

Correct tension and pressure in zigzag stitching produces stitches in which the interlocking link of threads falls at the corner of each stitch, midway between fabric layers. Stitches lie flat and fabric does not pucker.

Too tight tension causes fabric to pucker. The thread link falls near the top fabric layer. To correct, decrease the tension. Incorrect pressure is not as apparent in zigzag as in straight stitching. But if the pressure is not accurate, stitches will not be of even length.

Too loose tension causes the bottom layer to pucker and the thread link to fall near the bottom fabric layer. Increase tension to balance stitch. The zigzag stitch should be properly balanced in normal sewing. Loosen tension slightly for decorative stitches, and the top stitch pattern will become more rounded.

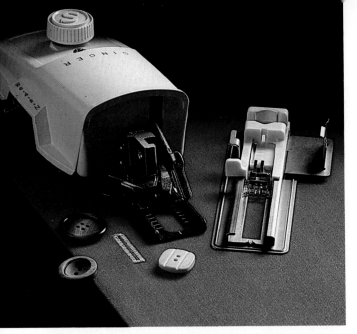

Machine Accessories for Special Tasks

Every sewing machine has accessories that allow it to perform a variety of special tasks. There are universal accessories that fit any machine, such as the zipper foot, buttonhole attachment and various hemming feet. Other accessories, such as a ruffler attachment, are designed to save time and effort for special types of sewing.

When adding a special accessory or foot to a machine you must know if your machine has a high shank, low shank or slanted shank. The *shank* is the distance from the bottom of the presser foot to the attachment screw. Attachments are specifically designed to fit one of these three styles.

The zigzag plate and the general-purpose foot usually come with the machine. Other accessories often included are the straight-stitch plate and foot, buttonhole foot or attachment, zipper foot, seam guide, various hemming feet, and Even Feed™ or roller foot. The machine manual explains how to attach the various accessories and achieve the best results with each.

Buttonhole attachments allow you to stitch complete buttonholes in a single step. One type stitches and adjusts the buttonhole length to fit the button placed in a carrier behind the foot. When the button is larger than 1½" (3.8 cm), or of an unusual shape or thickness, the gauge lines can be used instead of the carrier. Another type of buttonholer for straight-stitch machines makes buttonholes automatically using templates of various sizes. Keyhole buttonholes can be made with this accessory.

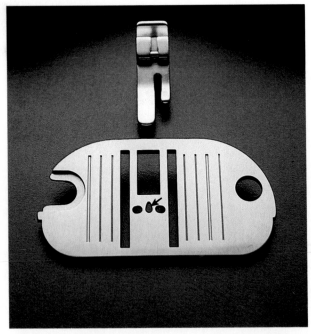

Straight-stitch plate and foot are used for straight stitching only. The needle hole (arrow) in the plate is small and round. The straight-stitch plate and foot do not allow for any sideways needle movement. Use these features when your fabric or sewing procedure requires close control, such as edgestitching or making collar points. They are also good for sheers and delicate fabrics, because the small needle hole helps keep fragile fabrics from being drawn into the feed.

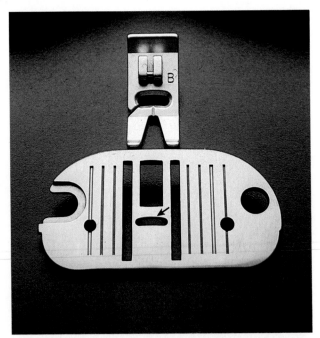

Zigzag plate and foot are the general-purpose plate and foot on a zigzag machine at time of purchase. They are used for zigzag and multi-needle work as well as plain straight stitching on firm fabrics. The needle hole (arrow) in the plate is wider, and the foot has a wider area for the needle to pass through, allowing for side-to-side needle motion. Use this plate and foot for general-purpose sewing.

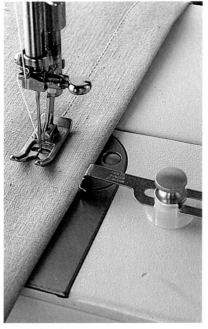

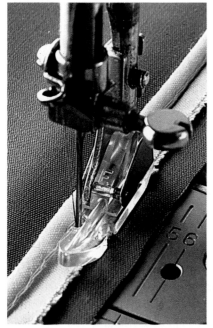

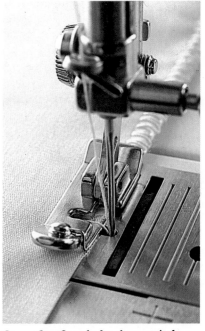

Zipper foot is used to stitch cording, insert zippers, sew bound buttonholes and stitch any seam that has more bulk on one side than the other. It adjusts to either side of the needle.

Seam guide attaches to the machine bed and helps keep seam allowances even. It adjusts to any seam width and swivels for sewing curved seams.

Blindstitch hem foot positions the hem for blindstitch hemming on the machine. This is a fast alternative to hemming by hand.

Even Feed™ foot feeds top and bottom layers together so seams start and end evenly. Use it for vinyl, pile fabrics, bulky knits or other fabrics that tend to stick, slip or stretch. This foot is also useful for topstitching and stitching plaids.

Button foot holds flat buttons in position for attaching with machine zigzag stitch. This foot saves time when sewing several buttons on a garment.

Overedge foot helps keep stitches at full width and prevents curling of flat edges when sewing overedge stitches. Stitches are formed over a hook on the inside edge of the foot.

The Overlock Machine

An overlock machine, also called a serger, is a special-purpose sewing machine that supplements a conventional machine. It is similar to the speed-sewing equipment used by garment manufacturers. An overlock cuts sewing time considerably, because it trims and overcasts raw fabric edges as it sews the seam. In addition, it performs this three-in-one operation at high speed. Overlocks form 1,500 or more stitches a minute — about twice the rate of conventional sewing machines. As another benefit, all fabrics feed evenly so that even traditionally difficult-to-handle fabrics, such as slippery silks and thin sheers, will not take any extra sewing time.

Because of its unique capabilities, an overlock machine streamlines garment construction. It eliminates time-consuming steps and encourages efficient sewing habits such as flat construction, pinless sewing, and continuous seaming. It also dispenses with routines such as raising and lowering the presser foot, backstitching, and filling bobbins.

Functions & Parts

An overlock excels at making self-finished narrow seams, rolled hems, blindstitched hems, and overcast edge finishes. It is also the machine to choose for applying elastic, ribbing, ribbons, and lace. Use a conventional machine whenever straight or zigzag stitching is necessary, such as for topstitching, inserting a zipper, or making buttonholes.

Each overlock model makes a distinctive stitch and is identified by the number of threads it uses. The principal parts of an overlock machine are shown on a 4-thread model (opposite). Because it can also be adjusted to sew with three threads, it is called a 4/3-thread convertible overlock. Other commonly used models are: 3-thread, 4/2-thread, and 5/4/3/2-thread overlocks (pages 18 and 19). Check the manufacturer's manual for specific information on the model you own.

Needles may be an industrial type with short or long shaft, or a standard type used on a conventional sewing machine. Use the needle specified for your machine. Industrial needles are stronger and last longer than conventional needles, but may be more expensive and less widely available. Change conventional needles frequently. Use the finest needle possible to avoid damaging the fabric. Size 11/80 works for most fabric weights.

Knives work like blades of scissors to trim the fabric for the stitch width selected. One knife is high-carbon steel and may last several years. The other knife is less durable and may require replacement three or four times annually. When knives seem dull, first clean them with alcohol; then reposition and tighten the screw. Test by sewing slowly. If a problem remains, replace the less durable knife and test again. As a last resort, replace the other knife.

Care & Maintenance

Because an overlock machine trims fabric as it sews, it creates more lint than a conventional machine and needs to be cleaned inside and out frequently. Use a lint brush or canned air to remove lint from the looper and throat plate area. Wipe off tension discs, needles, knives, and feed dog with alcohol.

To keep an overlock running smoothly and quietly, oil it often. Overlocks are lubricated by a wick system and can lose oil by gravity even when idle.

Overlock Thread

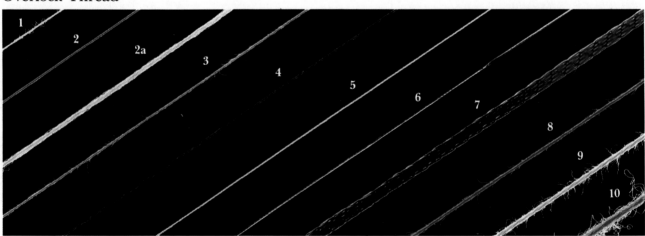

Thread that is fine and strong will perform best. Long-staple polyester (1) is a good, all-purpose choice; woolly nylon (2 and 2a) has exceptional strength and resilience. Cotton and cotton/polyester thread (3) also give satisfactory results but create more lint and may break with tighter tension adjustments and high speed. Decorative rayon (4), silk (5), and metallic (6) threads can be used for special effects, as can narrow ribbon (7), buttonhole twist (8), pearl cotton (9), and lightweight yarn (10).

Principal Parts of an Overlock Machine

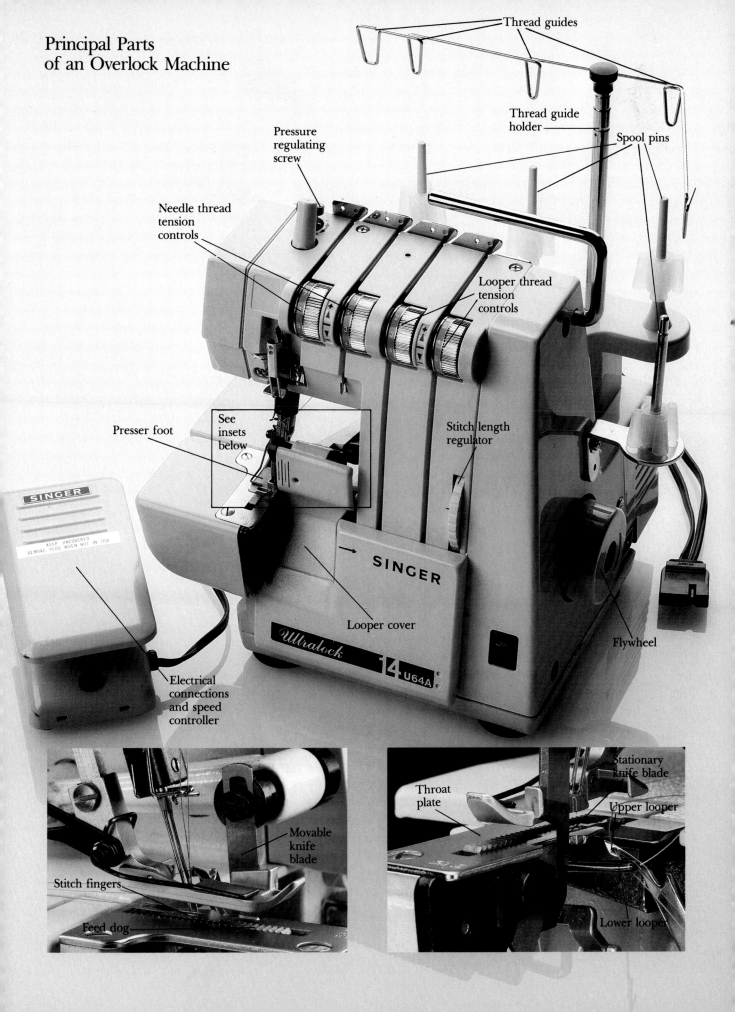

Thread guides

Thread guide holder

Spool pins

Pressure regulating screw

Needle thread tension controls

Looper thread tension controls

Presser foot

See insets below

Stitch length regulator

SINGER

KEEP UNCOVERED
REMOVE PLUG WHEN NOT IN USE

SINGER

Looper cover

Ultralock 14·U64A

Flywheel

Electrical connections and speed controller

Movable knife blade

Stitch fingers

Feed dog

Throat plate

Stationary knife blade

Upper looper

Lower looper

The Stitches & Their Uses

Types of Overlocks	Types of Stitches				
	2-Thread Overedge Stitch • lightweight seam finishes • used for wovens	**3-Thread Overlock Stitch** • stretch seams • durable seams or seam finishes • used for knits and wovens	**2-Thread Chainstitch** • stable basting stitch • decorative topstitching • used primarily for wovens	**4-Thread Safety Stitch** • stable seams with lightweight seam finishes • used primarily for wovens	
3-Thread Overlock	on some models				
4/2-Thread Overlock					
4/3-Thread Overlock	on some models				
5/4/3/2-Thread Overlock	on some models			on some models	

4-Thread Mock Safety Stitch	Wrapped Overedge Stitch	5-Thread Safety Stitch	Flatlock Stitch	Rolled Hem Stitch
• durable stretch seams • used for knits and wovens	• decorative stitching for edges • used for knits and wovens	• stable seams with durable seam finishes • used primarily for wovens	• flat, nonbulky stretch seams • decorative stitching • used primarily for knits	• narrow hems and seams • decorative stitching • used for knits and wovens

on some models

Creating the Perfect Stitch

The tension controls on an overlock machine are actually stitch selectors. Each thread has its own tension control. Changing one or more tension settings affects the character of the stitch, because it changes how the threads loop together. With tension adjustments, the overlock can stitch a wide range of threads, fabrics, seams, hems, and decorative treatments.

A good way to become comfortable with overlock tension adjustments is to thread each looper and needle with a contrasting thread color. Copy the color code used for the machine's threading diagram. Make several stitch samples, tightening and loosening the tensions in sequence. You will see the effect of each tension adjustment and learn how to use the tension controls to create a balanced overlock stitch. Most of the stitch samples shown below and opposite were made on a 3-thread overlock; stitch samples made on other models look similar and are adjusted in the same way.

Correctly Balanced Tensions

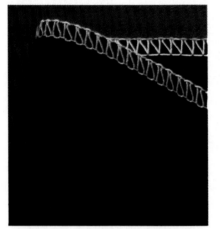

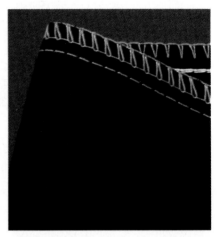

3-thread stitch is formed by two loopers and one needle. Upper (orange) and lower (yellow) looper threads form neat, smooth chain at raw edge. Needle thread (green) forms flat stitches without puckers.

4/3-thread stitch is formed by two loopers and two needles. Upper (orange) and lower (yellow) looper threads chain neatly at raw edge. Both needle threads (blue, green) form flat stitches that interlock with looper threads.

4/2-thread stitch makes double row of stitches with two loopers and two needles. Left needle thread (blue) interlocks with lower looper thread (yellow) to make neat, pucker-free chainstitch. Upper looper thread (orange) and right needle thread (green) interlock over raw edge.

Common Tension Adjustments

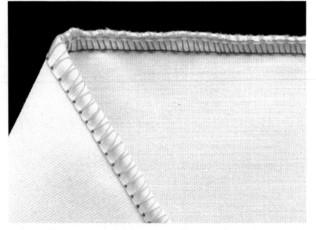
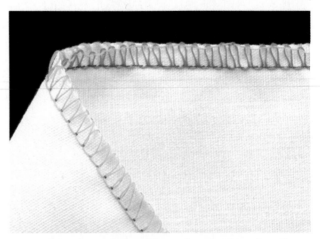

Upper looper too tight. Upper looper thread (orange) pulls lower looper thread (yellow) to top side of fabric. Loosen upper looper tension so threads interlock at raw edge.

Lower looper too loose. Lower looper thread (yellow) rides loosely on top of fabric. Tighten lower looper tension until stitches lie flat and smooth on fabric.

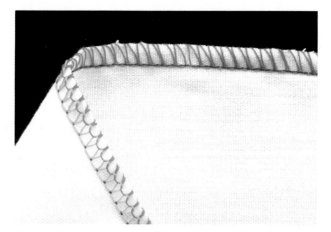

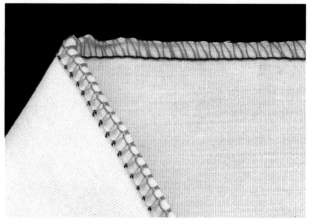

Upper looper too loose. Upper looper thread (orange) interlocks with lower looper thread (yellow) underneath fabric. Tighten upper looper tension so threads interlock at raw edge.

Lower looper too tight. Lower looper thread (yellow) pulls upper looper thread (orange), causing stitches to interlock under fabric. Loosen lower looper tension so threads interlock at raw edge.

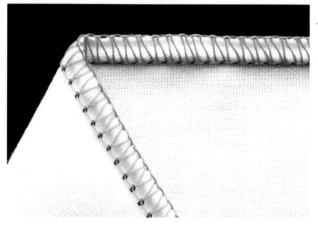

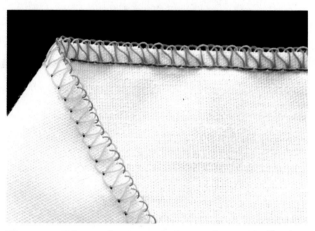

Upper and lower loopers too tight. Fabric bunches and puckers within stitches. Loosen upper and lower tensions until fabric relaxes.

Upper and lower loopers too loose. Lower (yellow) and upper (orange) looper threads interlock beyond raw edge and form loose loops. Tighten both looper tensions so stitches hug raw edge.

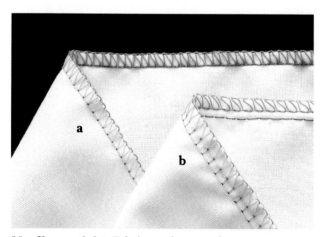

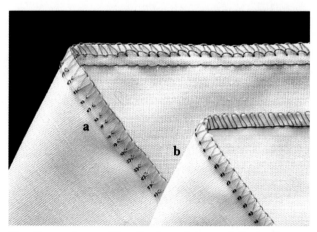

Needle too tight. Fabric puckers or draws up lengthwise when needle thread (green) is too tight **(a)**. Loosen needle tension until fabric relaxes. Test knits for thread breakage, loosening needle thread if necessary. On 4/3-thread machine **(b)**, adjust each needle thread (blue, green) individually.

Needle too loose. Needle thread (green) forms loose loops underneath fabric **(a)**. Tighten needle tension for flat, smooth stitches. On 4/3-thread serger **(b)**, adjust each needle thread (blue, green) individually.

Overlock Basics

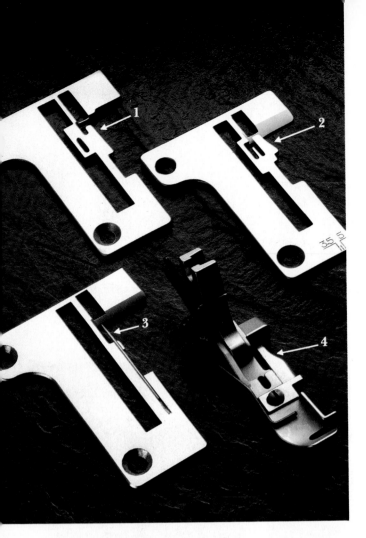

To begin overlock stitching, run the machine without fabric under the presser foot to create a chain of stitches about 2" (5 cm) long. A thread chain at the start and end of seams prevents stitches from raveling. Operating an overlock machine without fabric does not damage the machine or break threads, because stitches are formed on the stitch fingers (prongs).

The throat plate on most overlock machines has one (1) or two (2) stitch fingers. Stitches are formed around the stitch finger so that, with the correct tension, the width of the stitch finger determines the width of the stitch. A special throat plate with a narrow stitch finger (3) is used to sew a rolled hem or seam.

The presser foot may also contain a stitch finger (4). Machines with this type of presser foot use a special presser foot for a rolled hem or seam.

How to Change Thread

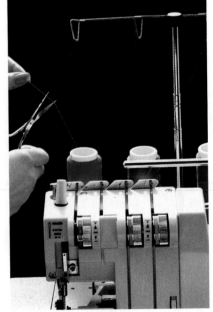

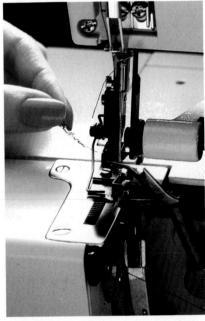

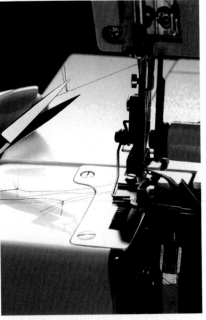

1) Cut each thread near cone, and remove cone. Tie new thread onto each thread in machine, using small overhand knot. Clip thread ends ½" (1.3 cm) from knot.

2) Release tensions, or set tension controls on 0. Cut needle thread in front of needle. Pull on tail chain to separate threads.

3) Pull threads one at a time through thread guides, upper looper, and lower looper. Pull needle thread until knot reaches needle eye. Cut off knot; thread needle with tweezers.

How to Clear the Stitch Fingers

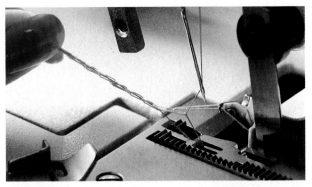

1) Raise presser foot. Turn flywheel to raise needle. Place left hand on thread chain behind presser foot. To slacken needle thread, pull it gently above last thread guide before needle. (Presser foot has been removed to show detail.)

2) Pull straight back on thread chain behind presser foot until threads separate and stitch fingers (prongs) of throat plate or presser foot are empty.

How to Start a Seam

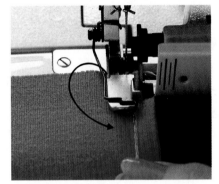

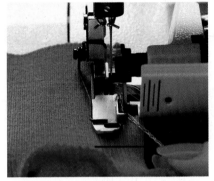

1) Make thread chain. Stitch seam for one or two stitches. Raise presser foot; turn flywheel to lift needle. Clear stitch fingers. Run your fingers along thread chain to make it smooth. (Presser foot has been removed to show detail.)

2) Bring thread chain to the left, around and under presser foot. Place thread chain between needle and knife. Hold thread chain in position, and lower presser foot.

3) Stitch seam over thread chain for about 1" (2.5 cm); then swing thread chain to the right so it is trimmed off as you continue to stitch seam.

How to End a Seam

1) Stitch past end of seam by one stitch, and stop. Raise presser foot and needle to clear stitch fingers. (Presser foot has been removed to show detail.)

2) Turn seam over, and rotate it to align edge of seam with edge of knife. Lower presser foot. Turn flywheel to insert needle at end of seam and at left of edge the width of stitch.

3) Stitch over previous stitches for about 1" (2.5 cm). Stitch off edge, leaving thread chain. With scissors or serger knife, trim thread chain close to edge of seam.

How to Stitch Inside Corners and Slits

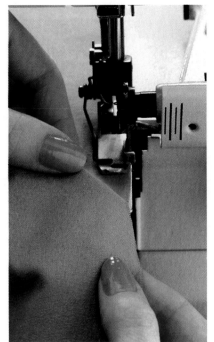

1) Finish seams of inside corners by aligning raw edge of fabric with knife of serger. Stitch, stopping before corner.

2) Fold the fabric to the left to straighten edge. This may create a tuck, which will not be stitched.

3) Resume stitching, holding fabric in straight line. Once past corner, fabric can be relaxed.

How to Stitch Curved Edges

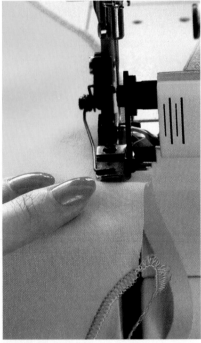

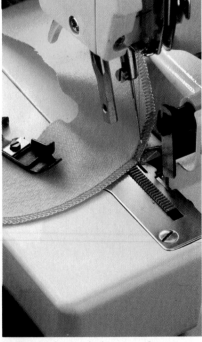

1) Begin cutting at an angle, until you reach the desired cutting or stitching line.

2) Guide fabric in front of presser foot so knives trim raw edge to curved shape. While stitching, watch knife, not needle.

3) Stop when stitches overlap previous stitches. Lift presser foot. Shift fabric so it is behind needle; stitch off edge to prevent gradual looping over edge of fabric. (Presser foot has been removed to show needle position.)

How to Stitch Outside Corners

1) Trim off seam allowance past corner for about 2" (5 cm). If making napkins, placemats, or similar projects, you can cut fabric to finished size and omit this step.

2) Sew one stitch past end of the corner, and stop. Raise presser foot and needle to clear stitch fingers and slacken needle thread slightly. (Presser foot has been removed to show needle position.)

3) Pivot fabric to align raw edge of trimmed seam allowance with knife. Insert needle at serged edge. Lower presser foot, and continue stitching.

How to Remove Stitches

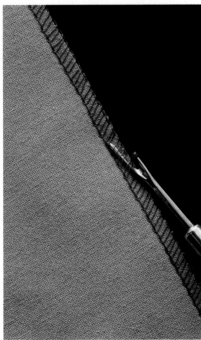

2-thread stitch. Cut threads by sliding seam ripper or blade of scissors under the stitches. Remove cut threads.

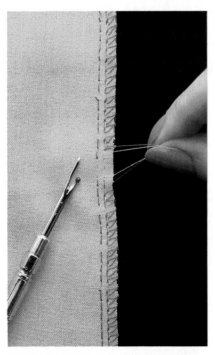

3-thread or 4/3-thread stitch. Clip needle threads every three or four stitches, working from upper side. Pull both looper threads straight out at edge. Remove cut threads.

4/2-thread stitch. Working from under side, pull on looper thread to remove chainstitching. Remove overedging as described for 2-thread stitch, left.

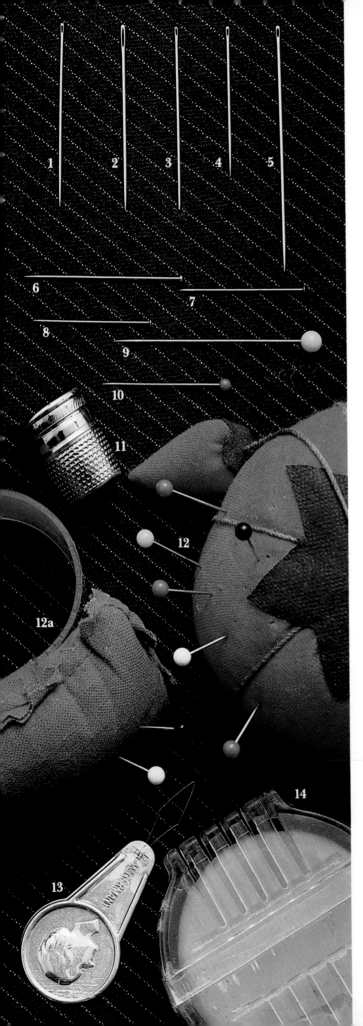

Essential Equipment

Basic sewing is divided into five processes: measuring, cutting, marking, stitching by hand or machine, and pressing. For each of these tasks, there are essential tools to make the steps easier and the results superior. Build an equipment inventory as you add to your sewing skills.

Hand Sewing Equipment

Needles and pins are available in a variety of sizes and styles for different uses. Look for rustproof needles and pins made of brass, nickel-plated steel or stainless steel. Pins with colored ball heads rather than flat heads are easier to see in fabric and less likely to get lost.

1) Sharps are all-purpose, medium length needles used for general sewing.

2) Crewels are generally used for embroidery. They are sharp and of medium length.

3) Ballpoint needles are used on knits. Instead of a sharp point which may pierce the fabric, the rounded end pushes the knit loops apart.

4) Betweens are very short and round-eyed. They help make fine stitches in heavy fabric or quilting.

5) Milliner's needles are long with round eyes, used for making long basting or gathering stitches.

6) Silk pins are used for light to mediumweight fabrics. Size #17 is 1 1/16" (2.6 cm) long; #20 is 1 1/4" (3.2 cm). Both are also available with glass or plastic heads. Extra fine 1 3/4" (4.5 cm) silk pins are easier to see in fabric because of their length.

7) Straight pins in brass, steel or stainless steel are used for general sewing. They are usually 1 1/16" (2.6 cm) long.

8) Pleating pins are only 1" (2.5 cm) long, for pinning delicate fabrics in the seam allowance.

9) Quilting pins are 1 1/4" (3.2 cm) long, used for heavy materials because of their length.

10) Ballpoint pins are used for knits.

11) Thimble protects your middle finger while hand sewing. It is available in sizes 6 (small) to 12 (large) for individual, snug fit.

12) Pin cushion provides a safe place to store pins. Some pin cushions have an emery pack (an abrasive material) attached for cleaning pins and needles. A wrist pin cushion (**12a**) keeps pins handy.

13) Needle threader eases threading of hand or machine needles.

14) Beeswax with holder strengthens thread and prevents tangling for hand sewing.

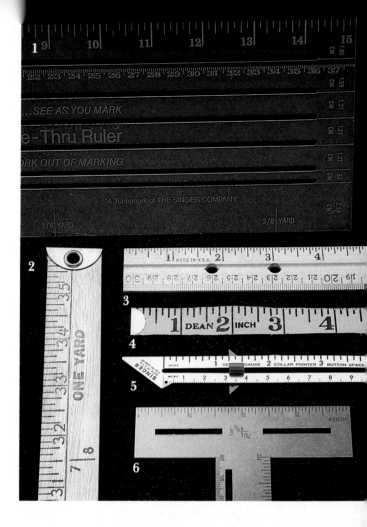

Marking Tools

The symbols on a pattern piece are guides for the accurate construction of the garment. Transferring these symbols from pattern to fabric is essential to fitting and sewing. Because you will be working with several types of fabrics, you will need a variety of marking tools.

1) Tracing wheels come in two types: serrated or smooth edge. The serrated edge makes a dotted line marking. It is suitable for most fabrics but may pierce delicate ones. The smooth-edge tracing wheel protects delicate, smooth fabrics such as silk and chiffon. It makes a solid line marking.

2) Dressmaker's tracing paper is a special waxed carbon paper which transfers the tracing wheel's line to the fabric. Choose a color close to that of the fabric, making sure it can be seen easily.

3) Tailor's chalk or marking pencil marks quickly and easily, directly on the fabric. Chalk rubs off quickly, so use it only when you plan to sew immediately. A tailor tacker **(3a)** holds two pieces of chalk and marks from both sides.

4) Liquid marking pencils make quick work of marking tucks, darts, pleats and pocket locations. One type disappears within 48 hours. The other washes off with water but should not be used on fabrics that show water marks. Pressing may set the marks permanently, so remove marking before pressing the area.

Measuring Tools

Body and pattern measurements both require measuring tools. To ensure a good fit, measure often and accurately with the best tool for the job.

1) See-through ruler lets you see what you measure or mark. This ruler is used to check fabric grainline and to mark buttonholes, tucks, and pleats.

2) Yardstick is for general marking and for measuring fabric grainline when laying out the pattern. It should be made of smooth, shellacked hardwood or metal.

3) Ruler is for general marking. The most useful sizes are 12" or 18" (30.5 or 46 cm) long.

4) Tape measure has the flexibility required to take body measurements. Select a 60" (152.5 cm) long tape with metal tips, made of a material that will not stretch. It should be reversible, with numbers and markings printed on both sides.

5) Seam gauge helps make quick, accurate measurements for hems, buttonholes, scallops, and pleats. It is a small, 6" (15 cm) metal or plastic ruler with a sliding marker.

6) See-through T-square is used to locate cross grains, alter patterns, and square off straight edges.

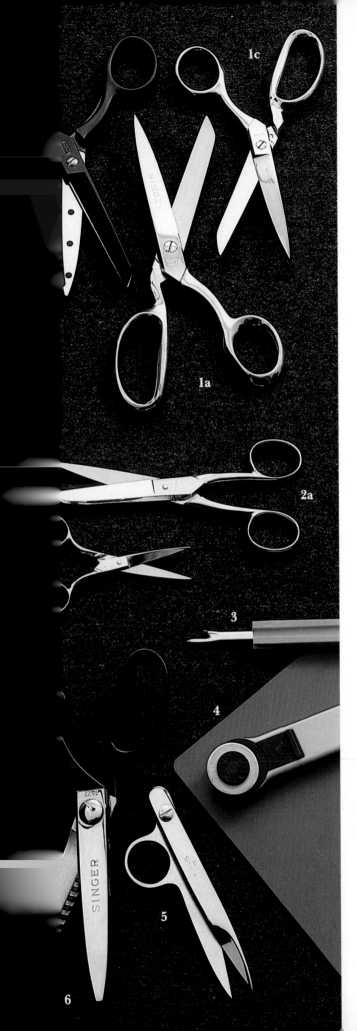

Cutting Tools

Buy quality cutting tools and keep them at their best with periodic sharpening by a qualified professional. Scissors have both handles the same size; shears have one handle larger than the other. The best quality scissors and shears are hot-forged, high-grade steel, honed to a fine cutting edge. Blades should be joined with an adjustable screw (not a rivet) to ensure even pressure along the length of the blade. Sharp shears make clean cuts and well-defined notches. More important, they do not damage fabric. Dull shears slow the cutting process, and make your hand and wrist tire easily. Sewing shears should not be used for other household tasks such as cutting paper or twine. Scissors and shears last longer if you occasionally put a drop of oil on the screw assembly, wipe them clean with a soft dry cloth after use, and store them in a box or pouch.

1) Bent-handled dressmaker's shears are best for pattern cutting because the angle of the lower blade lets fabric lie flat on the cutting surface. Blade lengths of 7" or 8" (18 or 20.5 cm) are most popular, but lengths up to 12" (30.5 cm) are available. Select a blade length appropriate to the size of your hand — shorter lengths for small hands, longer lengths for large hands. Left-handed models are also available. If you sew a great deal, invest in a pair of all-steel, chrome-plated shears (**1a**) for heavy-duty cutting. The lighter models with stainless steel blades and plastic handles (**1b**) are fine for less-frequent sewing or lightweight fabrics. For synthetic fabrics and slippery knits, a serrated-edge shears (**1c**) gives maximum cutting control.

2) Sewing scissors (2a) have one pointed and one rounded tip for trimming and clipping seams and facings. The 6" (15 cm) blade is most practical. Embroidery scissors (**2b**) have 4" or 5" (10 or 12.5 cm) finely-tapered blades. Both points are sharp for use in hand work and precision cutting.

3) Seam ripper quickly rips seams, opens buttonholes and removes stitches. Use carefully to avoid piercing the fabric.

4) Rotary cutter is an adaptation of the giant rotary cutters used by the garment industry. It works like a pizza cutter and can be used by left or right-handed sewers. Use the rotary cutter with a special plastic mat available in different sizes. The mat protects both the cutting surface and the blade. A special locking mechanism retracts the blade for safety.

5) Thread clipper with spring-action blades is more convenient than shears and safer than a seam ripper.

6) Pinking shears or scalloping shears cut a zigzag or scalloped edge instead of a straight one. Used to finish seams and raw edges on many types of fabric, they cut a ravel-resistant edge.

Pressing Tools

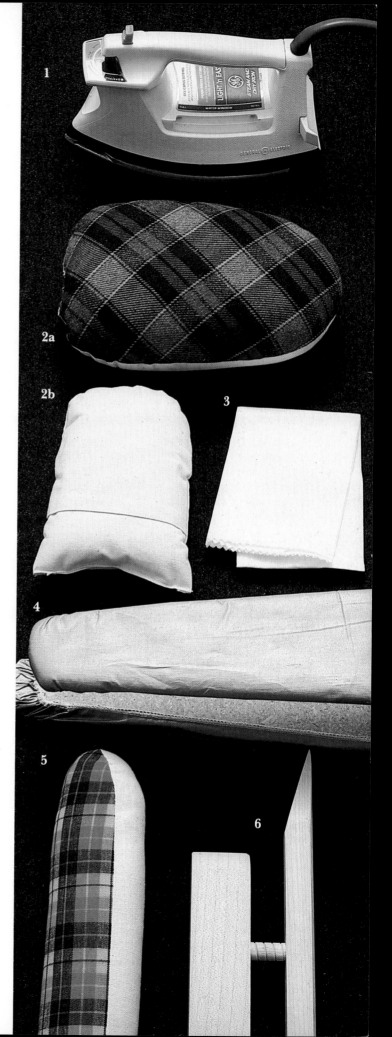

Pressing as you sew is one important procedure that is often neglected. It may seem like a needless interruption, but pressing at each stage of construction is the secret to a perfectly finished garment.

If you need help getting into the pressing habit, locate your pressing equipment near your sewing area. It also helps to press in batches. Do this by stitching as much as possible at the machine. Then press all the stitched areas at one time.

Pressing does not mean ironing. In ironing, you glide the iron over the fabric. In pressing, you move the iron very little while it is in contact with the fabric. Use minimum pressure on the iron, and press in the direction of the fabric grain. Lift the iron to move to another section.

Your pattern directions usually tell when to press, but the general rule is: Press each stitched seam before crossing with another. Press on the wrong side to prevent iron shine, and protect the iron's soleplate by removing pins before pressing.

1) **Steam/spray iron** should have a wide temperature range to accommodate all fabrics. Buy a dependable, name-brand iron. An iron that steams and sprays at any setting, not just the higher heat settings, is helpful for synthetic fabrics.

2) **Tailor's ham or pressing mitt** is used when pressing shaped areas such as curved seams, darts, collars or sleeve caps. The ham (2a) is a firmly-packed cushion with rounded curves. One side is cotton; the other side is covered with wool to retain more steam. The mitt (2b) is similar to the ham but is especially handy for small, hard-to-reach areas. It fits over the hand or a sleeve board.

3) **Press cloth** helps prevent iron shine and is always used when applying fusible interfacing. The transparent variety allows you to see if the fabric is smooth and the interfacing properly aligned.

4) **Sleeve board** looks like two small ironing boards attached one on top of the other. It is used when pressing seams and details of small or narrow areas such as sleeves, pants legs or necklines.

5) **Seam roll** is a firmly-packed cylindrical cushion for pressing seams. The bulk of the fabric falls to the sides and never touches the iron, preventing the seam from making an imprint on the right side of the fabric.

6) **Point presser/clapper** is made of hardwood and used for pressing seams open in corners and points. The clapper flattens seams by holding steam and heat in the fabric. This tool is used in tailoring to achieve a flat finish and sharp edges on hard-surfaced fabrics.

Timesaving Aids

Many kinds of special equipment are designed to save time in layout, construction and pressing. The more you sew, the more these aids will become necessities. Just as you would invest in timesaving devices for cooking and cleaning, invest in sewing equipment to make your wardrobe and home decorating projects go faster.

Before using a new product, read all instructions carefully. Learn what special handling or care is required, and what fabrics or techniques it is suited for. Here is an overview of some of these specialized sewing products.

Table-top ironing board is portable and saves space. It is easy to set up near your sewing machine. This ironing board keeps large pieces of fabric on the table so they do not stretch out or drag on the floor. It also helps cultivate the habit of detail pressing while you sew.

Hand steamer is a lightweight steam iron, providing a concentrated area of steam at a low temperature setting. No press cloth is needed, even when pressing on the right side of the fabric. It heats to a steam temperature in less than two minutes and is useful for darts, seams, pleats and hems.

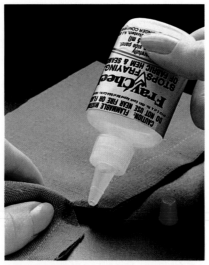

Glue substitutes for pinning or basting by holding fabric, leather, vinyl, felt, trims, patch pockets and zippers in place for permanent stitching. Use it for craft work as well as general sewing. Glue stick is water soluble, so it provides only a temporary bond. Liquid glue can be dotted in seam allowances to hold layers of fabric together.

Liquid ravel preventer is a colorless plastic liquid which prevents fraying by stiffening fabric slightly. It is helpful when you have clipped too far into a seam allowance or want to reinforce a pocket or buttonhole. It darkens light colors slightly, so apply cautiously. The liquid becomes a permanent finish that will withstand laundering and dry cleaning.

Basting tape is double-faced adhesive tape that eliminates pinning and thread basting. Use it on leather and vinyl as well as on fabric. The tape is especially helpful for matching stripes and plaids, applying zippers, and positioning pockets and trims. Do not machine-stitch through the tape, because the adhesive may foul your machine needle.

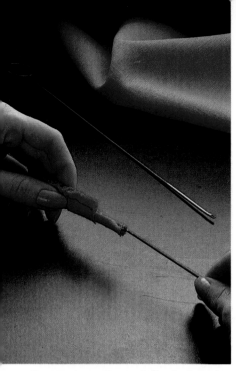

Loop turner is specially designed with a latch hook device at one end to grasp bias tubing or cording and turn it to the right side. It is quicker and easier than attaching a safety pin to one end and working the pin through. Because the wire is so fine, it can be used for very narrow tubing and button loops.

Bodkin threads ribbon, elastic or cord through a casing without twisting. Some bodkins have an eye through which ribbon or elastic is threaded; others have a tweezer or safety pin closure which grabs the elastic. The bodkin above has a ring which slides to tighten the prongs of the pincers.

Point turner pokes out the tailored points in collars, lapels and pockets without risking a tear. Made of wood or plastic, its point fits neatly into corners. Use the point to remove basting thread and the rounded end to hold seamlines open for pressing.

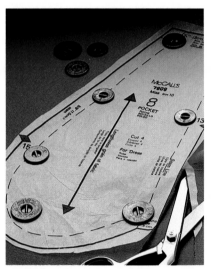

Folding cutting board protects a fine table's finish from pin or shears scratches. It also prevents fabric from slipping while cutting, and holds fabric more securely. Stick pins into it for faster pinning, square off fabric against marked lines, and use the 1" (2.5 cm) squares as an instant measure. The folding feature makes storage easy.

Weights hold a pattern in place for cutting. They eliminate time-consuming pinning and unpinning of the pattern and protect fabrics that would be permanently marked by pins. Weights are most easily used on smaller pattern pieces. Some sewers use items like cans of vegetables in place of retail weights.

Magnetic pin catcher and pin cushion keep all-steel pins in their place. The pin catcher attaches to the throat plate of the machine to catch pins as you pull them out while stitching. The magnetic, weighted pin cushion is more convenient than an ordinary one, and is especially handy for picking pins off the floor.

Timesaving Layout & Cutting Aids

Save time during pattern layout and cutting by using the fewest possible pins or eliminating pins entirely. For cutting, use weights to hold the pattern on the fabric. Purchase sets of sewing weights, or improvise by using canned goods. To lay out a pattern with weights, arrange large pattern pieces first, then small ones. Pin through grainline markings on large pattern pieces. Place weights on one pattern piece at a time, inside the cutting line.

Use a rotary cutter instead of shears to speed the work. This tool works like a pizza cutter. The sharp wheel cuts easily through multiple layers of fabric so patterns can be cut out in a few, swift motions. Protect the cutting edge and work surface by using a special plastic mat under the fabric. Mats are available in several types and sizes. The most practical is as large as your layout surface. Those printed with a grid and bias lines can save time, because you can use the printed lines to help you measure accurately. Also use the rotary cutter to trim pattern margins before cutting and to trim seam allowances from interfacings.

How to Use a Rotary Cutter

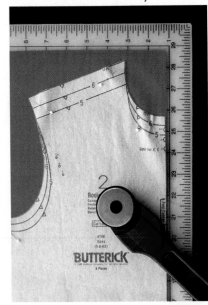

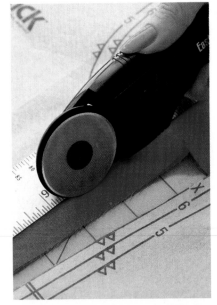

1) Slide protective plastic mat under pattern piece to be cut. Shift mat under pattern pieces as needed, so work surface is always covered as you cut.

2) Use a metal ruler as a guide for cutting straight edges. Hold rotary cutter so thumb is on blade side of handle. Trim off notches as you cut. Blades are adjustable for cutting lightweight fabric or heavy, bulky, and multiple layers.

3) Use small rotary cutter for short, straight lines and sharp curves. Small wheel is easier to maneuver than large one when cutting lines have complex shapes.

Timesaving Basting Aids

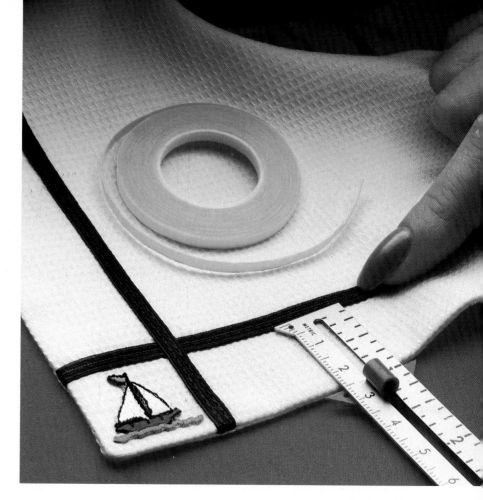

Basting can be a time-consuming preparation for final stitching. Yet it becomes especially important if you are sewing a garment on an overlock machine, because you may want to baste first to check the fit. After seams are overlocked, there is no seam allowance left to provide a margin for error if the seams have to be let out.

Adhesives, fusibles, and dissolvable basting thread (page 34) are fast alternatives to hand sewing or pinning. Use these techniques for making seams and hems, inserting zippers, and positioning trims.

How to Use Timesaving Basting Aids

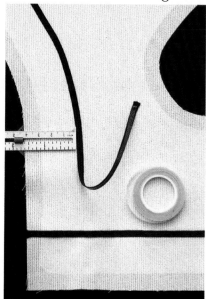

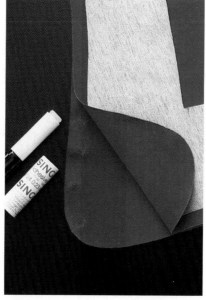

Basting tape. Use to position trims, appliqués, zippers, and pockets. With adhesive side down, finger press in position desired. Remove paper backing from face of tape to expose adhesive. Position detail, and stitch in position; do not stitch through tape. Water-soluble tape will dissolve in first washing.

Glue stick. Apply dots of glue to seam allowances of first fabric layer so glue is next to, but not on, stitching line. While glue is still tacky, position second layer. Use glue sparingly. Refrigerate stick in warm or humid weather to keep it firm.

Fusible web. Fold ¼ yd. (.25 m) of fusible web several times to cut ⅛" (3 mm) strips. To attach patch pockets, slip strip under edge of pocket, and press onto garment before stitching. Pocket will not shift as you stitch. You can also use web to baste appliqués and trims.

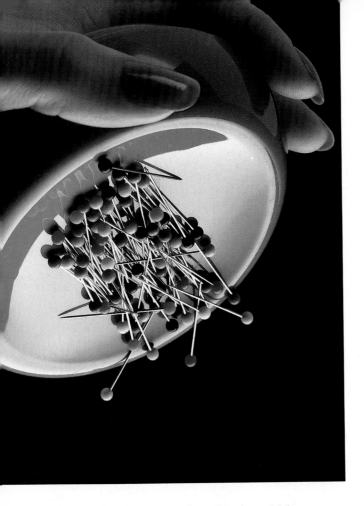

Timesaving Sewing Aids

Timesaving sewing aids solve specific sewing problems or make techniques easier. Many of these aids are versatile and can save time in ways other than the specific purposes for which they were designed. A magnetic pin cushion, for example, not only holds steel pins and needles but is handy for cleanup, too; just slide it along the sewing surface or nearby floor area to attract stray pins and needles. Hook and loop tape, often used for closures, can also be used to attach shoulder pads.

Sewing aids are continually being developed. Many, such as liquid fray preventer and fusible web, rely on adhesive, chemical, or heat-sensitive formulations to replace handwork. When using one of these sewing aids for the first time, test on scraps to develop a feeling for using the aid.

Periodically check fabric stores and notions counters for newer products, such as dissolvable basting thread; and look for new designs of products that are updated often, such as iron-on appliqués. Not all timesaving sewing aids are recent innovations, however. Do not overlook the timesaving capabilities of tried-and-true tools such as the seam ripper, button spacer, and thread snips.

How to Use Timesaving Sewing Aids

Iron-on appliqués. Position the appliqué on fabric, right side up, and cover with a press cloth. Apply pressure with iron, using the heat setting and time recommended by manufacturer.

Dissolvable basting thread. To machine-baste, thread machine needle and bobbin with dissolvable thread, and set machine for longest stitch. To hand-baste, use 18" to 24" (46 to 61 cm) length to prevent tangling. Use water or steam pressing to dissolve thread.

Hook and loop tape. Use hook side on shoulder pads with matching loops on garment shoulder seam to make pads easy to detach. On sweater knits, use hook side of tape on shoulder pad only; it clings to knit fabric.

Three Uses for Liquid Fray Preventer

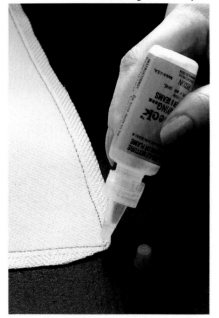

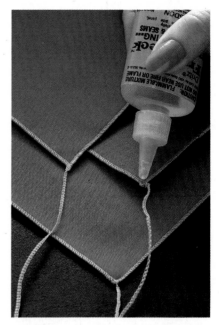

Reinforce edges that are clipped or trimmed close to a stitching line, using a single drop of fray preventer. After the liquid dries, the raw edge becomes firm and resists raveling.

Seal cut edges of machine-made buttonholes by coating them lightly with fray preventer. Test first on sample, because product can make fabric darker and stiffer. Remove excess with rubbing alcohol before it dries completely.

Finish row of overlock stitches by dabbing end with liquid fray preventer. Trim thread chains after liquid dries. Hasten drying with hand-held blow dryer.

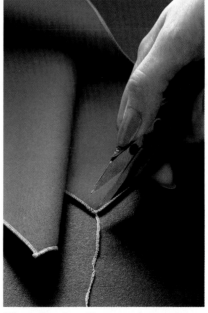

Button spacer. When sewing on buttons, adjust the movable U-shaped parts at end of gauge to make uniform thread shanks. Choose from three shank lengths, using thickness of one, two, or three parts at end of gauge.

Thread snips. Press spring-action blades between thumb and fingers to clip threads. Single hand motion takes less time than opening and closing scissor blades. To save even more time, tie thread snips on a ribbon around your neck.

Seam ripper. Insert prong of seam ripper under single stitches at 1" (2.5 cm) intervals to break stitch. Pull thread from other side of seam. To keep fabric taut, use presser foot as third hand to hold one end of seam. Pull edges gently apart to open seam. Do not slide ripper along seam.

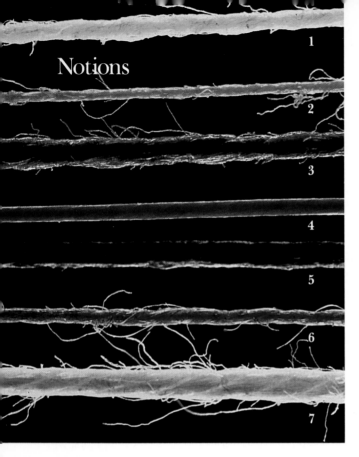

Thread

Select high-quality thread according to the fiber and weight of the fabric and the purpose of the stitching. As a general guideline, use a natural fiber thread for natural fiber fabrics and synthetic fiber thread for synthetic fabrics. Photo above has been enlarged 20 times to show detail.

1) Cotton-wrapped polyester thread is an all-purpose thread designed for hand and machine sewing on all fabrics: natural fibers and synthetics, wovens and knits.

2) Extra fine cotton-wrapped polyester thread reduces fabric puckering on lightweight fabrics, and does not build up or break during machine embroidery.

3) Topstitching and buttonhole twist is designed for topstitching, decorative programmed stitching, cording in machine-worked buttonholes and stitching hand-worked buttonholes.

4) Hand quilting thread is a strong cotton or polyester/cotton thread that does not tangle, knot or untwist while hand sewing through layers of fabric.

5) Button and carpet thread is suitable for hand sewing where extra strength is required.

6) Long-fiber polyester thread is smooth and even, and suitable for hand or machine stitching.

7) 100% mercerized cotton thread is used for natural fiber woven fabrics like cotton, linen and wool; it does not have enough stretch for knits.

Trims & Tapes

Choose trims and tapes that are compatible with your fabric and thread. Most trims and tapes can be machine stitched, but some must be applied by hand. Preshrink trims for washable garments.

1) Single-fold bias tape, ½" (1.3 cm) wide, and wide bias tape, ⅞" (2.2 cm) wide, available in prints and solid colors, are used for casings, trim and facings.

2) Double-fold bias tape binds a raw edge. It comes in ¼" (6 mm) and ½" (1.3 cm) folded widths.

3) Lace seam binding is a decorative lace hem finish or lace insertion for all fabrics.

4) Seam tape is 100% rayon or polyester, ⅜" (1 cm) wide, used to stay seams, finish hems and reinforce clipped corners.

5) Rickrack comes in ¼" (6 mm), ½" (1.3 cm), and ⅝" (1.5 cm) widths for accent trim and edging.

6) Braid is available in loop (shown), soutache and middy styles. Use it for accent, scroll motifs, drawstrings, ties or button loops.

7) Twill tape is used to stay seams or roll lines.

8) Corded piping is an accent trim inserted in seams to define and decorate edges.

9) Elastic is inserted in casings to shape waistbands, wrists and necklines. Knitted **(9a)** and woven **(9b)** elastics are softer then braided elastics **(9c)**, curl less, and can be stitched directly onto the fabric. Non-roll waistband elastic has lateral ribs to keep it from twisting or rolling.

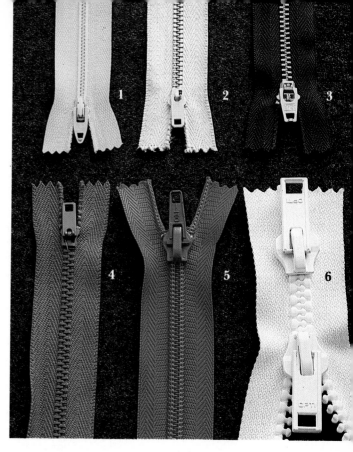

Buttons & Closures

Select these notions either to blend with the garment or stand out and make a fashion statement. Closures can be decorative as well as functional.

1) Sew-through, two-hole or four-hole buttons are commonly-used, all-purpose buttons.

2) Shank buttons have a "neck" or shank underneath the button.

3) Self-covered buttons can be covered with the same fabric as the garment for an exact color match.

4) Toggles are loop-and-bar fasteners with leather or leather-like trim, used on lapped areas.

5) Frogs are loop-and-ball fasteners that lend a dressy look to special outfits.

6) Snap and Velcro® tapes are used as closures on lapped areas of jackets, shirts or casual dresses.

7) Heavy-duty hooks and eyes are used to close waistbands on skirts or pants.

8) Hooks and eyes are inside closures available in sizes appropriate to various fabric weights.

9) Snaps are inside closures for areas that do not receive much stress, such as cuffs.

10) Jumbo snaps are hammered on or applied with a plier-like tool on the outside of a garment for a decorative effect.

Zippers

Zippers have metal or plastic teeth, or a synthetic coil of polyester or nylon attached to a woven tape. Both types come in all-purpose weights. Coil zippers are lightweight, more flexible, heat-resistant and rustproof. Metal zippers come in heavier weights for heavy fabrics and sportswear. Although zippers are usually designed to blend into the garment, some are big, colorful and made to be shown off.

1) Polyester all-purpose zippers are suitable for fabrics of all weights in skirts, pants, dresses and home decorating items.

2) Metal all-purpose zippers are strong, durable zippers for sportswear as well as pants, skirts, dresses and home decorating items.

3) Brass jean zippers are stamped metal zippers with a closed bottom, designed for jeans, work and casual wear in medium to heavyweight fabrics.

4) Metal separating zippers, available in medium and heavy weights, are used in jackets, sportswear and home decorating. Reversible separating zippers have pull tabs on the front and back of the zipper.

5) Plastic molded separating zippers are lightweight yet strong and durable, designed with extra fullness to give a smooth, straight finish to the application. Their decorative appearance makes them a natural for skiwear and outdoor wear.

6) Parka zippers are plastic molded separating zippers with two sliders, so they can be opened from the top and bottom.

A Place to Sew

Sewing is more enjoyable and much easier when you have a permanent place to sew with everything close at hand. Whether you can dedicate a large or small space to sewing, use it wisely by organizing your collection of equipment and supplies.

An efficient way to organize is according to sewing task. Sewing involves three major activities: layout/cutting, stitching, and pressing. Therefore it is practical to arrange three work stations in your sewing area similar to the work triangle kitchen planners use to locate range, sink, and refrigerator. Assemble all the equipment and supplies that relate specifically to each sewing activity, and keep them handy to the area where they will be used.

You also need storage space. Sewing naturally encourages a stockpile of fabrics, trims, interfacings, notions, and patterns earmarked for future sewing projects. Storage hardware and modular units, like those used for kitchens and closets, work well in a sewing area. Plastic-coated wall shelves, for example, keep supplies out of the way but within reach. Select components suitable to the size of your sewing space. Allow room for hanging garments and projects in progress; the edge of open shelving can provide a hanging surface. Hang folded fabric over padded suit hangers, or place in drawers.

Use wall-mounted racks and hooks for small items such as scissors, lint brush, and rolls of tape. A hanging thread rack keeps thread upright and visible. Other small items can be stored in a sportsman's tackle box with stepped trays or a utility box with clear plastic drawers.

A sewing machine should have ample flat work surface around it to support the fabric. An office chair rolls easily between machines and other work areas, and it adjusts for your height and comfort.

Organizing a Sewing Area

Layout/cutting area. A padded work surface, made from plywood or a hollow door, is large enough for laying fabric flat. Square corners aid in straightening grainlines; a muslin covering prevents the fabric from sliding. You can also pin into the work surface and use it as a pressing table for large projects. A magnetic pin cushion grabs pins for faster cleanup. A handy basket with hooks holds shears and other cutting aids.

Stitching area. Store machine attachments, presser feet, replacement needles, instruction manual, and maintenance tools nearby. If you have an overlock machine, keep it next to your conventional machine. Both should be ready to use when you're working on a sewing project. A bulletin board can hold the pattern guide sheet for ready reference. Keep thread near the machines.

Pressing area. A tabletop ironing board can be placed near the sewing machines or on a padded work surface; large pieces of fabric will not stretch out or drag on the floor. Steam/spray iron, hand steamer, and pressing tools (such as tailor's ham, sleeve board, point presser/clapper, seam roll, and press cloths) can be stored within arm's reach. A well-organized pressing station encourages the good habit of pressing as you sew.

Storage. Group similar items such as buttons, trims, zippers, and threads; put each group in see-through containers so you can see at once what you have and where it is. Cover fabric with sheeting or acid-free tissue paper, not plastic, to store on a long-term basis. Roll fusible interfacings on cardboard tubes for storage without wrinkling.

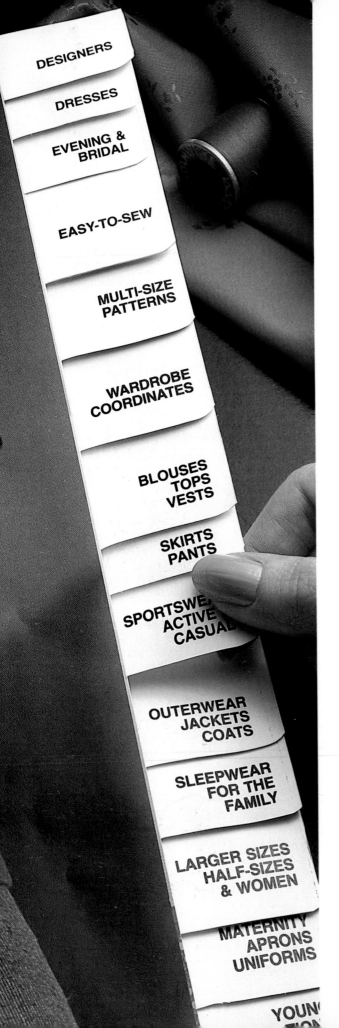

The Pattern

Shopping a pattern catalog is more creative than shopping a ready-to-wear catalog. In a pattern catalog, you aren't limited to the fabric, color, skirt length or buttons you see on the pages. You are the designer of your own fashion. You can choose the combination that flatters you and expresses your own personal style.

Pattern selection has never been better. Designer styles are available in the same season that they appear in ready-to-wear. There are easy patterns for the sewer with limited time. You will find patterns for accessories, home decoration, evening wear, men's and boys' fashions, and almost every kind of women's or children's garment.

The pattern catalog is divided into categories by size or fashion look, marked by index tabs. The newest fashions usually appear in the first few pages of each category. Pattern illustrations are accompanied by information on recommended fabrics and yardage requirements. An index at the back of the catalog lists patterns in numerical order along with their page numbers. The back of the catalog also includes a complete size chart for every figure type: male, female, children, and infants.

Match the pattern's level of sewing difficulty to your sewing experience. For success, select a pattern appropriate to your sewing skill. If your time or patience is limited, stay with simpler styles.

The number of pattern pieces listed on the back of the pattern is a clue to the complexity of the pattern. The fewer the pieces, the easier the pattern. Details like shirt cuffs, collar bands, pleats, and tucks also make a pattern more difficult to sew. Easy-to-sew patterns feature few of these details.

All pattern companies follow a uniform sizing based on standard body measurements. This is not exactly the same as ready-to-wear sizing. To select the right pattern size, first take your standard body measurements. Wear your usual undergarments and use a tape measure that doesn't stretch. For accuracy, have another person measure you. Record your measurements and compare them with the size chart on page 43.

How to Take Standard Body Measurements

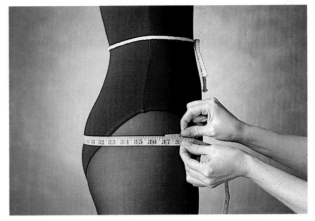

1) Waistline. Tie a string or piece of elastic around your middle and allow it to roll to your natural waistline. Measure at this exact location with tape measure. Leave string in place as a reference for measuring hips and back waist length.

2) Hips. Measure around the fullest part. This is usually 7" to 9" (18 to 23 cm) below the waistline, depending on your height.

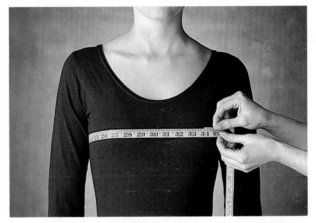

3) High bust. Place tape measure under arms, across widest part of back and above full bustline. Pattern size charts do not include a high bust measurement, but this measurement should be compared with the full bust to choose the right size pattern.

4) Full bust. Place tape measure under arms, across widest part of the back and fullest part of bustline. Note: If there is a difference of 2" (5 cm) or more between high and full bust, select pattern size by high bust measurement.

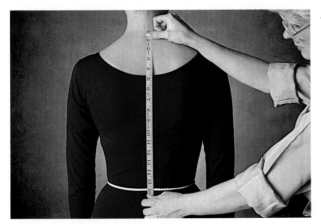

5) Back waist length. Measure from middle of the most prominent bone at the base of the neck down to waistline string.

6) Height. Measure without shoes. Stand with your back against a wall. Place a ruler on top of your head and mark the wall. Measure from the mark to the floor.

Female Figure Types

Young Junior Teen
About 5'1" to 5'3" (1.55 to 1.60 m) tall. Developing teen or preteen figure, with small, high bust. Waistline is larger in proportion to bust.

Junior Petite
About 5' to 5'1" (1.53 to 1.55 m) tall. Well-developed, shorter figure, with smaller body build and shorter back waist length than a Junior.

Junior
About 5'4" to 5'5" (1.63 to 1.65 m) tall. Well-developed figure, slightly shorter in height and back waist length than a Miss.

Miss Petite
About 5'2" to 5'4" (1.57 to 1.63 m) tall. Well-developed and well-proportioned shorter figure, with a shorter back waist length and slightly larger waist than a Miss.

Miss
About 5'5" to 5'6" (1.65 to 1.68 m) tall. Well-developed and well-proportioned in all areas. Considered the average figure.

Half-size
About 5'2" to 5'3" (1.57 to 1.60 m) tall. Fully-developed but shorter than the Miss. Shoulders are narrower than a Miss Petite. Waist is larger in proportion to bust than a Woman.

Woman
About 5'5" to 5'6" (1.65 to 1.68 m) tall. Same height as Miss, but larger and more fully mature, making all other measurements proportionately larger.

Maternity
Corresponds to Miss sizes. Measurements are for a figure five months pregnant, but patterns are designed to provide ease through the ninth month.

Female Figure Size Chart

To choose the right size pattern, take your measurements as directed on page 41. Then determine your figure type using the descriptions on the opposite page. Find your figure type on the chart below. Locate the column of numbers that most closely matches your measurements. Choose dress, blouse, and suit patterns by bust size; pants and skirt patterns by hip size.

Inches

Young Junior/Teen:

Size	5/6	7/8	9/10	11/12	13/14	15/16
Bust	28	29	30½	32	33½	35
Waist	22	23	24	25	26	27
Hip	31	32	33½	35	36½	38
Back Waist Length	13½	14	14½	15	15⅜	15¾

Junior Petite:

Size	3jp	5jp	7jp	9jp	11jp	13jp
Bust	30	31	32	33	34	35
Waist	22	23	24	25	26	27
Hip	31	32	33	34	35	36
Back Waist Length	14	14¼	14½	14¾	15	15¼

Junior:

Size	5	7	9	11	13	15
Bust	30	31	32	33½	35	37
Waist	22½	23½	24½	25½	27	29
Hip	32	33	34	35½	37	39
Back Waist Length	15	15¼	15½	15¾	16	16¼

Miss Petite:

Size	6mp	8mp	10mp	12mp	14mp	16mp
Bust	30½	31½	32½	34	36	38
Waist	23½	24½	25½	27	28½	30½
Hip	32½	33½	34½	36	38	40
Back Waist Length	14½	14¾	15	15¼	15½	15¾

Miss:

Size	6	8	10	12	14	16	18	20
Bust	30½	31½	32½	34	36	38	40	42
Waist	23	24	25	26½	28	30	32	34
Hip	32½	33½	34½	36	38	40	42	44
Back Waist Length	15½	15¾	16	16¼	16½	16¾	17	17¼

Half-size:

Size	10½	12½	14½	16½	18½	20½	22½	24½
Bust	33	35	37	39	41	43	45	47
Waist	27	29	31	33	35	37½	40	42½
Hip	35	37	39	41	43	45½	48	50½
Back Waist Length	15	15¼	15½	15¾	15⅞	16	16⅛	16¼

Woman:

Size	38	40	42	44	46	48	50	52
Bust	42	44	46	48	50	52	54	56
Waist	35	37	39	41½	44	46½	49	51½
Hip	44	46	48	50	52	54	56	58
Back Waist Length	17¼	17⅜	17½	17⅝	17¾	17⅞	18	18⅛

Maternity:

Size	6	8	10	12	14	16
Bust	34	35	36	37½	39½	41½
Waist	28½	29½	30½	32	33½	35½
Hip	35½	36½	37½	39	41	43
Back Waist Length	15½	15¾	16	16¼	16½	16¾

Centimeters

Young Junior/Teen:

Size	5/6	7/8	9/10	11/12	13/14	15/16
Bust	71	74	78	81	85	89
Waist	56	58	61	64	66	69
Hip	79	81	85	89	93	97
Back Waist Length	34.5	35.5	37	38	39	40

Junior Petite:

Size	3jp	5jp	7jp	9jp	11jp	13jp
Bust	76	79	81	84	87	89
Waist	56	58	61	64	66	69
Hip	79	81	84	87	89	92
Back Waist Length	35.5	36	37	37.5	38	39

Junior:

Size	5	7	9	11	13	15
Bust	76	79	81	85	89	94
Waist	57	60	62	65	69	74
Hip	81	84	87	90	94	99
Back Waist Length	38	39	39.5	40	40.5	41.5

Miss Petite:

Size	6mp	8mp	10mp	12mp	14mp	16mp
Bust	78	80	83	87	92	97
Waist	60	62	65	69	73	78
Hip	83	85	88	92	97	102
Back Waist Length	37	37.5	38	39	39.5	40

Miss:

Size	6	8	10	12	14	16	18	20
Bust	78	80	83	87	92	97	102	107
Waist	58	61	64	67	71	76	81	87
Hip	83	85	88	92	97	102	107	112
Back Waist Length	39.5	40	40.5	41.5	42	42.5	43	44

Half-size:

Size	10½	12½	14½	16½	18½	20½	22½	24½
Bust	84	89	94	99	104	109	114	119
Waist	69	74	79	84	89	96	102	108
Hip	89	94	99	104	109	116	122	128
Back Waist Length	38	39	39.5	40	40.5	40.5	41	41.5

Woman:

Size	38	40	42	44	46	48	50	52
Bust	107	112	117	122	127	132	137	142
Waist	89	94	99	105	112	118	124	131
Hip	112	117	122	127	132	137	142	147
Back Waist Length	44	44	44.5	45	45	45.5	46	46

Maternity:

Size	6	8	10	12	14	16
Bust	87	89	92	95	100	105
Waist	72	75	77.5	81	85	90
Hip	90	93	95	99	104	109
Back Waist Length	39.5	40	40.5	41.5	42	42.5

The Pattern Envelope

The pattern envelope contains a wealth of information, from a description of the garment to the amount of fabric needed. It gives ideas for fabric and color selection. The envelope helps you determine the degree of sewing difficulty with labels that indicate whether the style is a designer original, easy-to-sew or only suitable for certain fabrics. On the pattern envelope, you'll also find all the information needed to select fabric and notions.

The Envelope Front

Size and figure type are indicated at the top or side of the pattern. If the pattern is multi-sized, such as 8-10-12, you will find cutting lines for all three sizes on one pattern.

Pattern company name and style number are prominently displayed at the top or along the side of the pattern envelope.

Designer original patterns, indicated by the designer's name, often contain more difficult-to-sew details such as tucks, topstitching, linings or underlinings. For sewers who have the time and skill, these patterns provide designer fashions that duplicate ready-to-wear.

Views are alternate designs of the pattern. They may show optional trims, lengths, fabric combinations or design details to appeal to a beginner, or challenge an experienced sewer.

Labels may identify a pattern that has easy construction methods, is designed for timesaving sewing, has special fitting or size-related information, or shows how to handle special fabrics like plaids, knits or lace. Each pattern company has special categories and names for these designs.

Fashion illustration or photograph shows the main pattern design. It suggests suitable fabric types such as wool or cotton, and fabric designs such as print or plaid. If you are unsure of your fabric choice, use the pattern illustration as your guide. It is the designer's interpretation of the fashion.

SIZE 10
/MISS

6157

$4.00 U.S.A.

PATTERN

Designer

BONUS—Pattern includes special chart on how to work with plaids.

The Envelope Back

Back views show the details and style of the back of the garments.

Number of pattern pieces gives an idea of how easy or complicated the pattern is to sew.

Style number is repeated on the back of the envelope.

Garment descriptions include style, fit and construction information.

Fabric types suitable for the garments are suggested. Use them as a general guide to fabric selection. The special advice, such as "unsuitable for stripes or obvious diagonals," alerts you to fabrics that are not appropriate.

Body measurement and size chart is a reference to determine if you need to make alterations. For a multi-sized pattern, compare your measurements with those in the chart to decide which cutting line to use.

Metric equivalents of body measurements and yardage are included for countries which use the metric system.

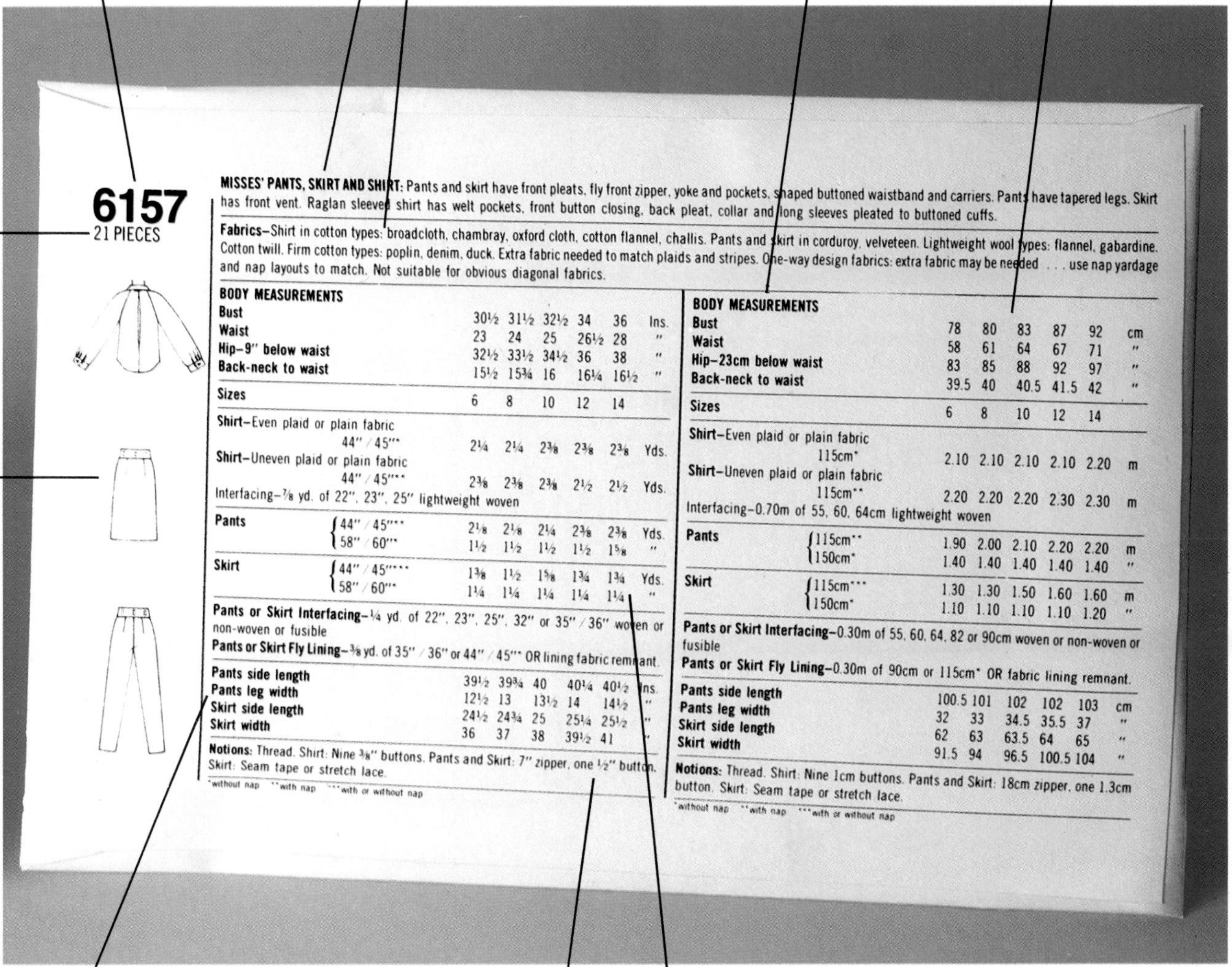

6157
21 PIECES

MISSES' PANTS, SKIRT AND SHIRT: Pants and skirt have front pleats, fly front zipper, yoke and pockets, shaped buttoned waistband and carriers. Pants have tapered legs. Skirt has front vent. Raglan sleeved shirt has welt pockets, front button closing, back pleat, collar and long sleeves pleated to buttoned cuffs.

Fabrics—Shirt in cotton types: broadcloth, chambray, oxford cloth, cotton flannel, challis. Pants and skirt in corduroy, velveteen. Lightweight wool types: flannel, gabardine. Cotton twill. Firm cotton types: poplin, denim, duck. Extra fabric needed to match plaids and stripes. One-way design fabrics: extra fabric may be needed . . . use nap yardage and nap layouts to match. Not suitable for obvious diagonal fabrics.

BODY MEASUREMENTS

Bust	30½	31½	32½	34	36	Ins.
Waist	23	24	25	26½	28	"
Hip–9" below waist	32½	33½	34½	36	38	"
Back-neck to waist	15½	15¾	16	16¼	16½	"
Sizes	6	8	10	12	14	
Shirt—Even plaid or plain fabric						
44" / 45""	2¼	2¼	2⅜	2⅜	2⅜	Yds.
Shirt—Uneven plaid or plain fabric						
44" / 45""	2⅜	2⅜	2⅜	2½	2½	Yds.
Interfacing—⅞ yd. of 22", 23", 25" lightweight woven						
Pants { 44" / 45"""	2⅛	2⅛	2¼	2⅜	2⅜	Yds.
{ 58" / 60"""	1½	1½	1½	1½	1⅝	"
Skirt { 44" / 45"""""	1⅜	1½	1⅝	1¾	1¾	Yds.
{ 58" / 60"""	1¼	1¼	1¼	1¼	1¼	"

Pants or Skirt Interfacing—¼ yd. of 22", 23", 25", 32" or 35" / 36" woven or non-woven or fusible
Pants or Skirt Fly Lining—⅜ yd. of 35" / 36" or 44" / 45"" OR lining fabric remnant.

Pants side length	39½	39¾	40	40¼	40½	Ins.
Pants leg width	12½	13	13½	14	14½	"
Skirt side length	24½	24¾	25	25¼	25½	"
Skirt width	36	37	38	39½	41	"

Notions: Thread. Shirt: Nine ⅜" buttons. Pants and Skirt: 7" zipper, one ½" button. Skirt: Seam tape or stretch lace.

*without nap **with nap ***with or without nap

BODY MEASUREMENTS

Bust	78	80	83	87	92	cm
Waist	58	61	64	67	71	"
Hip–23cm below waist	83	85	88	92	97	"
Back-neck to waist	39.5	40	40.5	41.5	42	"
Sizes	6	8	10	12	14	
Shirt—Even plaid or plain fabric						
115cm*	2.10	2.10	2.10	2.10	2.20	m
Shirt—Uneven plaid or plain fabric						
115cm**	2.20	2.20	2.20	2.30	2.30	m
Interfacing—0.70m of 55, 60, 64cm lightweight woven						
Pants { 115cm**	1.90	2.00	2.10	2.20	2.20	m
{ 150cm*	1.40	1.40	1.40	1.40	1.40	"
Skirt { 115cm***	1.30	1.30	1.50	1.60	1.60	m
{ 150cm*	1.10	1.10	1.10	1.10	1.20	"

Pants or Skirt Interfacing—0.30m of 55, 60, 64, 82 or 90cm woven or non-woven or fusible
Pants or Skirt Fly Lining—0.30m of 90cm or 115cm* OR fabric lining remnant.

Pants side length	100.5	101	102	102	103	cm
Pants leg width	32	33	34.5	35.5	37	"
Skirt side length	62	63	63.5	64	65	"
Skirt width	91.5	94	96.5	100.5	104	"

Notions: Thread. Shirt: Nine 1cm buttons. Pants and Skirt: 18cm zipper, one 1.3cm button. Skirt: Seam tape or stretch lace.

*without nap **with nap ***with or without nap

Finished garment measurements indicate finished length and width. You may need to make length adjustments. The "width at lower edge" is the measurement at the hemmed edge, indicating the fullness of the garment.

Notions, such as thread, zipper, buttons and seam binding, which are required for garment construction are listed. Purchase them at the same time as the fabric to ensure a good color match.

Yardage block tells you how much fabric to buy for the size and garment view you have selected. Yardage for lining, interfacing and trims is also listed. To determine how much fabric you need, match the garment or view and the fabric width at the left with your size at the top of the chart. The number where the two columns meet is the number of yards to buy. The most common fabric widths are given. If the width of your fabric is not given, check the conversion chart at the back of the pattern catalog. Some patterns list the extra yardage required for napped fabrics or uneven plaids.

Inside the Pattern

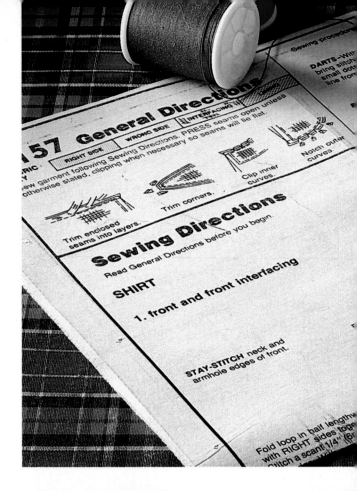

Open the pattern envelope to find the printed pattern pieces and the direction sheet which guides you, step-by-step, through the construction of the garment. Read through the direction sheet *before* cutting or sewing. Use it to plan and organize your sewing time, and alert you to the techniques you need to know as you progress.

Views of a single garment are labeled by number or letter. Patterns which include several different garments such as a skirt, jacket and pants (called *wardrobe patterns*) usually feature only one version of each. In this case, each garment is identified by name only. All pattern pieces are identified with a number and name, such as *skirt front*.

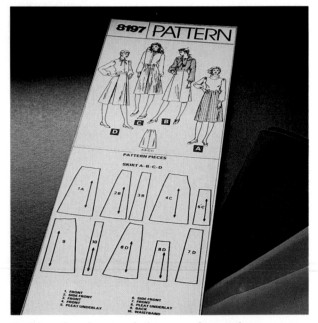

Fashion drawings and views are featured prominently on the direction sheet, sketched as they appear on the front of the envelope or as detailed line drawings. Some patterns illustrate each garment separately with the pattern pieces used in its construction. Most patterns illustrate all the pattern pieces together, with a key to identify the pieces used for each garment or view.

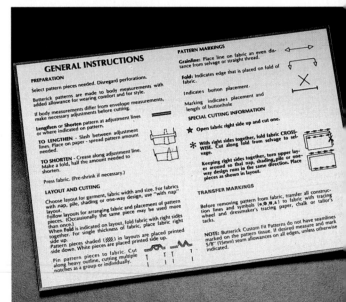

General instructions are given as a short refresher sewing course. These instructions may have a different name on each company's pattern, but they generally contain tips on how to use the pattern. Included is information on pattern and fabric preparation; explanation of pattern markings; cutting, layout and marking tips; and a short glossary of sewing terms. The easy-to-sew and beginner patterns often incorporate these tips into the step-by-step instructions.

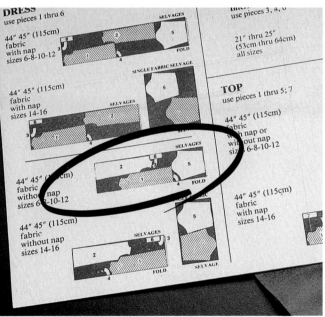

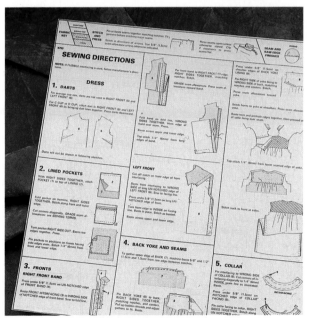

Cutting layouts are shown for each garment view. They differ according to the width of the fabric, pattern size and whether the fabric is with or without nap. Layouts for interfacing and lining are also included. When the fabric is to be cut in a single thickness or on the crosswise grain, the pattern layout indicates this with a symbol, explained in the general instructions. A pattern piece, right side up, is illustrated without shading; wrong side up, it is shaded or scored. Circle the layout for the correct pattern size, fabric width and view.

Sewing directions are a step-by-step guide to constructing the garment, arranged by views. Beside each instruction is a sketch illustrating the sewing technique. The right side of the fabric usually appears shaded; the wrong side, plain. Interfacing is indicated with dots. Together, the sketch and the directions give you a clear picture of exactly what to do. Remember that these are only general directions. An alternative technique may be more effective for the fabric you are using.

Fabric Essentials

All fabrics are based on two kinds of fibers: *natural* or *man-made*. Natural fibers are those derived from plants or animals: cotton, wool, silk and linen. Man-made fibers are produced by chemical processes. They include polyester, nylon, acetate, spandex and many others.

Combining natural and man-made fibers produces *blends* which give you the best qualities of several fibers. For example, the strength of nylon may be added to the warmth of wool, the easy care of polyester to the comfort of cotton.

There is an almost endless variety of blends available, and each one behaves differently. Check the fiber content on the bolt end for the kinds and quantities of fibers used. Care instructions are also listed. Examine the *hand* of the fabric — how it feels, how it drapes, whether it crushes easily or ravels, whether it stretches. Drape the fabric over your hand or arm to determine if it is as soft or crisp, heavy or light, as you need for a particular project.

Fabrics are also classified by *fabrication,* meaning how they are made. All fabrics are either *woven, knit* or *nonwoven.* The most common woven is the plain weave construction. This is found in fabrics like muslins, poplin and taffeta. Denim and gabardine are diagonal weaves. Cotton sateen is a satin weave. Knits also have several classifications. Jersey is an example of a plain knit. Sweater knits can be made by the purl, patterned or raschel knit processes. Felt is an example of a nonwoven fabric.

Selecting the right fabric for your sewing project takes a little practice. Refer to the back of the pattern envelope for suggestions, and learn to feel the hand of fabric. Quality fabric doesn't have to be expensive. Choose well-made fabric that will wear well and stay looking good.

Easy-to-Sew Fabrics

Poplin   Cotton broadcloth   Shirtings   Linen-likes   Firm knits   Firm wool   Denim

There are many fabrics that are easy and quick to sew. These fabrics are generally plain weave or firm knit, of medium weight. Most do not require complicated seam finishes or special handling, since they ravel little or not at all.

Small prints, overall prints and narrow stripes are easy to sew because they do not require matching at the seams. Prints, especially if they are dark, can hide stitching imperfections.

Plain weave fabrics like poplin or cotton broadcloth are always good choices. Stable or moderate-stretch knits do not need seam finishing, and their stretchability makes fitting easier. Natural fiber fabrics, such as cottons and lightweight wools, are easy to sew because stitching easily blends into these fabrics.

For more examples of easy-to-sew fabrics, consult the suggested fabrics that are listed on the backs of easy-to-sew patterns.

Handling Special Fabrics

Certain fabrics, because of their design or fabrication, need special attention during layout and construction. Some easy-to-sew fabrics fall into this category. The special handling required is usually not difficult. Often you need only add one more step, such as a seam finish, or exercise a little more care.

1) Napped and pile fabrics like velvet, velveteen, velour, flannel, and corduroy require special care in cutting out. These fabrics appear light and shiny when brushed in one lengthwise direction, and dark when brushed in the other direction. To prevent your garment from having a two-toned look, you must follow the "with nap" layouts on the pattern instruction sheet. Decide which way you want the nap to lie, and cut all pattern pieces with the top edges facing the same direction.

Although satin and moiré taffeta are not napped fabrics, their shiny surfaces reflect light differently in each lengthwise direction. Decide which effect you prefer, and use a one-way layout.

2) Sheer fabrics look best with special seams and seam finishes. Unfinished seam allowances detract from the fragile, see-through look of voile, batiste, eyelet, or chiffon. French seams are a classic choice, but other seam finishes can also be used.

3) Twill weave fabrics like denim and gabardine have diagonal ridges. If these ridges are very noticeable, use a "with nap" layout for cutting, and avoid patterns that are not suitable for obvious diagonals. Denim ravels easily and requires enclosed seams.

4) Plaids and stripes require special care in layout and cutting (pages 82 to 84). To match plaids and large stripes at seams, you need to buy extra fabric. Buy ¼ to ½ yard (.25 to .50 m) more than the pattern calls for, depending on the size of the design.

5) Knits must be handled gently during construction to keep them from stretching out of shape. Special stitches and seam finishes (page 116) are needed to maintain the right amount of stretch.

6) One-way design fabrics, such as some flower and paisley prints, require a "with nap" cutting layout so the design does not go up one side of the garment and down the other. Border prints are cut on the crosswise rather than lengthwise grain of the fabric. They usually require more yardage. Select patterns which show a border print view and specify the correct yardage.

Guide to Fabrics and Sewing Techniques

Type	Fabric	Plain Seam or Edge Finish	Seam	Machine Needle Size	Thread Type & Weight
Sheer to lightweight	Gauze, voile, chiffon, organza, crepe de chine, fine lace, tulle, net, georgette	Stitched and pinked, zigzag	French, mock French, self-bound, double-stitched	9/65	Extra fine: silk, mercerized cotton, or cotton/polyester
Lightweight	Silk, shirtings, gingham, broadcloth, oxford cloth, calico, lightweight linens, chambray, seersucker, tricot, eyelet, challis, organdy, muslin, batiste, dimity, lawn, piqué	Stitched and pinked, zigzag, selvage	French, mock French, self-bound	11/75	Extra fine: silk or mercerized cotton; all-purpose: cotton/polyester
Light to mediumweight knits	Cotton knits, tricot, cotton/polyester knits, jersey knits, light sweater knits, stretch terry, stretch velour	Zigzag, straight with overedge	Double-stitched, straight and zigzag, narrow zigzag, straight stretch, elastic stretch	14/90 Ballpoint	All-purpose: cotton/polyester or long-fiber polyester
Mediumweight	Cotton, wool, wool flannel, rayon, linen and linen types, chintz, wool crepe, gabardine, chino, poplin, denim, corduroy, velvet, velveteen, velour, taffeta, satin, double knits, sweatshirt knits	Stitched and pinked, zigzag, selvage, turned and stitched, bound finishes	Welt, lapped, flat-fell, mock flat-fell	14/90 (Ballpoint for knits)	All-purpose: cotton/polyester, long-fiber polyester or mercerized cotton
Mediumweight/suiting weight	Wool, wool blends, tweeds, flannels, gabardine, twill, mohair, boucle, heavy poplin, heavy denim, double knits, quilted fabric	Stitched and pinked, zigzag, selvage, bound finishes	Welt, lapped, flat-fell, mock flat-fell	14/90 16/100	All-purpose: cotton/polyester or mercerized cotton
Medium to heavyweight	Wool, wool blends, heavy wool flannel, fake fur, fleece, canvas, heavy cotton duck, coating, sailcloth, upholstery fabric	Stitched and pinked, selvage	Welt, lapped, mock flat-fell	16/100 18/110	Heavy-duty: cotton or cotton/polyester; topstitching and buttonhole twist
No grain (nonwoven)	Leather, suede, reptile (natural and man-made), buckskin, calfskin, plastic, felt		Welt, lapped, mock flat-fell	14/90 16/100 Wedge-point	All-purpose or heavy-duty (all types)

Sheer & Silky Fabrics

Sheer fabrics can have a soft or crisp hand; crisp sheers are easier to cut and sew. Soft sheers are batiste (1), chiffon (2), China silk (3), and georgette (4). Crisp sheers include fabrics such as organza (5), voile (6), and organdy (7).

The major consideration with sheer fabrics is their transparent quality. The stitches on the inside of a sheer garment show from the outside. Whether revealed clearly or as mere shadows, details such as seams, facings, and hems must be neat and narrow to look well made.

Silky fabrics are made from natural silk fibers or synthetic fibers that look like silk, such as polyester, nylon, rayon, and acetate. The polyester types are popular because they are less costly than silk fabrics. Most synthetic silk-like fabrics do not shrink or fade, and can be washed and dried by machine. This group of fabrics includes charmeuse (8), crepe de chine (9), lightweight jacquard weaves (10), lightweight satin-backed crepe (11), and tissue faille (12).

Even when silk and synthetic silk-like fabrics do not have the see-through character of sheers, they do have similar fine weaves and light weights. Inner construction can show as ridges on the outside of silky garments. That is why many of the same sewing supplies and techniques are suggested for both kinds of fabrics. An additional consideration with silk-like fabrics is their smooth, slick texture, which makes them slippery to handle. You will need to take special steps when laying out and cutting the pattern pieces to control these fabrics.

Guide to Sewing Sheer and Silky Fabrics

Equipment & Techniques	Soft Sheers Batiste, chiffon, China silk, georgette **Crisp Sheers** Organdy, organza, voile	Lightweight Silkies Charmeuse, crepe de chine, jacquard weaves, satin-backed crepe, tissue faille
Machine Needles	Size 8 (60), 9 (65), or 11 (75)	Size 8 (60), 9 (65), or 11 (75)
Stitch Length	12 to 16 per inch (2.5 cm)	12 to 16 per inch (2.5 cm)
Millimeter Stitch Setting	2.5 to 2	2.5 to 2
Thread	Extra-fine long staple polyester; silk or mercerized cotton. These threads are often sold as notions for lingerie, machine embroidery, or quilting. Use finest thread possible.	
Hand Needles	Betweens, sizes 8 to 12	Betweens, sizes 8 to 12
Interfacings	Sheer nonwoven fusible or sew-in, self-fabric, organza	Fusible tricot, sheer nonwoven fusible or sew-in, batiste, self-fabric, lining fabric, organza, organdy
Special Seams	French, hairline, overlocked, double-stitched	French, overlocked, double-stitched
Special Hems	Overlocked, rolled overlocked, hand-rolled, tricot-bound, hairline, narrow topstitched	

Lustrous Fabrics

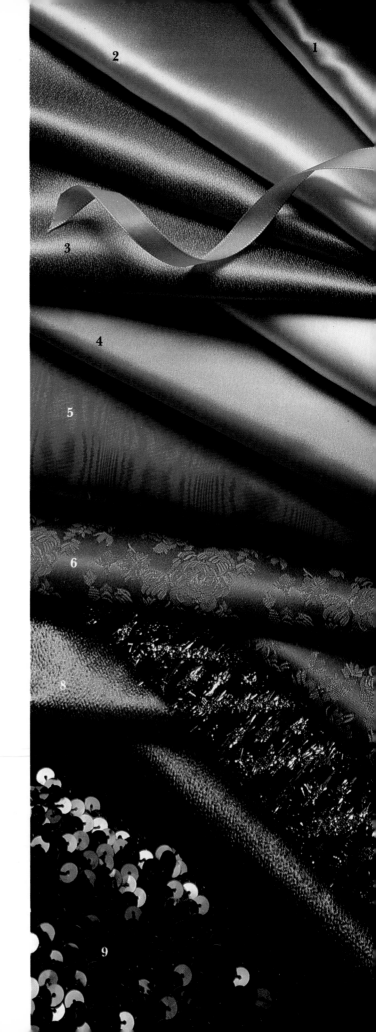

The lustrous surface of special occasion fabrics can come from the weave of the fabric, as is true for satin, or from fibers with sheen, such as silk and acetate. Special finishes also create surface luster, or metallic yarns or sequins can be added to give an ordinary fabric glamorous sparkle.

1) Satin is a weave that produces a shiny surface texture from floating yarns. The combination of fibers such as silk, rayon, or polyester with the distinctive weave makes the fabric likely to water-spot; protect the fabric with a press cloth, and use a dry iron when pressing. Use superfine pins to avoid snagging surface yarns.

2) Crepe-backed satin is also called satin-backed crepe because the fabric is reversible; one face has the matte, pebbly texture of crepe, and the other face has the smooth, shiny texture of satin. One side may be used as a binding or trim for the other.

3) Satin peau is a satin with a firm twill weave on the right side. Some peaus are double faced, with fine crosswise ribs on both sides. Because pins and ripped-out stitches can leave marks, pin only in seam allowance; test-fit to avoid ripping stitches.

4) Taffeta has a crisp hand and drapes stiffly. Test sewing techniques on scraps, because pins and ripped-out stitches can leave marks. When the fiber content includes acetate, steam can leave spots.

5) Moiré taffeta is passed between heated rollers to give it a watermarked surface texture.

6) Brocade comes in all weights, from light to heavy, and has raised tapestry-style motifs. The motifs should be balanced on major garment sections and matched at prominent seams. Most brocades are woven, but some are knit. Careful pressing on a padded surface preserves the surface texture. When brocades have shiny metallic threads, set the iron at a low temperature for pressing. To make metallic brocades more comfortable, underline with batiste.

7) Metallic fabrics have metallic yarns woven or knit into them. Most metallics are sensitive to heat and discolor when steam is used. Finger press seams with a thimble or blunt end of a point turner; or use a cool, dry iron.

8) Lamé is a smooth, shiny metallic fabric, either knit or woven. Knit metallics drape and ease better than the wovens. Besides traditional gold, silver, and copper tones, lamé is available in iridescent colors.

9) Sequined fabrics have a knit or sheer woven base. A simple pattern style is especially important for these fabrics. Or use sequined fabric for only a part of the garment, such as the bodice.

Techniques for Lustrous Fabrics

Many fabrics fit into the lustrous category, and some have unique sewing requirements. However, all of these fabrics are alike in two ways: A "with nap" pattern layout is used for uniform color shading in the finished garment, and the less handling, the better. Keep handling to a minimum by choosing patterns in simple styles with few seams and darts. Avoid buttoned closings and details such as shaped collars and welt pockets. Use a simple pinked finish on plain seams, or treat raw edges with liquid fray preventer instead of using elaborate dressmaker techniques. Take special care when pressing, using a light touch and covering the pressing surface with a scrap of self-fabric so nap faces nap. To prevent ridges when pressing seams, press over a seam roll or place strips of heavy brown paper between seam allowance and garment.

Guide to Sewing Lustrous Fabrics

Equipment & Techniques	Mediumweight Crepe-backed satin, lamé, satin, satin peau, silk, taffeta, moiré	Heavily Textured Brocade, sequined fabrics
Machine Needles	Size 11 (75)	Size 14 (90) or 16 (100)
Stitch Length	8 to 12 per inch (2.5 cm)	8 to 12 per inch (2.5 cm)
Millimeter Stitch Setting	3.5 to 2.5	3.5 to 2.5
Thread	All-purpose cotton or cotton/polyester, silk for silk fabrics	All-purpose cotton or cotton/polyester
Hand Needles	Betweens, size 7 or 8	Betweens, size 7 or 8
Interfacings	Sew-in nonwoven or woven	Sew-in nonwoven or woven
Special Seams	Plain seam: pinked, overedge, three-step zigzag, or liquid fray preventer finish	Plain seam or lined to edge
Special Hems	Catchstitched, topstitched, horsehair braid, faced	Faced

Tips for Handling Lustrous Fabrics

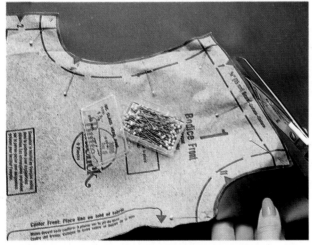

Layout. Pin only in seam allowances to prevent pin marks. Use extra-fine silk pins for finely woven fabrics such as satin and taffeta. Shears must be sharp or strokes will chew raw edges of fabric. Cut directionally for smoothest edges. Always use "with nap" layout for fabrics with luster.

Seams. Use plain seams with a simple edge finish. Raw edges can be pinked, overlocked, or finished with three-step zigzag. If fabric frays easily, apply thin coat of liquid fray preventer to raw edges. Slip envelopes between seam allowances and garment to protect garment from stray drops.

Knits

A knit is a fabric made from interlocking looped stitches. Because of this construction, knits shed wrinkles well, are comfortable to wear, and are easy to sew because they do not ravel. There are many kinds of knits, and most of those available for sewing can be grouped into five general categories.

Firm, stable knits do not stretch significantly and are handled similarly to woven fabrics. In this group are double knits (**1**), which have fine lengthwise ribs on both sides. It is difficult to tell the right and wrong side of a double knit unless the right side has a decorative design. Raschel knit (**2**) is a lacy or open knit texture that does not stretch because lengthwise threads are locked into some of the knitted loops. Some raschel knits are made from bulky yarns and look like bouclé wovens or hand knits. Others are made from finer yarns and look crocheted.

Lightweight single knits have fine ribs running lengthwise on the right side and loops running crosswise on the wrong side. Pull the crosswise edge of a single knit and it will roll to the right side. Single knits such as jersey (**3**), tricot (**4**), and interlock (**5**) do not stretch lengthwise, but they do have crosswise give.

Textured knits may be single or double knits. This category is distinguished by a surface texture, usually on the right side. Knitted terry (**6**) and velour (**7**) are pile knits that look like their woven namesakes; however, they usually have a great deal of crosswise stretch. Also in the category of textured knits are sweater knits (**8**). Patterned sweater knits have floats on the wrong side where colored yarns are carried from one motif to another. This limits their crosswise stretch. Comfortable sweatshirt fleece (**9**) looks like a single knit on the right side; the wrong side has a soft, brushed surface. It is usually fairly stable with little stretch in either direction.

Two-way stretch knits have a great degree of stretch crosswise and lengthwise and a high percentage of resilient spandex fibers. Absorbent cotton/spandex and cotton/polyester/spandex knits (**10**) are favored for active sportswear such as leotards, body suits, and aerobic exercise outfits. Strong nylon/spandex knits (**11**) are resilient, even when wet, and are usually selected for swimwear.

Ribbing is a very stretchy knit that can be used for tops and for finishing knit garments at wrists, ankles, neck, and waist. One type is tubular ribbing (**12**), which is sold by the inch (2.5 cm) and must be cut open along one lengthwise rib for sewing. Another type is rib trim (**13**), which is color coordinated with sweater knits; one edge is prefinished, and the other is sewn to the garment.

Techniques for Knits

Patterns for knits depend on the stretch characteristics and weight of the knit. The list of suggested fabrics on the back of a pattern envelope usually includes a combination of knit and woven fabrics. If a knit is soft and lightweight, such as jersey, it is suitable for patterns that have gathers, draping, and similar features. If it is firm, such as double knit, a pattern with tailoring or a shaped, fitted silhouette is suitable. If it is bulky or textured, such as a sweater knit, a pattern with few seams and details works best to show off the knit texture.

Certain patterns, however, require knits that stretch. These are closely fitted pattern styles, such as swimsuits and leotards, which would be too small to wear if made from a fabric without elasticity, or tops and pants that use the knit for a comfortable close-to-the-body fit. Most patterns designed for knits have a stretch gauge printed on the back of the envelope. Test the knit that you have selected against the ruler gauge. When the pattern specifies "two-way stretch knit," test the crosswise and lengthwise stretchability of the knit.

Patterns designed for knits often have ¼" (6 mm) seam allowances. If the pattern you have selected has ⅝" (1.5 cm) seam allowances, trim them to ¼" (6 mm) when using knit sewing techniques.

Fabric Preparation

For best results, preshrink knits. Wash and dry them if they will be washed as part of their routine care. Use a bulk drycleaner if the finished garment will be drycleaned. It is not necessary to preshrink ribbing unless using a dark-colored ribbing on a light-colored garment.

If, after preshrinking, a knit still has a crease where it was folded on the bolt, steam the crease. If the crease cannot be removed by steaming, it is permanent. Refold the knit for pattern layout to prevent the crease from showing on the garment.

To straighten the ends of knits, draw a chalk line across the cut crosswise edges at right angles to the ribs. Cut the fabric on the chalk line.

How to Use a Stretch Knit Gauge

Correct knit for pattern stretches easily to right-hand side of the gauge printed on pattern envelope. To test, fold crosswise edge of knit over 3" to 4" (7.5 to 10 cm), and test fold against gauge. Knit that stretches even more than gauge requirements may still be used for pattern.

Wrong knit for pattern is forced beyond reasonable limits to satisfy gauge printed on pattern envelope. Ribs of knit are distorted, and stretched edge folds over on itself because of too much stress on fabric. Knit does not have enough natural elasticity for this pattern style.

Pressing

Press knits on the lengthwise ribs by lifting and lowering the iron. Use a low iron temperature setting, and raise the temperature as needed. Do not press across the ribs or handle the fabric until it is completely cooled. Either action can stretch knits out of shape.

Block sweater knits instead of pressing. To block, pat the fabric or the garment into shape on a flat surface. Steam with a hand steamer, or hold a steam iron above the knit surface. Allow the fabric to dry and cool completely before further handling.

Pattern Layout

Always use a "with nap" pattern layout on knits. Because of knit construction, they have a directional quality that shows up as a difference in color shading in the completed garment.

Stretch both crosswise edges of a knit before pattern layout to see if the knit runs. If so, the runs will occur more readily along one edge than the other. Position the run-prone edge at the garment hemline during pattern layout. The hem is subject to less stress, so the knit will be less likely to run after the garment is sewn.

When laying out and cutting a knit fabric, do not allow it to hang off the work surface. The weight of the fabric can distort the portion on the work surface, pulling it off-grain.

On bulky or textured knits, it is easier to lay out the pattern on a single layer of fabric. Position the textured side down; pin and mark on the smoother, wrong side of the knit. Use weights instead of pins on knits with open or lacy textures.

Interfacings

Interface knits to stabilize details, such as buttonholes, plackets, and patch pockets, and to support shaped areas such as collars. Select a supple interfacing that does not change the character of the knit. Two types of interfacings especially suitable for knits are fusible tricot and stretch nonwoven.

Tips for Interfacing Knits

Fusible tricot interfacing adds support and body to fashion knits without adding stiffness. It also allows for some crosswise stretch. Use tricot to stabilize detail areas such as cuffs, pockets, and plackets.

Stretch nonwoven interfacing stabilizes knit lengthwise but allows knit to stretch crosswise. Use this interfacing for flexible shaping in collars, necklines, facings, tabs, and zipper openings.

Classic Fabrics

Whether or not you have had much sewing experience, this group of fabrics probably looks familiar because it includes fabrics that are always in fashion. Some require out-of-the-ordinary sewing techniques, and some need special handling because they have unique surface textures. Others rate extra attention because they have woven, knitted, or printed designs that affect pattern layout.

1) Loose weaves have coarse or uneven textures and tend to fray. The primary sewing challenge with loosely woven fabrics is to control raveling.

2) Plaids require careful pattern layout. Study the fabric before pattern layout to decide which bars are dominant, where to position them on the pattern pieces, and whether the design has a one-way direction. Arrange the pattern pieces so the fabric design matches at the most noticeable seams. Careful pinning or basting ensures against mismatches.

3) Stripes require handling similar to that of plaids. Careful layout and basting is necessary to match stripes attractively.

4) Large prints are among the most dramatic types of fabric designs. Print repeats can be as large as 24" (61 cm). With prints this size, position the print motifs for pleasing balance.

5) Diagonal fabrics are woven, knitted, or printed designs that cross the straight fabric grain on a slant. To sew diagonals, it is necessary to adapt patterns for special layouts so the diagonal lines flow around the body in the same direction.

6) Gabardine is a firmly woven fabric with a twill weave, usually of wool or polyester. Characteristic of this weave are the fine diagonal ribs on the right side. The surface is hard and long wearing, but easily damaged during sewing unless special pressing techniques are used. This texture needs a "with nap" pattern layout for uniform color shading in the completed garment.

7) Velvet is similar to velveteen because the pile covers the entire surface, but it is made a different way. A velvet pile is formed from warp (lengthwise) yarns woven into the base. This creates a deep, straight, erect pile that does not show as great a difference in color shading as does velveteen. Velvet is handled the same way as corduroy and velveteen.

8) Velveteen is made by shearing pile loops, but unlike corduroy, the loops cover the entire surface. Velveteen requires techniques for layout, stitching, and pressing similar to those for corduroy.

9) Corduroy has a ribbed pile, formed by sheared rows of loops or ribs that contrast with the flat base of the fabric. Use a "with nap" layout and sewing techniques that keep the fabric from shifting while it is being stitched. Special pressing techniques are also necessary.

Loose Weaves

Loosely woven fabrics are frequently made from unusual yarns, which are thick and lightly spun to preserve natural irregularities and create a hand-loomed look. Two sewing considerations are to control the raveling and to maintain the soft, loose hand of the fabric.

The loosely woven basketweave (**1**) has two or more yarns woven together in a basket effect. Heavy raw silk (**2**) is ravel-prone because of the thick and thin crosswise yarns. Gauze fabrics (**3**), lightweight and crinkly, should be handled with sewing techniques for sheer fabrics. The homespun look (**4**) is achieved with lightly spun yarns that ravel easily. A pulled thread look (**5**) creates a novelty windowpane effect.

Pattern Selection

Choose a pattern that has the potential for omitting linings, facings, and interfacings, as well as closures such as buttons and zippers. Many jacket, blouse, and skirt patterns, especially pullover or wrap styles, can be adapted this way. The less stable the fabric, the more loosely fitted the pattern selected should be, but in most cases simple styles are the best. The stability of loosely woven fabrics varies. Test the stability by draping the fabric over your hand and letting a length hang freely. See how much it stretches and whether it drapes softly. Gently tug on the true bias grain to get a feeling for the amount the fabric gives in this direction.

Fabric Preparation

Preshrink all loose weaves, using the care method planned for the finished garment. To prevent excessive raveling, zigzag crosswise cut ends or bind them with sheer bias tricot binding before washing. To wash, treat loose weaves like delicate fabrics. Air dry to prevent shrinkage from the heat of a dryer. Roll the fabric in towels to remove excess moisture. Spread on a flat surface, and straighten the grain.

Layout, Cutting & Marking

Because the individual yarns of the fabric stand out, it is important to arrange the fabric straight and on-grain for pattern layout. Any wavy grainlines will show clearly on the finished garment. When the fabric texture comes from nubby, irregular yarns, use a "with nap" layout so the texture in all the garment sections looks the same. Space pins closely to anchor the pattern pieces securely to the fabric.

If you are working with a fabric that frays readily, cut out the pattern with 1" (2.5 cm) seam allowances. Wider seam allowances are easier to handle for special seam and edge finishes, and they provide ample fabric for clean cuts on raw edges that must be trimmed. Transfer pattern markings with marking pen or thread basting.

Special Seam Techniques

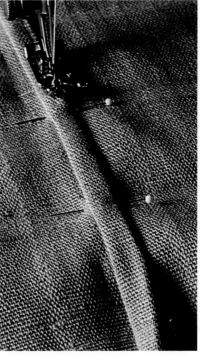

Plain seam with raw edges enclosed in sheer tricot bias binding is quick, neat treatment. Use zigzag, 3-step zigzag, or long straight stitches, 10 to 12 per inch (2.5 cm).

Flat-fell seam, formed on right side of garment, makes reversible seam which is ideal for roll-up sleeves or other areas showing both faces of seams.

Overlocked seam, sewn on 4-thread overlock machine or 3-thread machine with a row of straight stitches, covers raw edges with thread.

Special Hem Techniques

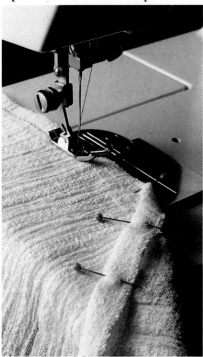

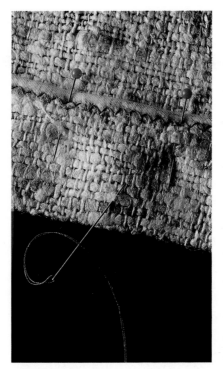

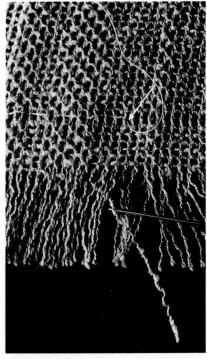

Topstitch to stabilize hem edges. This method is fast and attractive. Finish raw edge before hemming; use a zigzag stitch or a 2-thread or 3-thread overlock stitch.

Bind edge with sheer tricot bias binding. Hand hem with blind catchstitch or blind hem, worked loosely between garment and hem.

Fringe edge. Pull a thread at desired depth of fringe. Stitch on thread-pulled line (arrow); then one by one remove fabric yarns below stitching.

Synthetic Fur, Suede & Leather

Synthetic fur has a deep pile texture on the right side, which can imitate the coloring and texture of natural pelts, such as mink **(1)**, seal **(2)**, fox **(3)**, or sheepskin **(4)**. Or a synthetic fur fabric can have a novelty texture **(5)** that looks man-made. Synthetic furs are usually made from modacrylic or polyester fibers and can be washed and dried by machine. Most have a knitted backing.

Synthetic suede is a nonwoven, softly napped polyester/polyurethane fabric that closely resembles genuine sueded leather. Unlike real leather, it is an easy-care fabric that can be washed and dried by machine. The main difference between synthetic suedes is weight. Lightweight synthetic suedes **(6)** drape softly and do not require special patterns. Mediumweight types **(7)** are more like real suede.

With conventional sewing methods, you may need to take extra finishing steps, such as fusing the seam allowances and topstitching the edges because suedes are difficult to press flat with conventional pressing techniques. Or you can use flat construction techniques, such as lapped seams and faced hems. Besides solid colors, the synthetic suedes can be embossed **(8)** or printed **(9)** to add textural interest.

Synthetic leather/vinyl fabrics can be smooth **(10)** or textured **(11)**. Like suedes, vinyls have different weights. Lightweight, supple vinyls have a knitted or woven backing. When handling vinyls, use many of the same methods used for synthetic suedes, except vinyls are damaged by heat and steam so they cannot be pressed.

Guide to Sewing Synthetic Fur, Suede and Leather

Equipment & Techniques	Synthetic Fur	Synthetic Suede	Synthetic Leather/Vinyl
Machine Needles	Size 14 (90) or 16 (100)	Size 11 (75); 16 (100) for topstitching/buttonhole twist	Size 11 (75)
Stitch Length	10 to 12 per inch (2.5 cm)	8 to 10 per inch (2.5 cm)	8 to 10 per inch (2.5 cm)
Millimeter Stitch Setting	3 to 2.5	3.5 to 3	3.5 to 3
Thread	All-purpose polyester or polyester/cotton; topstitching/buttonhole twist or two strands of all-purpose for topstitching.		
Interfacings	Omit	Fusible	Sew-in
Special Seams	Butted	Lapped, topstitched, welt	Topstitched, welt
Special Hems	Faced or lined to the edge	Topstitched, faced, fused	Topstitched

The same kinds of garments furriers create from luxury pelts can be sewn from synthetic fur: coats, jackets, vests, and capes with simple seams and a loose fit. Synthetic fur can also be used for details on a garment, such as the collar or hood lining on a coat or jacket. Because synthetic furs are bulky, avoid details such as pleats, gathers, darts, and patch pockets. Replace buttonholes with alternative closures such as loops, snaps, or hooks and eyes.

Layout, Cutting & Marking

Simplify the pattern wherever possible. Lap the seamlines of the front facing and jacket front, for example, to cut the facing in one with the body of the garment. Omit interfacing pattern pieces; synthetic furs rarely need this extra strength and support. Cut inner garment sections, such as in-seam pockets or a back neckline facing, from coat lining fabric to reduce bulk. Undercollars can be cut from the fur fabric, lining, or synthetic suede.

For easier handling, trim off the extra tissue margins from the pattern pieces on the cutting lines if using a plain seam. Trim the pattern on the seamlines for butted seams (opposite).

Lay out the pattern on a single layer of fabric, backing side up, and use a "with nap" layout. If using fabric that looks like real fur, run the pile down toward the hem of the garment. For a natural look, balance and match color shadings on the major pattern pieces. Novelty furs can be cut with the nap running up, down, or across the garment.

Use long pins with large plastic heads to hold the pattern on the backing; long, quilting, or super pins work well. Cut through the backing only, using the tips of shears or a single-edged razor blade or blade cutting tool. Avoid cutting into the pile on the right side. Transfer pattern markings to the backing of cutout garment sections, using pins and chalk or marking pen.

Pressing

Rarely do synthetic furs need pressing; steam can be damaging to the pile. Usually you can smooth seams and garment edges into place with your fingers. A soft, rolled edge is more appropriate on these fabrics than a sharp crease. To renew flattened pile, tumble the garment in a clothes dryer.

Two Ways to Cut Synthetic Fur

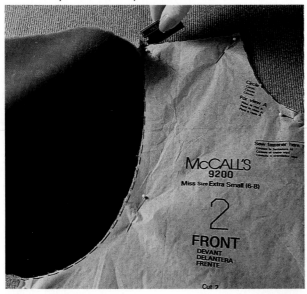

Single-edged razor blade makes clean, quick cuts without damaging pile on right side. Hobby knife can also be used to cut synthetic fur.

Shears can be used to cut synthetic fur, using tips to snip through backing alone. Shears must be sharp and close at tips for successful cutting.

Seams

Because synthetic furs are bulky, adjust your sewing machine pressure and tension for straight and zigzag sewing. Use fabric scraps to test the stitch, decreasing the pressure on the presser foot and loosening the needle tension until the stitch is balanced. For even feeding of the layers, smooth the pile away from the raw edges and stitch in the direction of the nap.

For long-haired synthetic furs with a knit backing, the butted seam is ideal. It resembles the seam used by furriers and joins garment sections with minimum bulk. Butted seams can be used throughout the garment, even on enclosed seams at collars and facings. For synthetic furs with shallow pile, you can use a plain seam. To reduce bulk, shear the pile from the seam allowances after stitching.

How to Sew a Butted Seam on Synthetic Fur

1) **Brush** pile away from raw edges to make them easier to handle when sewing. Pin seam with raw edges together. (Pattern pieces have been cut out on the seamline.)

2) **Stitch** with short, wide zigzag stitch. Position fabric so needle swings past cut edges on right-hand side. Or use 2-thread flatlock seam on the serger.

3) **Open out** both layers, and pull them gently apart until cut edges meet. Seam should lie flat with slight ridge along stitches.

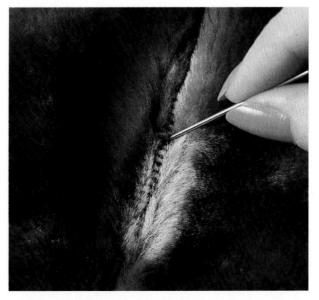

4) **Lift out** pile caught in seam, using T-pin or blunt tapestry needle and working from right side. Finished seam is barely visible.

Lace & Embroidered Fabrics

Laces look fragile and delicate but are actually easy to sew. True laces have a net or mesh background, which has no grainline and does not ravel. You can cut into the fabric freely for creative pattern layouts, seams need no time-consuming edge finishes, and hemming requires little more than trimming close to the edges of prominent motifs.

The openwork designs of lace fabrics have rich histories. Some laces still bear the names of the European localities where they were once made by hand from silk, cotton, or linen fibers. Today, many laces are made by machine from easy-care cotton blends, polyester, acrylic, or nylon.

1) Alençon lace has filled-in motifs outlined by soft satin cord on a sheer net background. One or both lengthwise edges usually have a finished border.

2) Chantilly lace has delicate floral motifs worked on a fine net background and outlined with silky threads. A popular bridal fabric, Chantilly lace usually has an allover pattern.

3) Eyelet is a finely woven cotton or polyester/cotton fabric embroidered with a satin-stitched openwork design. Even though eyelet embroideries are not true laces, they require pattern layout and pressing techniques similar to those for laces.

4) Peau d'ange is a form of Chantilly lace made with a flossy yarn to give it a soft texture.

5) Venice lace is made from heavy yarns and unique stitches that give it a three-dimensional texture. Picot bridges join the motifs. Venice lace does not have the net background that is typical of most laces.

6) Point d'esprit has an open net or fine tulle background with a pattern of embroidered dots.

7) Cluny lace is made from heavy cotton-like yarns and looks hand-crocheted. It usually has paddle or wheel motifs and may have raised knots as part of the design.

8) Schiffli is an embroidered sheer or semi-sheer fabric decorated on a Schiffli machine, which imitates hand embroidery stitches.

Guide to Sewing Laces

Equipment & Techniques	Delicate Chantilly, peau d'ange, point d'esprit	Embroidered Eyelet, Schiffli	Textured Alençon, Cluny, Venice
Machine Needles	Size 8 (60) or 9 (65)	Size 9 (65) or 11 (75)	Size 11 (75)
Stitch Length	12 to 16 per inch (2.5 cm)	10 to 12 per inch (2.5 cm)	10 to 12 per inch (2.5 cm)
Millimeter Stitch Setting	2.5 to 2	3 to 2.5	3 to 2.5
Thread	Extra-fine	All-purpose	All-purpose
Hand Needles	Betweens, size 7 or 8	Betweens, size 7 or 8	Betweens, size 7 or 8
Interfacings	Omit	Omit	Omit
Special Seams	Lapped, overlocked, double-stitched	Overlocked, double-stitched	Lapped, double-stitched
Special Hems	Self-hem, appliquéd	Self-hem	Self-hem, appliquéd, horsehair braid

Select a pattern that suits the texture and weight of the lace fabric. Use heavy laces such as Alençon and Cluny for simple, fitted pattern silhouettes. Select lightweight laces, such as Chantilly, for patterns with full skirts and sleeves, and details such as ruffles.

Patterns for bridal and evening gowns that are illustrated in lace fabrics may require specific forms of lace, such as edgings of specific widths or a wide allover lace. Check the back of the pattern envelope to see if the lace fits the pattern requirements.

When considering a pattern that is not illustrated in laces, select a pattern with sections sized to fit the fabric width. If planning to use a bordered lace on sleeves, you may have to use a short-sleeved pattern if the lace is not wide enough for long sleeves, or place the lace at the lower edge of an organza sleeve. Facings, hems, and pockets are usually eliminated so you may need less fabric. Because lace has no grainline, it is possible to turn the pattern pieces to use an edge or border as a finished edge.

Fabric Preparation

Lace rarely requires any preparation for sewing. Most laces must be drycleaned. Although shrinkage is rare, if the care label on a lace fabric indicates it is washable, and you are combining it with other fabrics and trims to make a washable garment, then you should preshrink the lace. Add it to the other components of the garment as you preshrink them.

Facings, Interfacings & Underlinings

Facings and interfacings are not used on lace garments. Finish outer edges with lace trim, lace borders, or sheer tricot bias or French binding. Cut collars and cuffs as single layers, and finish the outer edges with lace trim or appliqué. Use a narrow seam to join them to the garment.

If you need to add body or support to lace, underline the lace with tulle netting. For example, you may choose to underline a fitted lace bodice or sleeves. The tulle netting adds strength without showing through or changing the character of the lace. A lining fabric in a contrasting color can also be used as an underlining. Although this makes the lace opaque, it shows off the lace design and hides seams, darts, and other details of inner construction.

Layout & Cutting

Pattern layout is an important preliminary step for lace fabrics. Begin by studying the details of the lace design. Unfold the fabric fully on the work surface,

laying contrasting fabric underneath if necessary to make the design easier to read.

Note the placement of prominent motifs, the spacing of the repeats, and the depth of any borders. These affect pattern layout because the most noticeable motifs should be matched at the seams and centered or otherwise balanced on major garment sections, just like large fabric prints. If the design has one-way motifs, use a "with nap" pattern layout.

Plan at this point how to use the motifs creatively. Some laces have large primary motifs and smaller secondary motifs or borders that can be cut out and used as appliqués. To use borders as prefinished hems, determine the finished skirt and sleeve lengths before pattern layout. If you plan to trim the border from the fabric and sew it to the garment as a decorative edging, you do not need to determine lengths in advance so precisely.

Before cutting, decide which seam treatment you will be using. Allover laces can be sewn like sheer fabrics, with narrow seams. However, if you are working with a re-embroidered lace or a special heirloom lace with a large motif, lapped seams may be better. They will not interrupt the flow of the lace design around the garment because the seam is nearly invisible. With this method, pattern sections must be pinned in place and cut out one by one in sequence. You may use a combination of seams in one garment, with lapped seams at shoulder and side seams and narrow zigzag or double-stitched seams for set-in sleeves.

Once lace is cut, there is little margin for fitting changes. Fit the pattern before layout to avoid ripping out stitches later. Cut the pattern from lining or underlining fabric to use for fitting, as well as for the inside of the finished garment. Another method is to make a muslin trial garment. A third method is to make a full pattern from pattern tracing fabric and baste the sections together for a fitting. You can then use this pattern to cut out the lace.

Pressing

Avoid overhandling lace with pressing. If a light touch-up is needed, press with right side down on a well-padded surface to avoid flattening the lace texture. Use a press cloth to prevent the tip of the iron from catching or tearing the net background. If you are working with lace made from synthetic fibers, such as polyester or nylon, use a low temperature setting on the iron. Finger press seams, darts, and other construction details. Wear a thimble and press firmly. If further pressing is necessary, steam lightly, then finger press.

Interfacing

Interfacing plays a supporting role in almost every garment. It is the inner layer of fabric used to shape and support details like collars, cuffs, waistbands, pockets, lapels and buttonholes. Even simple styles often need interfacing to add stability to necklines, facings or hems. Interfacing adds body to garments and helps keep them crisp through repeated washings and wearings.

Interfacings come in many different fibers and weights. The pattern may require more than one kind. Choose interfacing according to the weight of the fashion fabric, the kind of shaping required and the way the garment will be cleaned. Generally, interfacing should be the same weight or lighter than the fashion fabric. Drape two layers of the fabric and the interfacing together to see if they hang well. Areas like collars and cuffs usually need stiffer interfacing. For sheer fabrics, another piece of the fashion fabric may be the best interfacing.

Interfacings are available in *woven* or *nonwoven* fabrics. Woven interfacing has a lengthwise and crosswise grain. It must be cut with the same grain as the part of the garment to be interfaced. Nonwoven interfacing is made by bonding fibers together; it has no grain. Stable nonwovens can be cut in any direction and will not ravel. Stretch nonwovens have crosswise stretch, most effective for knits.

Both woven and nonwoven interfacings are available in *sew-in* and *fusible* versions. Sew-in interfacing must be pinned or basted, and is ultimately held in place by machine stitching. Fusibles have a coating on one side which, when steam-pressed, melts and fuses the interfacing to the wrong side of the fabric. Fusibles come in plastic wrappers which have directions for applying. Follow them precisely, since each fusible is different. When applying fusibles, use a damp press cloth to protect the iron and provide extra steam.

Choosing between fusible and sew-in interfacing is usually a matter of personal preference. Sew-ins require more hand work. Fusibles are quick and easy, and give more rigidity to the garment. However, some delicate fabrics cannot take the heat that fusing requires. Textured fabrics such as seersucker cannot be fused because the texture would be lost.

Interfacings are made in weights from sheer to heavy and usually come in white, gray, beige or black. There are special timesaving interfacings for waistbands, cuffs and plackets. These have pre-marked stitching lines to keep edges even.

Another interfacing aid is *fusible web*, available in strips of various widths. It bonds two layers of fabric together, making it possible to bond a sew-in interfacing to the fashion fabric. Fusible web can also be used to put up hems, hold appliqués in place and secure patches before stitching.

Guide to Interfacings

Fusible woven interfacings are available in different weights and crispness, from medium to heavyweight. Cut them on the same grain as the garment piece, or on the bias for softer shaping.

Fusible nonwoven interfacings come in all weights, from sheer to heavyweight. Stable nonwovens have little give in any direction and can be cut on any grain.

Fusible knit interfacings are made of nylon tricot, which is stable in the lengthwise direction and stretches on the crosswise grain to be compatible with lightweight knit and woven fabrics.

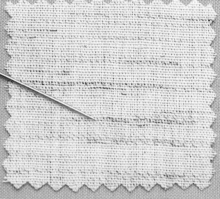

Sew-in woven interfacings preserve the shape and qualities of the fabric, and should be used for natural shaping with woven fabrics. Weights range from sheer organza and batiste to heavyweight hair canvas.

Sew-in nonwovens provide a choice of weight, color, stretch, stable or all-bias combinations. They are appropriate for knits and stretch fabrics as well as for wovens. Preshrink all nonwoven interfacings.

Fusible web is a bonding agent used to join two layers of fabric without stitching. Although it is not an interfacing, it adds some stiffness to the fabric but does not prevent stretching.

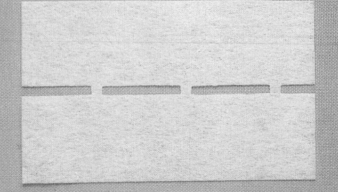

Nonwoven fusible waistbanding is precut in widths or strips to be used for extra firm, crisp edges such as waistbands, cuffs, plackets and straight facings. It has premarked stitching or fold lines.

Nonwoven sew-in waistbanding is a heavyweight, very firm finished strip for stiff, stable waistbands or belts. It is available in several widths. It can be sewn to the back or facing of a waistband, but is too stiff to sew into a waistband seam.

Fusible Interfacings

Dozens of fusible interfacings are available, and all can be timesaving. They allow you to build shape and support into garments or to add a backing to home decorating projects with minimal effort.

Some fusible interfacings have been developed for a special use, such as shaping waistbands, adding crisp body to shirt collars and cuffs, or tailoring. Some are designed for a specific fabric, such as stretch knits or sheers. Manufacturers print guidelines on plastic interleaving and the ends of the bolts to help you purchase the right product. Follow their suggestions to simplify shopping.

Test-fuse a sample of interfacing and fabric to make sure you have made a good interfacing choice and to determine how much heat, pressure, moisture,

and time is required for sound bonding. Because you may require more than one type of interfacing in the same garment, it is convenient to have several fusible interfacing weights and types on hand and ready to use.

Fusible interfacings suit a wide variety of fabrics, but they should not be used on fabrics that are damaged by heat, pressure, and moisture. Fabrics that are unsuitable include rayon velvet, silks that water-spot or that cannot be preshrunk, heavily textured fabrics, and acetates. Also, it may not be satisfactory to use fusibles on fabrics that have a glazed surface or that have been treated for water repellency or stain resistance; these fabrics resist the penetration of fusing resins and prevent acceptable bonding.

How to Test-fuse a Sample

1) Cut fabric sample at least 6" (15 cm) square. Cut interfacing sample half that size. Place fabric wrong side up; place interfacing, with resin side down, on one side of square. Resin side either looks slightly shiny or has tiny raised dots. Cut small triangle of lightweight fabric, and slip under one corner of interfacing to provide unfused tab, which can be used later to check bonding.

2) Fuse, covering sample with nonstick iron soleplate or dampened press cloth. Use iron setting and time recommended by interfacing manufacturer. Use clock or watch with a second hand to measure the time accurately. Lean firmly on iron. It is necessary to bear down on iron to melt fusing resins completely and to force them into the woven or knitted structure of the fabric.

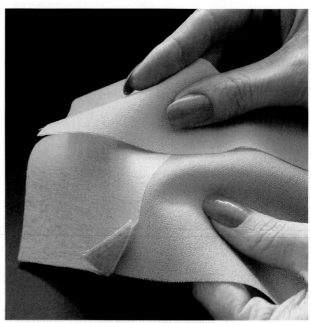

3) Turn sample over so fabric layer is right side up. Protect with nonstick soleplate or press cloth, and press thoroughly. Fusing resins are attracted to heat, so pressing on right side draws adhesive deeper into fabric structure for better bonding. Also, most iron heat is concentrated near steam vents. The second pressing helps fuse any areas not totally covered the first time. Let sample cool completely.

4) Pull corner tab, and try to peel away interfacing. Interfacing should feel permanently laminated to fashion fabric. Fold fabric over the interfacing to see if it creates the effect you desire. Handle sample to judge draping qualities. Look at right side to see if interfacing causes discoloration or if ridge shows through along edge. If desired, machine wash and dry sample to see how bond reacts to laundering.

How to Apply Fusible Interfacing

1) Position interfacing on warm fabric, resin side down; smooth into place. Lightly mist interfacing with water, or steam shrink. Position press cloth and dampen with liberal misting, even when using steam iron.

2) Start at center of large or long pieces of interfacing, and work toward each end to fuse. Do not slide iron from one position to the next. To ensure complete coverage, overlap fused areas with iron.

3) Use two-handed pressure, and lean on iron; fuse for recommended time, 10 to 15 seconds for most fusible interfacings. Otherwise, bond will not be permanent and will eventually separate from fabric.

4) Press the fused area from right side of fabric for better bonding. Use a press cloth or iron soleplate guard to protect fabric surface. Cool and dry fused fabrics before moving them; interfacing is easily reshaped or distorted while warm.

Preparing the Fabric

Before laying out the pattern, take the necessary steps to prepare the fabric for cutting. The label on the bolt tells whether the fabric is washable or dry-cleanable and how much, if any, the fabric will shrink. If the fabric has not been preshrunk by the manufacturer, or if the label says it will shrink more than one per cent, you must preshrink the fabric before cutting. It is often advisable to preshrink knits, since this removes the sizing that sometimes causes skipped stitches. Zippers and trims may also need preshrinking. Dry-cleanable fabrics can be preshrunk by steam pressing or by a professional dry,cleaner. This is especially important if you plan to use fusible interfacing, which requires more steam

than normal pressing and may cause shrinkage. To make sure the fabric is on-grain, begin by straightening the crosswise ends of your fabric. This may be done by pulling a crosswise thread, or cutting along a woven design or crosswise rib of a knit. Next, fold the fabric lengthwise, matching selvages and crosswise ends. If the fabric bubbles, it is off-grain. Fabric that is slightly off-grain can be straightened by steam pressing. Pin along selvages and both ends, matching edges. Press from the selvages to the fold. Fabric that is very much off-grain must be straightened by pulling fabric in the opposite direction from the way the ends slant. Permanent-finish fabrics cannot be straightened.

How to Preshrink Fabric

Preshrink washable fabric by laundering and drying it in the same manner you will use for the finished garment. You may also immerse it in hot water. After 30 minutes to one hour, gently squeeze water out and dry fabric as you would the finished garment.

Steam press to preshrink dry-cleanable fabrics. Steam evenly, moving iron horizontally or vertically (not diagonally) across the grain. After steaming, let fabric dry on smooth, flat surface for four to six hours, or until thoroughly dry.

How to Straighten Crosswise Ends of Fabric

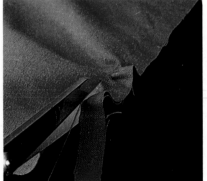

Pull threads to straighten woven fabric. Clip one selvage and gently pull one or two crosswise threads. Push fabric along threads with your other hand until you reach opposite selvage. Cut fabric along pulled thread.

Cut on a line to straighten a stripe, plaid, check or other *woven* design. Simply cut along a prominent crosswise line. Do not use this method for *printed* designs, because they may be printed off-grain.

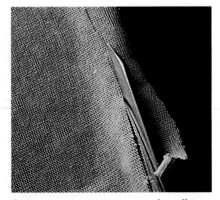

Cut on a course (a crosswise rib) to straighten ends of a knit. It may be easier to follow along the course if you first baste-mark it with contrasting thread, or mark with marking pencil or chalk.

Laying Out the Pattern

Get ready to lay out the pattern by preparing a large work area such as a table topped with a cutting board, or other large flat surface. Assemble all the pattern pieces for the view you are making and press them with a warm, dry iron to remove wrinkles.

Locate the correct layout diagram on the pattern direction sheet. Pattern layouts are reliable guides for laying out the pattern quickly and efficiently. Find the layout for the view, fabric width, and pattern size you are using. When working with a napped or other directional fabric (page 85), choose a "with nap" layout. Circle the layout with a colored pen to make sure you refer to the correct layout each time.

Fold the fabric as indicated on the layout. Most fabrics are cut with the right side folded in. This makes it easier to mark and faster to stitch, since some pieces will be in position to sew. Cottons and linens are usually folded right side out on the bolt; wools, wrong side out. The right side of the fabric may appear shinier or flatter, or have a more pronounced weave. Selvages look more finished on the right side. If you cannot tell which is the right side, simply pick the side you like best and consistently use that as the right side. A slight difference in shading that is not apparent as you cut may be noticeable in the finished garment if two different sides are used.

The layout diagram indicates the placement of the selvages and fold. Most garments are cut with the fabric folded along the lengthwise grain. If the fabric is to be cut folded on the crosswise grain, the fold is labeled "crosswise fold" on the layout. The crosswise fold should not be used on napped or other directional fabrics.

Place the pattern pieces on the fabric as indicated in the layout. The symbols and markings used in layout diagrams are standardized for all major pattern companies. A white pattern piece indicates that this piece is to be cut with the printing facing up. A shaded piece should be cut with the printing facing down. A dotted line indicates that a pattern piece should be cut a second time.

When a pattern piece is shown half white and half shaded, it should be cut from folded fabric. Cut the other pieces first and refold the fabric to cut this piece. A pattern piece shown extending beyond the fold is cut from a single layer rather than the usual double layer of fabric. After cutting the other pieces, open the fabric right side up and position this piece by aligning the grainline arrow with the straight grain of the fabric.

After all pattern pieces are in place, pin them to the fabric according to the directions below. Do not begin cutting until all pattern pieces are in place.

How to Pin Pattern Pieces in Place

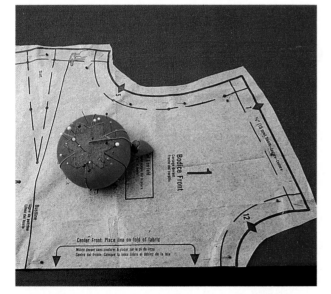

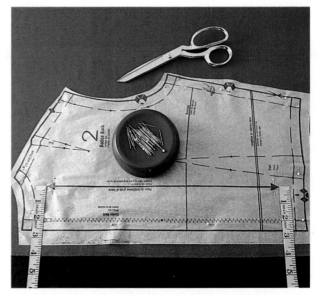

1) Position pattern pieces to be cut on the fold first. Place each directly on folded edge of fabric. Pin corners of pattern diagonally. Continue pinning in the seam allowance, placing pins parallel to the cutting line. Space pins about 3" (7.5 cm) apart, closer together on curves or on slippery fabrics.

2) Place straight-grain pattern pieces on fabric with grainline arrow parallel to the selvage of woven fabrics, parallel to a rib for knits. Measure from each end of the arrow to the selvage or rib, shifting the pattern until the distances are equal. Pin both ends of the grainline so pattern will not shift. Continue pinning as directed in step 1.

Laying Out Plaids & Stripes

Select simple styles for plaids and stripes. Complicated fashions can detract from or distort the fabric design. Avoid diagonal bustline darts, long horizontal darts and patterns designated "not suitable for plaids and stripes."

Always buy extra yardage to allow for matching the design at the seams. The extra amount needed depends on the size of the *repeat* (the four-sided area in which the pattern and color of the design are complete) and the number and lengths of major pattern pieces. Usually an extra ¼ to ½ yard (.25 to .50 m) is sufficient.

It is easier to work with even plaids and balanced stripes than uneven plaids and unbalanced stripes. *Even plaids* have the same arrangement of colors and stripes in both lengthwise and crosswise directions. The area of repeat is perfectly square. In *uneven plaids,* the color and stripes form a different arrangement in the lengthwise or crosswise direction, or both. *Balanced stripes* repeat in the same order in both directions; *unbalanced stripes* do not. To match at the seams, all uneven plaids and some unbalanced stripes must be cut from a single layer of fabric, using each pattern piece twice. This doubles the cutting time.

To determine if a plaid is even or uneven, fold back one corner diagonally through the center of a repeat (opposite). In an even plaid, the lengthwise and crosswise color bars will match. An uneven plaid will not match in one or both directions. If the color bars match diagonally, test the plaid one more way to make sure it is even. Fold the fabric vertically or horizontally through the center of a repeat. The halves will form a mirror image if the plaid is even. Some uneven plaids will pass the diagonal test, but fail the vertical/horizontal test.

To make the finished garment look blanced, make sure the dominant color bars, lengthwise and crosswise, are correctly placed. Follow these guidelines:

Position prominent vertical color bars at the center of sleeves, yokes and collars.

Place dominant horizontal bars on or close to garment edges such as hemline and sleeve edges, except in flared styles. Avoid placing dominant horizontal bars across the fullest part of the bust or hips, or at the waistline, because this makes these figure areas look larger.

Match vertical bars of the jacket to vertical bars of the skirt in a two-piece outfit. Place the dominant vertical bar at the center front and back of each piece.

Although it is not always possible to match the design at every seam, try to match: crosswise bars at vertical seams such as center front and back, and side seams; set-in sleeves to the bodice front at armhole notches; lengthwise stripes where possible; and pockets, flaps and other details to the area of the garment they will cover.

When laying out plaids and stripes, match *stitching* lines, not cutting lines. If fabric tends to shift during cutting, pin or use basting tape to keep fabric in place along matched color bars before pinning pattern in place.

How to Determine If Plaid Is Even or Uneven

Even plaid has matching stripes and colors when fabric is folded diagonally through center of any repeat. Halves also form a mirror image when plaid is folded vertically or horizontally.

Uneven plaid creates unmatched stripes and colors in one or both directions when folded diagonally through the center of repeat. Some uneven plaids match when folded diagonally, but do not form a mirror image when folded vertically or horizontally through a repeat.

How to Match Even Plaids

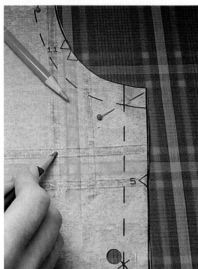  

1) Position a front or back pattern piece on the fabric. Trace design of plaid onto pattern piece in the area of a side seam notch. Identify the colors.

2) Place adjoining pattern piece on top of first piece, matching notch and lapping seamlines. Trace plaid design onto reverse side of the second piece.

3) Position second pattern piece on fabric so traced design matches design of fabric. Pin in place. Repeat with other pattern pieces to be matched.

How to Lay Out Plaids

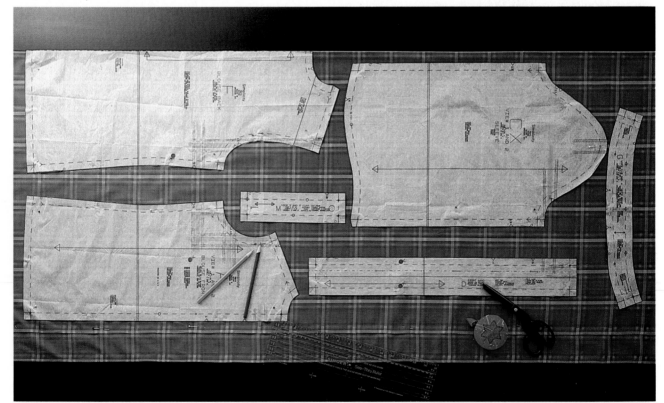

Layout for even plaids can follow either "without nap" or "with nap" diagram on pattern directions, but "with nap" often works best. Notches and symbols along stitching lines should match at sideseams and centers of front and back pieces. Place straight center seams so seamline is directly in the center of the plaid repeat. Place cuffs and pockets so they match the plaid on the portion of the garment they will cover. For two-piece garments, place center fronts and backs of both pieces along the same dominant color bar of the plaid.

Laying Out Directional Fabrics

Directional fabrics include *napped* fabrics such as corduroy, velveteen and flannel; *plush* fabrics such as fake fur; *shiny* fabrics such as taffeta and satin; and *print* fabrics which have one-way designs. Other fabrics which can be directional include some *twill weave* fabrics such as denim and gabardine, and *knits* such as jersey, single or double knits which appear lighter or darker depending on the direction of the grain.

To prevent the garment from having a two-toned look or having its design running in two different directions, all pattern pieces must be laid out with their tops facing the same direction. Napped fabrics can be cut with the nap running either up or down. Nap running up gives a darker, richer look. Nap running down looks lighter and usually wears better. Plush fabrics look best with the nap running down. Shiny fabrics can be cut in whichever direction you prefer. One-way designs should be cut so that the design will be right side up when the garment is completed.

How to Lay Out Directional Fabrics

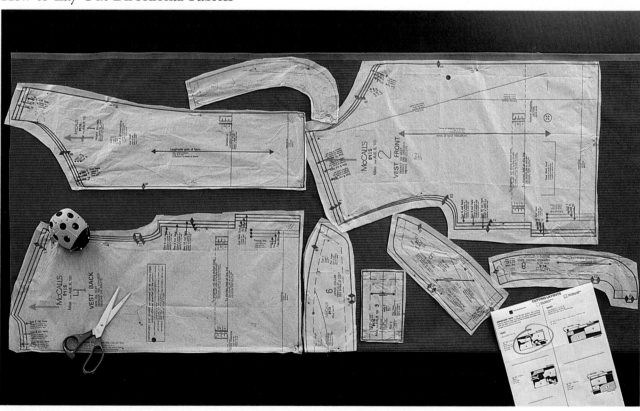

Choose the direction your fabric will run, then lay out the pattern pieces according to the "with nap" layout on the pattern direction sheet. To ensure proper placement, mark each pattern piece with an arrow pointing to the top of the piece. Sometimes the pattern calls for a crosswise fold. In this case, fold the fabric as the layout indicates, then cut along the foldline. Turn the top layer of fabric around so the nap runs in the same direction as the nap of the lower layer of fabric, and cut both layers at the same time.

Cutting Tips

Arrange your cutting table so you can move around it to get at the pattern from all angles. If your cutting surface is not this accessible, cut groups of pattern pieces apart from the rest of the fabric so you can turn these smaller pieces around.

Accuracy is important, since a mistake in cutting cannot always be corrected. Before cutting, double check placement of pattern pieces and alterations. Before cutting plaids, one-way designs, or directional fabrics, make sure the fabric is folded and laid out correctly. Basting tape (page 30) may be helpful to keep fabric from shifting. Heavy or bulky fabric can be cut more accurately one layer at a time. Slippery fabric is easier to cut if you cover the table with a sheet, blanket, or other non-slip material.

Choose sharp, plain, or serrated blade, bent-handled shears, 7" or 8" (18 or 20.5 cm) in length. Take long, firm strokes, cutting directly on the dark cutting line. Use shorter strokes for curved areas. Keep one hand on the pattern near the cutting line to prevent the pattern from shifting and to provide better control.

The rotary cutter (page 28) is especially useful for cutting leather, slippery fabrics, or several layers of fabric. The rotary cutter can be used by either right or left-handed sewers. Use a cutting mat to protect the cutting surface.

Notches can be cut outward from the notch markings, or with *short* snips into the seam allowance (page 89). Be careful not to snip beyond the seamline. Use snips to mark the foldlines and stitching lines of darts and pleats, and the center front and center back lines at the top and bottom. Mark the top of the sleeve cap above the large dot on the pattern with a snip. On bulky or loosely woven fabric where snips cannot be easily seen, cut pattern notches out into the margin. Cut double or triple notches as one unit, not separately.

After you finish cutting, save scraps to test stitching or pressing techniques, make trial buttonholes, or cover buttons. For accurate marking and easy identification, leave each pattern piece pinned in place until you are ready to sew that piece.

Your pattern may call for *bias strips* of fabric to enclose raw edges such as necklines or armholes. Ideally, these are cut from a piece of fabric long enough to fit the area to be enclosed. Bias strips may also be pieced together to form a strip of the correct length.

How to Cut & Join Bias Strips

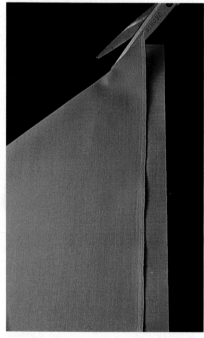

1) Fold fabric diagonally so that a straight edge on the crosswise grain is parallel to the selvage or lengthwise grain. The foldline is the true bias. Cut fabric along the foldline to mark the first bias line.

2) Mark successive bias lines with a marking pencil or chalk, and yardstick or see-through ruler. Cut along marked lines. When a bound finish is called for in a pattern, the pattern will specify the length and width of bias strips needed.

3) Join bias strips if piecing is necessary. With right sides together, pin strips together with shorter edges aligned. Strips will form a "V." Stitch a ¼" (6 mm) seam. Press seam open. Trim points of seams even with edge of bias strip.

Marking Tips

In marking, key pattern symbols are transferred to the wrong side of the fabric after cutting and before the pattern is removed. These markings become continuous reference points to help you through all stages of garment construction. Pattern symbols that should be marked include construction symbols and position marks for placement of details.

Marking is usually done on the *wrong* side of the fabric. Some pattern symbols, such as pocket placement and buttonholes, should be *transferred* from the wrong side to the right side of the fabric (not *marked* on the right side). To do this, hand or machine-baste through the marking on the wrong side. The thread becomes the marking on the right side. Foldlines can be marked by pressing.

There are several ways to transfer markings, each suitable for different fabrics. Choose whichever gives you the fastest, most accurate marking.

Pins are a quick way to transfer markings. They should not be used on fine fabrics or those on which pin marks would be permanent, such as silk or synthetic leathers. Use pin marking only when you plan to sew immediately, since pins may fall out of loose weaves or knits.

Tailor's chalk or dressmaker's pencil, used with pins, is suitable for most fabrics.

Tracing wheel and tracing paper provide a quick, accurate method. It works best on plain, flat-surfaced fabrics. The wheel may damage some fabrics, so always test on a scrap first. Before marking, place a piece of cardboard under the fabric to protect the table. On most fabrics, both layers can be marked at one time.

Liquid markers are felt-tip pens designed especially for fabric. The marker transfers through the pattern tissue onto the fabric. The ink rinses out with water or disappears on its own, so liquid markers can be used on the right side of most fabrics.

Machine basting transfers markings from the wrong side of the fabric to the right side. It can also be used to mark intricate matching points or pivot points. After marking on the wrong side, machine-stitch through the marking. Use a long stitch length or speed-basting stitch, with contrasting color thread in the bobbin. The bobbin thread marks the right side. To mark a pivot point, stitch on the seamline with regular-length stitching and matching thread. Leave the stitching in place as a reinforcement.

Snips or clips can be used on most fabrics except very loosely woven tweeds and some bulky wools. With the point of scissors, snip about ⅛" to ¼" (3 to 6 mm) into the seam allowance.

Pressing can be used to mark foldlines, tucks, or pleats. It is a suitable method for any fabric that holds a crease.

How to Mark with Chalk, Pencil or Liquid Marker

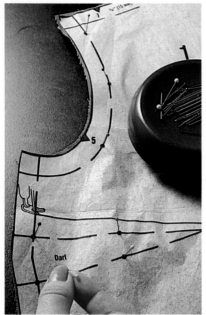

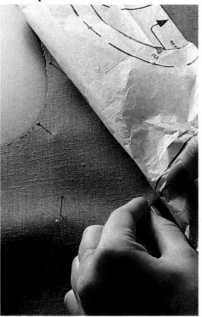

1) Insert pins straight down through pattern and both layers of fabric at marking symbols.

2) Remove pattern carefully by pulling over pin heads. Mark top layer with chalk, pencil or marker at pinpoints on wrong side.

3) Turn fabric over and mark other layer at pinpoints. Remove pins and separate layers.

How to Mark with Basting or Pressing

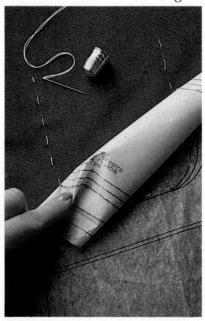

Hand-baste with long and short stitches to mark one layer of fabric. Stitch through pattern and fabric along a solid line, using short stitches on the tissue side and long stitches through fabric. Carefully pull pattern tissue away.

Machine-baste to transfer pencil, chalk or tracing paper markings from the wrong side to the right side. Use contrasting thread in the bobbin, longest stitch on machine. Do not use machine basting on fabrics which mar. Do not press over machine basting.

Press to mark foldlines, tucks and pleats. Pin pattern to a single layer of fabric. Fold pattern and fabric along marking line. Press along the fold with a dry iron.

How to Mark with Tracing Wheel and Tracing Paper

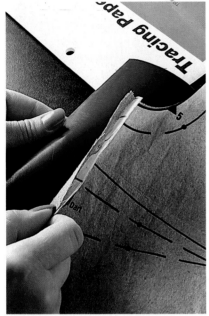

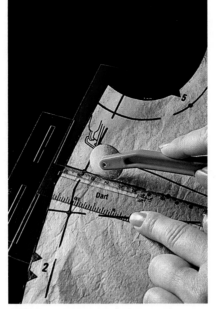

1) Place tracing paper under pattern, with carbon sides facing the wrong side of each fabric layer.

2) Roll tracing wheel over lines to be marked, including center foldlines of darts, using a ruler to help draw straight lines.

3) Mark dots and other large symbols with short lines perpendicular to the stitching line, or an "X." Use short lines to mark the ends of darts or pleats.

Timesaving Marking Techniques

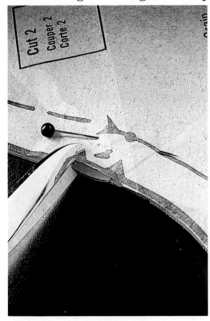

Snips can be used to mark notches, ends of darts, foldlines, or center front and back locations. Make tiny snips, ⅛" (3 mm) deep, into seam allowance. Snip through pattern and both fabric layers with point of scissors.

Pins can mark darts, dots or foldlines without the help of marking pencil. Insert pins through pattern and fabric. Pull pattern carefully over heads. Mark bottom layer with second set of pins. Secure first set of pins to mark top layer.

Tailor tacker has tailor's chalk inserted in two holders. One side has a pin which is inserted through pattern marking to meet chalk on the other side. Twist both sides of tacker so chalk marks two fabric layers in one timesaving step.

Sewing Techniques

Fit

The most basic element in fitting is having the right pattern size. To eliminate many fitting problems, use your body measurements to select pattern size. Those measurements include high bust, bust, waist, hips, back waist length, and height. Also, use the pattern appropriate to your figure type. If you are petite, for example, you can avoid most fitting headaches if you work with a Miss Petite size pattern rather than a Miss.

Fashion styles vary in the way they fit the body. Fit is part of the design. Some styles follow the figure closely, others are full cut and barely echo the figure at all, and there are fitting variations in between. Patterns for coats and jackets are sized to fit over other garments. If the pattern shows a coat worn over a jacket worn over a blouse, the three items will have a graduated fit for comfort.

Finally, your choice of fabric makes a difference in the way a garment fits. A pattern sewn in a soft jersey knit will fit in a completely different way from the same pattern sewn in a crisp taffeta. Some patterns require stretch knits or two-way stretch knits because the garment fit takes advantage of fabric elasticity. If you satisfy the pattern's fabric requirements, your garment will fit the way it should.

Be particular about how your garments fit. Fitting as you sew takes a little extra time, but keep at it until you are satisfied. You will quickly learn which fitting changes you need consistently; then you can save time by making them early in a project.

Recognizing fitting problems is not always easy because we often see only what we want to see when we look at ourselves in a mirror. Also, checking your own view from the back is physically awkward. For both these reasons, you should, if possible, ask someone to help you fit your garments. Determine the source of any fitting problems and resolve to fix them.

Apply the fitting standards described on these two pages to judge how well garments fit. Stand normally to study seam alignment. In general, vertical seams should fall straight to the floor, and horizontal seams should be parallel to the floor. Look carefully to be sure there are no wrinkles. In addition, move around to judge how the garment feels. Walk, sit down, reach forward, and reach up to spot any poorly fitted areas. A well-fitted garment allows you to move freely and returns to its original position when you are stationary.

Armhole seams should look smooth and feel comfortable. On classic set-in sleeve, ease around sleeve cap should have no wrinkles or puckers. Sleeve cap can be rotated toward back or front for better fit and distribution of ease. If armhole seams feel tight and stressed in back, open seams up and restitch to add width across back. Use a narrower seam allowance on the bodice only.

Shoulder seams should stop at end of shoulders for classic set-in sleeves. On raglan, kimono, and dolman sleeves, shaped shoulder seams or darts should match your shoulder contours. Extended shoulder seams, a fashion detail, require shoulder pads for good fit. Dropped shoulder seams, another fashion detail, rest on upper arms; check pattern shoulder markings to see how far below the shoulders the dropped seams belong.

Bust shaping should fall at fullest part of your bustline. If there are darts, they should end ½" to 1" (1.3 to 2.5 cm) short of your bust point. For a shirtwaist style, position one buttonhole at fullest part of your bustline; space other buttonholes evenly.

Waistline, waistband, or waist shaping should fall at natural waist. Bend sideways to find your natural waistline. Skirt or pants waistband has enough ease, from ½" to 1" (1.3 to 2.5 cm), for your thumb to fit comfortably between waistband and your abdomen.

Neckline or collar seams should rest on collarbone. If there is gaping, neckline is too big. If there is strain and wrinkling, neckline is too small and high for your bone structure; make seam deeper so neckline is in proper position.

Long sleeves, whether finished with cuffs or hems, should end at the wrist. Sleeves should be long enough so you can bend your elbow without straining garment. Full, gathered sleeves should blouse gracefully. Fitted sleeves often have darts or easing at elbow; be sure this extra shaping falls at the right place.

Side seams should fall in a direct line from underarm seams. If seams pull toward the front, garment front needs additional room to cover abdominal contours. If seams pull toward the back, garment back needs extra girth. There should be 2" to 4" (5 to 10 cm) of ease at hipline.

Hemline should be even distance from floor all around. Make sure hem is in flattering place for your height. Experiment to find best location, raising and lowering hemline with pins. Avoid placing the hem across the fullest part of your calves.

Understanding Ease

Ease is extra room that has been designed into a pattern for two reasons — for comfort and for design. Ease ensures that the garment sewn from the pattern is larger than your figure. You can measure the ease in a pattern at key points. Subtract the standard body measurements for your size (given on the back of the pattern envelope) from the measurements of the pattern pieces at bust, waist, hips, and back waist length; exclude seam allowances, darts, self-facings, and similar details as you measure. The difference between the two numbers is the ease allowance.

Amount of Ease

The amount of ease designed into a pattern varies from style to style. Fashion trends often dictate the amount of ease. Some silhouettes fit the body closely; other fashions may feature a looser look or a floating, oversized fit. The amount of ease differs with the type of garment, too.

Sometimes the ease is purely functional. The crotch seam of a jumpsuit has more ease than a pants crotch seam because the one-piece garment requires more room when you sit down. Jackets must have enough ease to fit over a sweater or blouse. Strapless bodices have little or no ease so that they hug the figure without slipping down. The pattern pieces for swimsuits can be smaller than the body measurements, a kind of negative ease; the highly elastic two-way stretch knit fabric used for swimsuits must be draped tightly to fit well when wet.

Fabrics & Ease

Fabric influences the amount of ease in a pattern. If the pattern specifies heavy coatings, for example, the thickness of the fabric has been taken into account and enough ease has been added for the pattern to fit well. Patterns for pleated skirts usually suggest thin, smooth fabrics when pleats fold into four layers of fabric at the waist and hips. Extra room is included in the pattern to accommodate these folded layers so the skirt fits smoothly.

At times you may select a fabric that requires an adjustment in the ease. Loosely woven fabrics should not be fitted closely, for example, and neither should leather, clinging jerseys, or fragile fabrics such as lace. Too close a fit stresses these fabrics and weakens seams. Allow extra-wide seam allowances, as described on page 110, and let out seams to add ease, if necessary, as you sew.

Preserving Ease

To help you predict how much ease is included in a pattern, pattern companies provide a description on the back of the pattern envelope. Phrases such as "close fitting," "semi-fitted," and "very loose fitting" suggest the way the garment should drape on your body. These clues help you avoid fitting loose styles too closely or letting the seams out too much on fitted styles. You should adjust the garment to fit your figure, keeping in mind the amount of ease the pattern furnishes.

To preserve the ease in a pattern, compare your figure measurements to the standard body measurements for your size. Any differences, plus or minus, indicate how much change to make when fitting the garment. For example, if your hips are 1" (2.5 cm) larger than the standard hip measurement, let out each side seam ¼" (6 mm) to add a total of 1" (2.5 cm). You have enlarged the garment to fit your figure without changing the amount of ease provided by the pattern.

Three Types of Fit

Fitted sheath has closely fitted silhouette with minimal ease. Darts shape garment to reveal figure at bust, waist, and hips. Amount of ease at bust varies from none to about 3" (7.5 cm). Avoid tendency to fit too closely; preserve enough ease so garment is comfortable.

Semi-fitted shirtdress is shaped to follow figure outline but skims figure. Waist may not be defined but may be suggested by contoured side seams. Amount of ease at bust ranges from about 4" to 5" (10 to 12.5 cm). This fit generally flatters full figures.

Loosely fitted dress has deep armholes and dropped shoulders; waistline is not defined. Amount of bust ease is generous, sometimes 8" (20.5 cm) or more. Presence of gathers or bloused waistline also signals loose fit. In general, loose fit is attractive on slender figures.

General Guidelines for Pattern Adjustments

Pattern adjustments change the measurement and shape of standard pattern pieces to fit your figure. To streamline the entire fitting process, make as many fitting changes as you can before you cut. Step-by-step instructions for specific adjustments are given on the following pages. The basic guidelines below apply to most changes you are likely to make.

Press pattern pieces with a warm, dry iron before you start. It is not accurate to work with wrinkled tissue pieces.

Pin-fit the pattern to preview how well the fashion style fits your figure. Adjust the pattern on your body, or decide how extensively you need pattern adjustments. If you need many adjustments, reconsider your choice of pattern style. Another style may fit your figure with fewer adjustments. Also, pin-fit after making pattern adjustments as a fast check of their accuracy.

Work in a logical order, completing lengthening or shortening pattern adjustments first. Then work from the top of the pattern down to make additional adjustments to fit body width and contours.

Watch for chain reactions. Adjustments on one pattern piece usually require matching adjustments on adjoining pattern sections. If you change the neckline seam, for example, you must change the neck facing to match. Sometimes a compensating rather than a matching adjustment is necessary. For example, if you lower the shoulder seams to fit sloping shoulders, you must also lower the underarm seam to retain the armhole size.

Maintain the original grainline as printed on the pattern pieces, so the finished garment hangs properly. Extend the grainline from one edge of the pattern piece to the other before cutting. This helps preserve grainline as you make adjustments.

Blend the adjusted stitching and cutting lines back into the original lines. When adjustments are blended correctly, the original shape of the pattern piece will not be distorted.

To blend a seam, draw a continuous line where one has become broken during pattern adjustment. To blend a straight line, use a ruler or straight edge, connecting the beginning and end of the new line. To blend a curved line, use a curved ruler to reconstruct the original curve of the pattern, blending to each end from a point halfway between the broken seamline.

Blend the seamline first, then the cutting line. On multiple-sized patterns where no seamlines are marked, blend the cutting line only, and stitch the specified seam allowance, usually ⅝" (1.5 cm).

When there is a dart in the seamline, fold the dart out before blending the line. Be sure to mark all notches and darts on the new blended seamline.

Choosing an Adjustment Method

Wherever possible, two methods are given for the most common pattern adjustments: the minor, or in-seam, method and the major, or cut-and-slide, method. Choose one method or the other, depending on how much of an adjustment you need to make.

Minor in-seam pattern adjustments are quick and easy, because you can mark them directly on the printed pattern within the seam allowance or on the pattern tissue margin. In-seam methods have narrow limitations. Usually you can add or subtract no more than ⅜" to ½" (1 to 1.3 cm).

In the photos, to clarify where an addition would normally be marked on the margin of the tissue pattern, the margin has been trimmed and a contrasting tissue placed under the pattern. This procedure is not necessary on patterns that have not been used previously, because they have generous tissue margins around them.

Major cut-and-slide pattern adjustments allow you to add or subtract greater amounts than in-seam methods and to make adjustments exactly where they are needed to fit your figure. Cut-and-slide methods also have limits, usually to a maximum of 2" (5 cm). The specific amount is stated with the step-by-step instructions. Do not attempt to adjust beyond the stated maximums or you will distort the shape of the pattern pieces and cause the finished garment to hang off-grain. It will also be more difficult to make matching or compensating adjustments on adjoining pattern sections.

If you need a greater adjustment than cut-and-slide methods allow, consider working with another pattern size. Or distribute the adjustment over additional pattern seams and details instead of concentrating the adjustment in one area.

Basic Length Adjustments

Before making any other pattern adjustments, adjust the length of pattern pieces to fit your personal length proportions. If your figure is close to average, basic length adjustments may be the only changes needed on most patterns.

Basic length adjustments are made in two areas: above and below the waist. Use your back waist length measurement to determine the correct pattern length above the waist. To determine the correct pattern length below the waist, measure from the waist in back to the proposed hemline. Make these length adjustments using the adjustment lines printed on the pattern pieces.

Adjustments for Special Figures

Most people can make basic length adjustments by using the printed lengthening and shortening lines on the pattern. If your bust point does not match the placement on the pattern it may be necessary to adjust

the length above the bust or to adjust the darts so that they point to the fullest part of the bust. If you have a full bust, adjust the front pattern length above the waist, as on pages 100 and 101.

For Half-sizes or Miss Petite figure types, reduce the pattern length proportionately, by dividing the total adjustment into smaller amounts. Shorten the pattern at the chest and sleeve cap and at the hip adjustment line, in addition to using the printed adjustment lines above the bust and waist. Length may also be adjusted at the hemline.

Standard pattern shortening adjustments for Miss Petite remove ¼" (6 mm) at chest, ¾" (2 cm) above waist, 1" (2.5 cm) at hip adjustment line, and 1" (2.5 cm) at hem to shorten pattern by 3" (7.5 cm). Standard adjustments for Half-sizes are similar, but the chest adjustment is omitted because armhole size does not need to be reduced. Customize standard length adjustments to suit your personal proportions.

How to Determine Length Adjustments

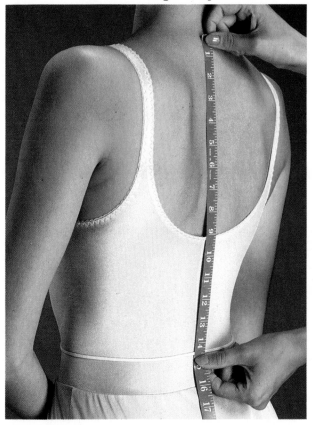

Above the waist. Measure back waist length from prominent bone at back of neck to natural waistline. Compare with back waist length measurement for your pattern size given on pattern envelope to determine how much to adjust bodice front and back patterns.

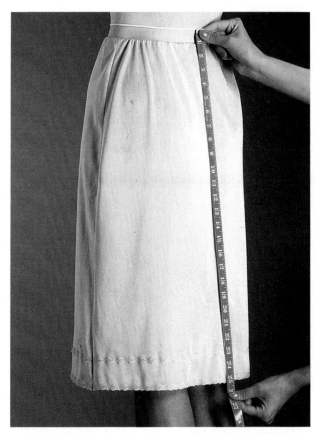

Below the waist. Measure at center back from waist to proposed garment hemline, or use a garment of correct length to determine this measurement. Compare with finished garment length given on back of pattern envelope to determine how much to adjust skirt front and back patterns.

How to Shorten Patterns

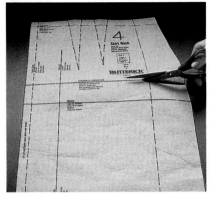

1) Cut pattern on the printed adjustment lines. If skirt pattern provides no adjustment lines, cut off excess length at bottom edge.

2) Lap cut sections. Overlap equals total amount pattern must be shortened. Tape sections together, keeping grainline straight.

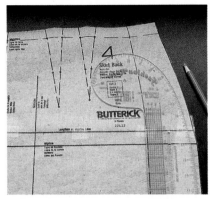

3) Blend stitching and cutting lines. Make matching adjustments on back and front pattern pieces.

How to Lengthen Patterns

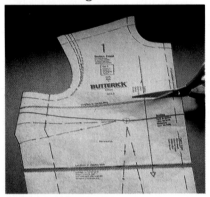

1) Cut pattern on the printed adjustment lines.

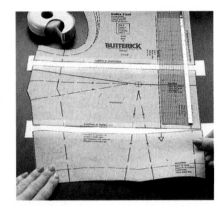

2) Spread cut sections the amount needed. Place paper underneath to bridge gap. Tape sections in place, keeping grainline straight.

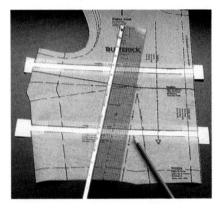

3) Blend stitching and cutting lines. Make matching adjustments on back and front patterns.

How to Shorten Patterns for Half-sizes and Petites

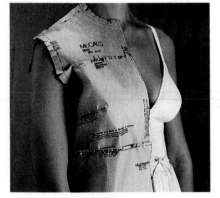

1) Pin-fit or measure pattern to determine how much length to remove across chest above armhole notches, at adjustment line above waist, at hipline, and at adjustment line below waist.

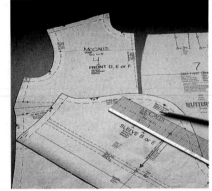

2) Draw adjustment lines on front and back, midway between armhole and shoulder seam notches. Draw similar line across sleeve cap. Draw hip adjustment line 5" (12.5 cm) below waist on skirt front and back.

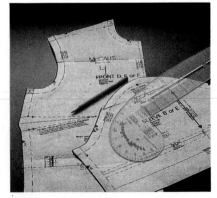

3) Cut pattern pieces on each adjustment line; lap to shorten. Shorten back and front patterns equally. Shorten sleeve cap by same amount removed from bodice at chest.

Fitting the Bust

When fitted correctly, the bodice of a garment drapes smoothly over the bust without pulling, and the waistline of the garment lies at natural waistline and is parallel to the floor. Adjust bodice back length according to back waist length measurement. Make similar adjustments on bodice front. In addition, front bodice seams or darts may need to be adjusted to fit your bust size and shape.

If your bust is fuller than standard, you may need to add additional length and width to the bodice front pattern. Keep in mind that bodice front and back side seam lengths must match. If you have selected a pattern featuring loose or oversized fit, you can use some of the design ease in the pattern to fit a full bust and make a lesser adjustment.

For an average or small bust, pin-fitting, as in step 3 below, will determine whether it is necessary to raise or lower darts. Repositioning the darts may be all that is needed to improve pattern fit.

If you make bust adjustments on the pattern beyond simply raising or lowering darts, you may want to test your adjustments by making a bodice fitting shell from the adjusted pattern. Many fitting solutions are easier to visualize in fabric, and this extra step can save time in the long run.

Ease, or extra room, is necessary for comfort at the bustline. Add the minimum amount of ease to your bust measurement, as shown on the chart below, before comparing with the pattern to judge whether pattern adjustments are needed.

The ease amounts given on the chart are general guidelines. At times you may want to fit with more or less ease. For example, thick fabrics require more ease than lightweight ones. Knits require less ease than wovens, and very stretchy knits require no ease at all or even negative ease for formfitting garments.

Minimum Ease

Garment	Minimum Bust Ease
Blouse, dress, jumpsuit	2½" to 3" (6.5 to 7.5 cm)
Unlined jacket	3" to 4" (7.5 to 10 cm)
Lined jacket	3½" to 4½" (9 to 11.5 cm)
Coat	4" to 5" (10 to 12.5 cm)

How to Determine Pattern Adjustments

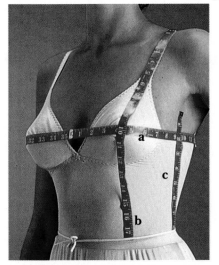

1) Measure bust (a) at fullest part, keeping tape measure parallel to floor. Add minimum ease to bust measurement. Measure the front waist length (b) from midpoint of shoulder, over bust point, straight down to waist. Measure the side length (c) from 1" (2.5 cm) below underarm to waist. Use two fingers under arm to determine distance.

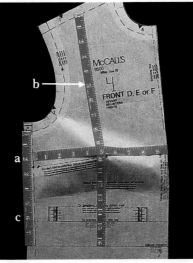

2) Measure pattern front and back at bustline (a). Measure bodice front pattern from midpoint of shoulder, over bust point, to waist (b). Note any differences to decide if pattern length must be adjusted above waist or bust (opposite). Measure side seam of bodice front pattern from underarm to waist (c). Note any differences to decide if pattern length must be adjusted.

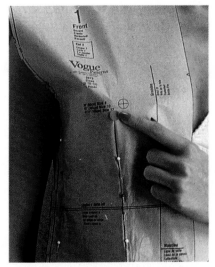

3) Pin-fit pattern to mark the bust point. Note if bust shaping or darts on the pattern should be raised or lowered for good fit. Compare pattern measurement with body measurement plus minimum ease to determine how much width to add for full bust or how much to remove for small bust.

High Bust

Poor fit, when the bust is higher than average, shows in pulls across the fullest part of the bust and in wrinkles under the bust. Dart does not point to fullest part of curve. Underarm dart must be raised; dart from the waistline (if any) needs to be lengthened.

Low Bust

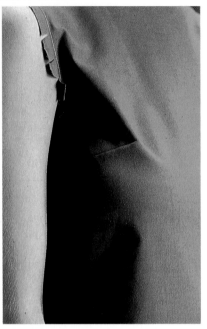

Poor fit, when the bust is lower than average, shows in pulls across the fullest part of the bust and in wrinkles above the bust. Darts are too high and need to be lowered and shortened.

How to Raise or Lower Darts

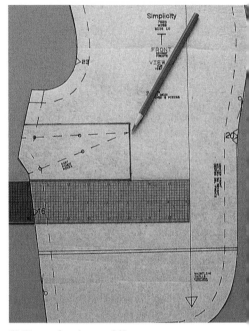

1) Draw horizontal lines on pattern ½" (1.3 cm) above and below the underarm dart, at right angle to grainline. Connect the lines with a vertical line through dart point. Cut out dart on marked lines.

How to Fit a Full Bust without Darts

Accommodate full bust on less closely fitted pattern styles by making an adjustment that does not create a dart. This method can be used to increase the pattern a limited amount. Exceeding the maximum adjustment distorts the fabric grain at the lower edge of the garment. This adjustment is not appropriate on plaids, checks, or stripes.

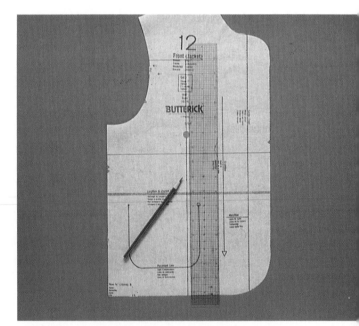

1) Draw line across bodice front midway between armhole notch and shoulder seam, at right angle to grainline. Draw second line 2" to 4" (5 to 10 cm) below armhole, at right angle to grainline. Draw third line through bust point, parallel to grainline to connect first two lines; extend line to lower edge.

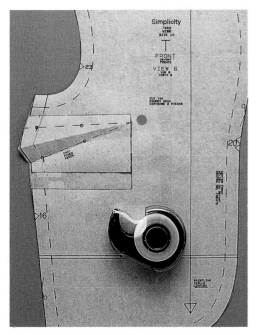

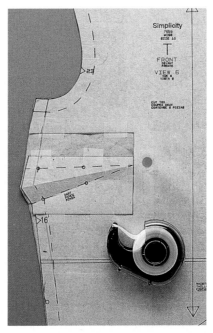

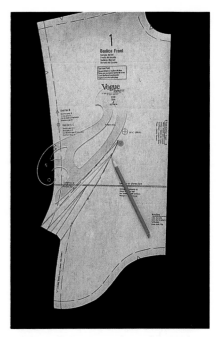

2) Raise dart the amount needed for a high bust. Position dart so that it points to the bust point (dot) or fullest part of figure. Place paper under pattern. Tape cut edges in place, keeping edges even. Redraw side seam.

2a) Lower dart the amount needed for a low bust. Position dart so that it points to the bust point (dot) or fullest part of figure. Place paper under pattern. Tape cut edges in place, keeping edges even. Redraw side seam.

Diagonal dart requires change in direction so that it points to bust point. Mark new dart point on pattern. Redraw dart, connecting side seam ends of the dart and new dart point.

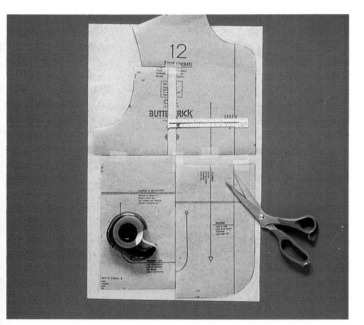

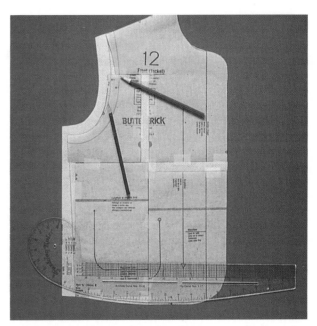

2) Cut pattern on adjustment lines. Slide armhole portion *out* a maximum of ¾" (2 cm) to add total of 1½" (3.8 cm) to bodice width. Slide center front waist section *down* no more than 2" (5 cm) to add bodice length. Tape to paper.

3) Blend stitching and cutting lines at armhole and side seams. Use curved ruler to blend lower cutting line from the center front, tapering back to the original side seam.

Fitting the Waist & Abdomen

Although a waistband or waistline should fit snugly, it must be slightly larger than your waist for good fit. For wearing comfort, a finished waistband should be from ½" to 1" (1.3 to 2.5 cm) larger than your actual measurement. In addition, allow ½" (1.3 cm) of ease from pattern waist measurement to waistband. Apply the same fitting guidelines to garments with faced waistlines. If garment has a waistline seam and no band, allow the total amount, 1" to 1½" (2.5 cm to 3.8 cm), for basic ease.

One indication of good waist fit is the way the side seams hang. They should hang straight, visually bisecting the body, without being pulled to the front or the back. Figure and posture variations may cause distortion of the side seams and require separate adjustment of skirt front and back. For example, a body with a full abdomen will need additional width and length in front, while a person with swaybacked posture may need to shorten the skirt pattern at center back. Adjustments for full abdomen and swayback should be determined and made at the same time that the waist width adjustment is made.

How to Determine Pattern Adjustments

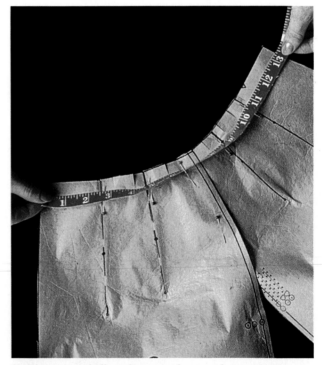

1) Measure your waist. Compare with the waist measurement for your pattern size. Minimum wearing ease is included in the pattern, so adjust the pattern accordingly, enlarging or reducing as needed.

2) Pin out waistline darts, tucks, or pleats to measure pattern to compare with body measurements plus ease. Measure at the waistline seam; on a garment without a waistline seam, measure at the waistline mark at the narrowest part of the waistline area. Double the pattern measurement to compare with your waist measurement.

Small Waist

Poor fit has waistline or waistband that is too large, although garment fits at hips and bust. A dress with a waistline seam is baggy, with loose vertical folds at the waist. On a skirt or pants, waistband stands away from waist and tends to slide down.

Minor Adjustment

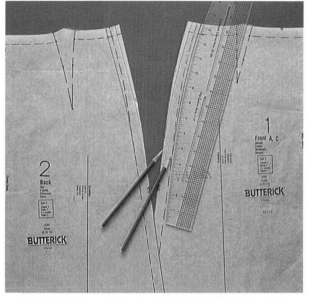

Remove one-fourth the amount needed at each seam. Maximum of ⅜" (1 cm) per seam allowance may be removed from pattern sizes smaller than 16. From size 16 and larger, remove maximum of ⅝" (1.5 cm). Blend stitching and cutting lines, using curved ruler. On dart-fitted skirts or pants, do not make darts deeper to reduce waistline unless additional garment contouring is needed to fit broad curvy hips or full round seat. Adjust width on adjoining pattern pieces.

Major Adjustment

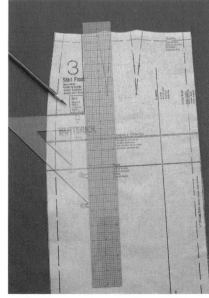

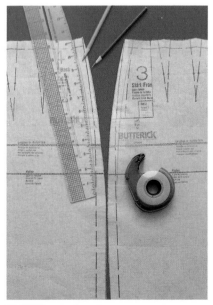

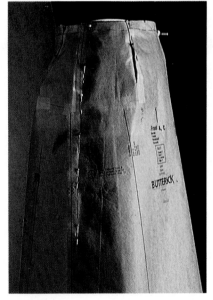

1) Draw a line 5" (12.5 cm) long, parallel to lengthwise grainline, between side seam and dart. Draw a second line from bottom of first line to side seam, at right angle to grainline.

2) Slide section *in* to remove up to 1" (2.5 cm) from waist seam. Tape paper underneath. Blend stitching and cutting lines. Make matching adjustment on back, removing up to 2" (5 cm) from each seam for a total reduction of 4" (10 cm).

3) Pin-fit pattern to check position of waistline darts. It may be necessary to reshape or move the darts closer to center front and back for good fit. Make a corresponding width adjustment to adjoining waistband, facing, or bodice pattern.

Large Waist

Poor fit is indicated by horizontal wrinkles near the waist, which cause the waistline of a dress to rise. A waistband on skirt or on pants creases from strain. Wrinkles fan out from waist or form horizontal folds below waistband.

Minor Adjustment

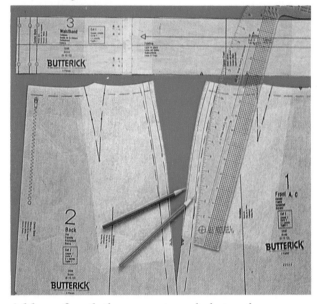

Add one-fourth the amount needed at each seam, adding up to ⅜" (1 cm) per seam allowance for total of ¾" (2 cm) per seam. On dart-fitted skirts, each dart can be reduced up to ¼" (6 mm) to enlarge waistline. Blend stitching and cutting lines, using curved ruler. Make corresponding width adjustment to adjoining waistband, facing, or bodice patterns.

Major Adjustment

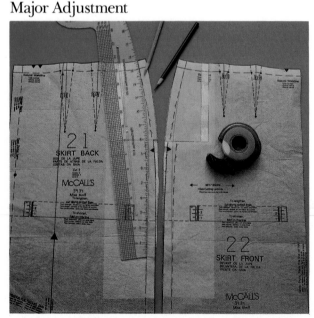

1) Draw adjustment lines and cut pattern as in step 1 for small waist (page 103). Slide section *out* up to 1" (2.5 cm). Tape paper underneath. Blend stitching and cutting lines to waist, using curved ruler, and to hem, using straightedge. Make matching adjustment on back pattern, adding up to 2" (5 cm) per seam for total of 4" (10 cm).

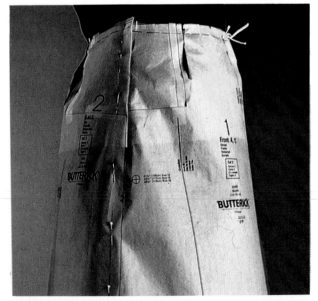

2) Pin-fit pattern to check position of waistline darts. It may be necessary to reshape darts or move them closer to the side seams for a better fit. Make a corresponding width adjustment to adjoining waistband, facing, or bodice sections.

Prominent Abdomen

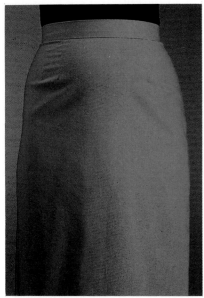

Poor fit is indicated by horizontal wrinkles across the front below the waistline. Diagonal wrinkles from abdomen to sides pull side seams forward. Waistline and hemline may ride up. Extra length and width are needed at center front.

Minor Adjustment

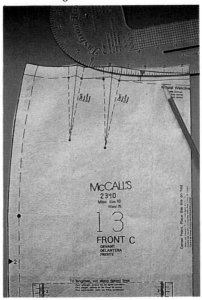

1) Raise waist stitching line on front skirt or pants pattern up to ⅜" (1 cm) at center front to add more length. Fold out darts, and blend stitching and cutting lines, using curved ruler.

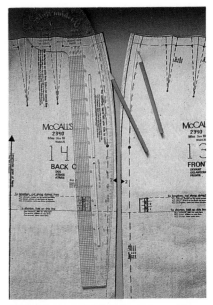

2) Add up to ½" (1.3 cm) at side seam of the front pattern piece. Remove same amount from back pattern piece to maintain the waist circumference. To further improve fit, convert front darts to gathers or unpressed pleats.

Major Adjustment

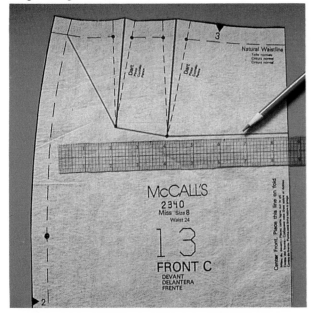

1) Draw diagonal adjustment lines on pattern from intersection of side seam and waistline seam through dart points, extending at right angle to center front. Cut on line. Cut on dart foldline to, but not through, dart point.

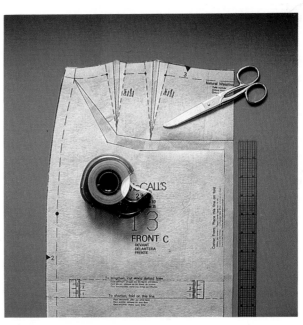

2) Slide center section *up* the amount needed and *out* half the amount needed, opening darts and diagonal slash. Extend center front line from new position to hemline. Darts can also be converted to gathers or unpressed pleats. Blend stitching and cutting lines at waistline.

Flat Abdomen

Poor fit is indicated by vertical wrinkles and excess fabric at center front. Hipbones may protrude. Darts are poorly located and too deep for flat abdomen contour.

Adjustments for Flat Abdomen

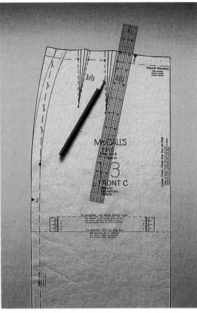

Redraw shallower darts by removing an equal amount on each side of dart foldline. To restore the original waistline measurement, remove the same amount from side seam, blending from a point on waistline seam to hipline with curved ruler.

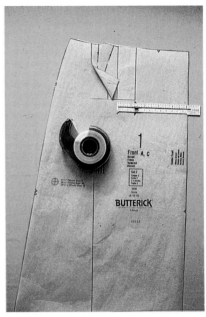

Move darts closer to side seam for prominent hipbones. Cut out dart as for raising or lowering bust dart (pages 100 and 101), and slide it to correct position after pin-fitting pattern. Fold out dart, and blend waistline stitching and cutting lines, using curved ruler.

Swayback

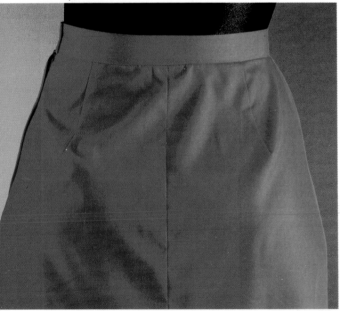

Poor fit is caused by posture variation; area directly beneath waist in back does not fit smoothly, or skirt bags in seat area, indicating that garment is too long at center back. Diagonal wrinkles form, indicating that dart width or length is wrong for body shape. Pin out excess to determine amount to shorten at center back.

Adjustment for Swayback

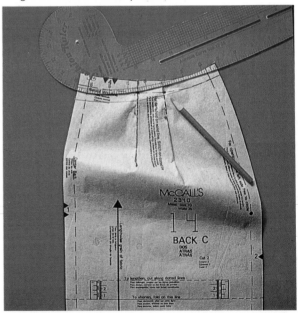

Adjust darts, if necessary, to accommodate protrusion of seat. If dart width is changed, make corresponding width adjustment at side seam to maintain waist size. Lower the waist stitching line on the back skirt pattern the amount needed. Fold darts toward center and blend stitching and cutting lines, using curved ruler.

Fitting Hips

When garments fit well at the hipline, they feel comfortable whether you are standing or sitting. They also look smooth, without strained wrinkles or excess fabric folds.

Before adjusting for width, make any basic lengthening or shortening adjustments below the waistline. Length adjustments may eliminate the need for adjusting pattern hip circumference. If you have one hip higher than the other, it may be necessary to make a copy of the pattern and adjust a separate pattern piece for each side of the body. If your hips are fuller or slimmer than the average, adjust the pattern to include the right amount of ease. For wearing comfort, there must be a minimum of 2" (5 cm) ease, or extra room, at the hipline of the garment for sizes smaller than 16. For size 16 or larger, there must be at least 2½" (6.5 cm) of ease. You may need more than minimum ease for good fit if you have full hips or are using a thick fabric. You may need less if you are working with a knit.

How to Determine Pattern Adjustments

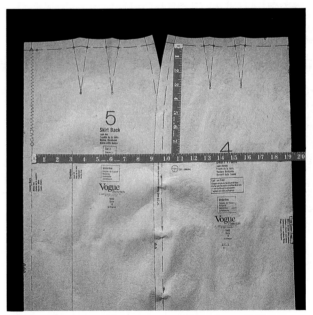

1) **Measure** hips, as viewed from the side, where seat protrudes most, keeping tape measure parallel to floor. Determine where hipline falls by measuring at side seam from waist to fullest part of hips. Add 2" to 2½" (5 to 6.5 cm) minimum ease to measurement.

2) **Mark** pattern side seam at point where fullest part of hipline falls. Lap the back and front pattern pieces at mark. Measure hipline from center front to center back at this position. Double this measurement to arrive at total finished circumference. Compare with hip measurement plus ease to determine if adjusment is needed.

Full Hips

Poor fit causes horizontal wrinkles across hips. Skirt cups under seat in back. Skirt tends to ride up, because there is not enough width at hip level to fit full hips. Pattern needs enlarging at hipline.

Minor Adjustment

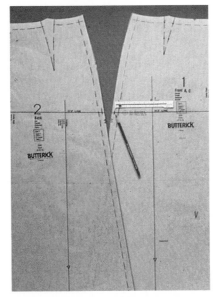

1) Mark hipline at side seam of back and front patterns. Add one-fourth the amount needed at each side seam, next to mark. Add maximum of ⅜" (1 cm) per seam allowance for total of ¾" (2 cm) per seam.

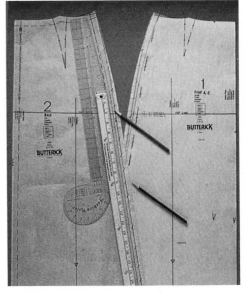

2) Blend stitching and cutting lines from hip to waist with curved ruler. Mark new stitching and cutting lines from hip to hem with straightedge.

Small Hips

Poor fit causes excess fabric to drape in folds and look baggy. Skirt hipline is too broad for figure with slender hips. Pattern width needs reduction at hipline, and darts may have to be reduced. If darts are reduced, side waist seam must be decreased equal amount, as on page 103.

Minor Adjustment

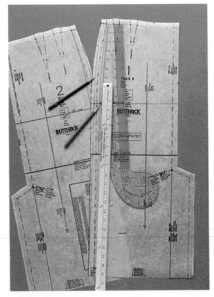

Mark hipline at side seam on back and front patterns. Remove one-fourth the amount needed at each side seam, next to mark. Remove up to ⅜" (1 cm) per seam allowance for total of ¾" (2 cm) per seam. Mark new stitching and cutting lines as in step 2, above.

Major Adjustment

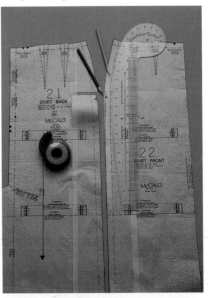

Reduce dart size as needed. Make side waist adjustment (page 103). Draw adjustment line and cut as for major adjustment for full hips, step 1, opposite. Slide section in to remove one-fourth of the extra width at the hipline. Blend stitching and cutting lines from waist to hip area with curved ruler. Mark hip area to hem with straightedge.

Major Adjustment

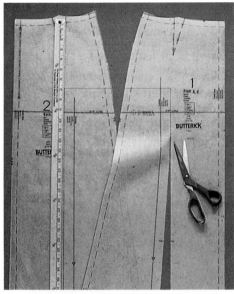

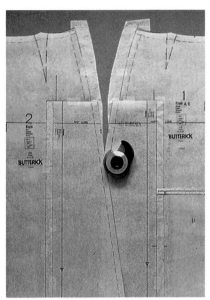

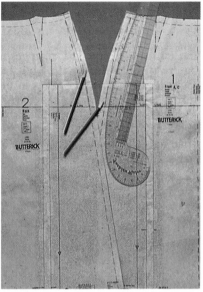

1) Draw a line parallel to the hipline approximately 5" (12.5 cm) below the waistline. Draw a second line parallel to lengthwise grainline from end of first line to hem. Cut on lines.

2) Slide section *out* to add one-fourth the amount needed. Add maximum of 1" (2.5 cm) to sizes under 16 for total of 2" (5 cm) per seam, and 1½" (3.8 cm) to sizes 16 and above for total of 3" (7.5 cm) per seam.

3) Blend stitching and cutting lines from hip to waist with curved ruler. Mark the hip area to the hem with a straightedge.

Uneven Hips

How to Adjust Pattern for One High Hip

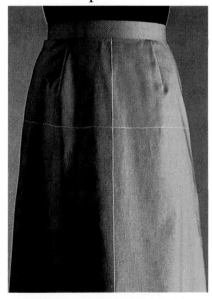

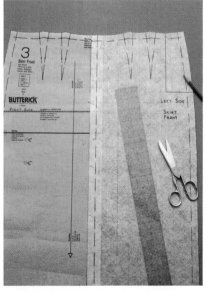

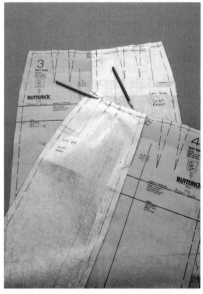

Poor fit causes diagonal wrinkles on one side. Fabric is off grain in hip area. One hip may be fuller, slimmer, or higher than other hip. Make necessary width adjustments in darts and side seam.

1) Trace front and back skirt pattern pieces. Label right and left sides. Draw adjustment line on poor fit side 5" (12.5 cm) long, parallel to lengthwise grainline, beginning midway between side seam and dart. Draw a second line at right angle from bottom of first line to side seam. Cut on adjustment lines.

2) Slide adjustment section up to add necessary length for fitting high hip. Tape paper underneath. Adjust skirt back and front to match. Fold darts or tucks as they will be pressed. Blend stitching and cutting lines at waist and side seams.

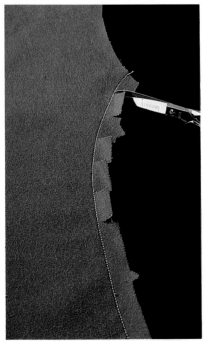

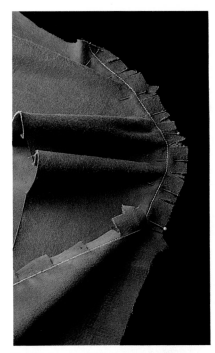

1) Stitch a line of reinforcement stitching just inside seamline of inner curve of center panel. Clip into seam allowance all the way to the stitching line at intervals along the curve.

2) Pin inner and outer curves, right sides together with clipped edge on top, spreading clipped inner curve to match all markings and fit outer curve.

3) Stitch on seamline with clipped seam on top, using shorter stitch than usual for the fabric and being careful to keep the lower layer of fabric smooth.

4) Cut out wedge-shaped notches in the seam allowance of outer curve by making small folds in seam allowance and cutting at slight angle. Be careful not to cut into stitching line.

5) Press seam flat to embed and smooth the stitches. Turn over and press on the other side.

6) Press seam open over curve of tailor's ham, using tip of iron only. Do not press into body of garment. If not pressed to contour, seam lines become distorted and look pulled out of shape.

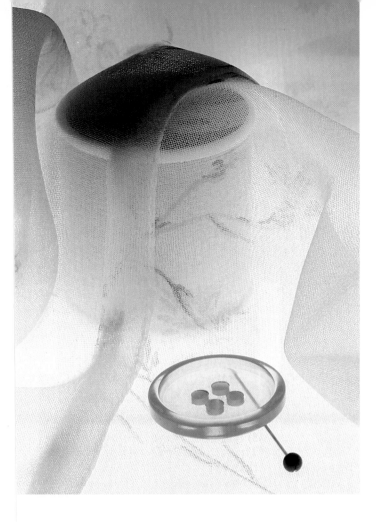

Encased Seams

Encased seams differ from bound seams in that no additional fabric or binding is used. The cut edges of seam allowances are enclosed within the seam itself. Encased seams are best suited to lightweight fabrics, since the additional bulk created is not a problem. These seams are especially appropriate for sheer fabrics, because no raw or contrasting edges show through. Use a straight-stitch foot and needle plate (page 14) to keep sheer fabric from being pulled into the feed.

Use encased seams for blouses, unlined jackets, lingerie or sheer curtains. They are also an excellent choice for children's clothes, because they stand up to rugged wear and repeated laundering.

Self-bound seam begins with a plain seam. One seam allowance is then folded over the other and stitched again.

French seam looks like a plain seam on the right side and a narrow tuck on the wrong side. It begins by stitching the wrong sides of the fabric together. This seam is difficult to sew in curved areas, so is best used on straight seams.

Mock French seam begins with a plain seam. Seam allowances are trimmed, folded to the inside and stitched along the folds. The self-bound and mock French seam can be used in curved or straight areas.

How to Sew a Self-bound Seam

1) Stitch a plain seam. Do not press open. Trim one seam allowance to ⅛" (3 mm).

2) Turn under the untrimmed seam allowance ⅛" (3 mm). Then turn again, enclosing the narrow trimmed edge and bringing the folded edge to the seamline.

3) Stitch on the folded edge, as close as possible to first line of stitching. Press seam to one side.

113

Stretch Seams

Stretch fabrics for casual or action wear include jersey, stretch terry, stretch velour and other knits. Stretch woven fabrics include stretch denim, stretch poplin and stretch corduroy. For swimwear and leotards, Lycra® knits are available. Seams in these fabrics must stretch or "give" with the fabric. Some sewing machines have special knit stitches that incorporate stretch.

Test the seam or knit stitch on a scrap of fabric to determine its appropriateness to the weight and stretchiness of the fabric. Some of the special knit stitches are more difficult to rip than straight stitching, so be sure the garment fits before stitching. Because knits do not ravel, they usually do not require seam finishing.

Double-stitched seam gives an insurance row of stitching to a seam. Use this method if your machine does not zigzag.

Straight and zigzag seam combines a straight seam with the stretchiness of zigzag. This is a suitable finish for knits that tend to curl along the raw edges.

Narrow zigzag seam is used for knits that do not curl along edges. It is a fast, easy stretch seam.

Straight stretch stitch is formed by a forward/backward motion of reverse-action machines. It makes a strong, stretchy seam appropriate for stressed areas such as armholes.

Straight with overedge stitch has a special pattern which combines a straight stretch stitch with diagonal stitching. It joins and finishes the seam in one step.

Elastic stretch stitch is an excellent choice for swimwear and leotards. The stitch combines a narrow and wide zigzag pattern.

Taped seams are used in areas where you do not want stretch, such as shoulder seams.

How to Sew a Taped Seam

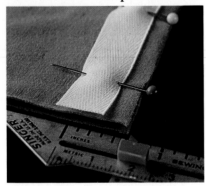

1) Pin fabric, right sides together, so that twill tape or seam binding is pinned over seamline. Position seam binding so it laps ⅜" (1 cm) into the seam allowance.

2) Stitch, using double-stitched, straight and zigzag, overedge or narrow zigzag seam. Press seam open or to one side, depending on selected seam.

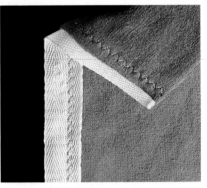

3) Trim seam allowance close to stitching, taking care not to cut into seam binding.

Conventional Edge Finishes

A seam finish lends a couture touch and improved appearance to any garment. Finish seams to prevent woven fabrics from raveling and knit seams from curling. Seam finishes also strengthen seams and help them stand up to repeated washings and wearing, making the garment look new longer.

Seams should be finished as they are stitched, before being crossed by another seam. A finish should not add bulk or show an obvious imprint on the right side of the garment after it is pressed. If you are not sure which seam finish to use, try several on a fabric scrap to see which works best.

The seam finishes shown here all begin with a plain seam. They can also be used as edge finishes for facings and hems.

Selvage finish requires no extra stitching. Appropriate for straight seams of woven fabrics, it requires adjusting the pattern layout so that the seam is cut on the selvage.

Stitched and pinked seam finish is suitable for firmly-woven fabrics. It is a quick and easy finish that prevents raveling and curling.

Turned and stitched finish (also called *clean-finished*) is suitable for light to mediumweight woven fabrics.

Zigzag seam finishes prevent raveling and are good for knits, because they have more give than straight-stitched finishes. These finishes use the built-in stitches on automatic zigzag machines.

Basic Seam Finishes

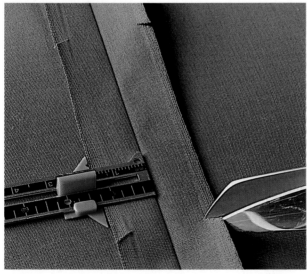

Selvage finish. Adjust pattern layout so that edges of seam are cut on selvage. To prevent shrinking and puckering, clip diagonally into both selvages at 3" to 4" (7.5 to 10 cm) intervals after seam is stitched.

Stitched and pinked finish. Stitch ¼" (6 mm) from edge of each seam allowance. Press seam open. Trim close to stitching with pinking or scalloping shears.

How to Sew a Turned and Stitched Finish

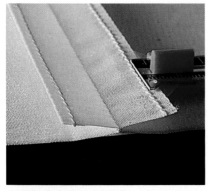

1) Stitch ⅛" to ¼" (3 to 6 mm) from edge of each seam allowance. On straight edges, this stitching may not be necessary.

2) Turn under seam allowance on stitching line. The stitching helps the edge turn under, especially on curves.

3) Stitch close to edge of fold, through seam allowance only. Press seam open.

How to Sew a Zigzag Finish

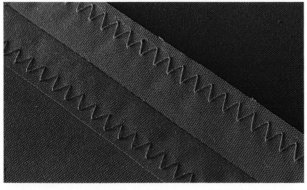

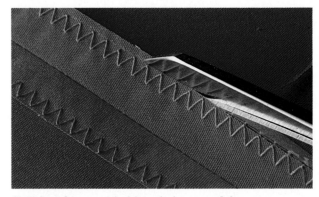

1) Set zigzag stitch for maximum width. Stitch near, but not over, edge of each seam allowance.

2) Trim close to stitching, being careful not to cut into stitching.

Other Zigzag Finishes

Overedge zigzag finish. Trim seam edges evenly, if necessary. Adjust zigzag stitch length and width to suit fabric. Stitch close to edge of each seam allowance so that stitches go over the edge. If fabric puckers, loosen tension by turning to a lower number.

3-step zigzag finish. Use stitch that puts three short stitches in space of one zigzag width. Set machine for pattern stitch and adjust length and width to suit fabric. Stitch close to edge of seam allowance, being careful not to stretch fabric. On some machines, a *serpentine* stitch gives same results. Trim close to stitching line.

Overedge stretch stitch finish. Trim seam edges evenly. Set machine for pattern stitch and attach overedge foot (page 15). Stitch over trimmed edge of seam allowance. If a narrow stitch width is desired on lightweight fabrics, use general-purpose foot.

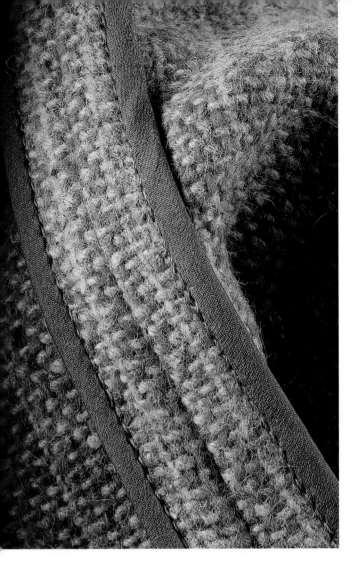

Bound Seam Finishes

These finishes totally enclose the cut edge of seam allowances and prevent raveling. They also enhance the appearance of the inside of the garment. Bound seam finishes are a good choice for unlined jackets, especially those made of heavy fabrics or those which ravel easily.

The most commonly used bound finishes are the bias bound, tricot bound and Hong Kong finishes. Mediumweight fabrics such as chino, denim, linen, gabardine and flannel, and heavyweight fabrics such as wools, velvet, velveteen and corduroy can utilize any of the three. Begin each of these finishes by sewing a plain seam. Bound finishes can also be used on hem or facing edges.

Bias bound is the easiest bound finish. Use purchased double-fold bias tape, available in cotton, rayon or polyester, to match the fashion fabric.

Tricot bound is an inconspicuous finish for delicate, sheer fabrics or bulky, napped fabrics. Purchase sheer bias tricot strips or cut ⅝" (1.5 cm) wide strips of nylon net or lightweight tricot. The nylon net must be cut on the bias; the tricot, on the crosswise grain for maximum stretch.

Bias Bound

Fold bias tape around cut edge of seam, with wider side of tape underneath. Stitch close to edge of inner fold, catching the wider fold edge underneath.

Tricot Bound

Fold sheer tricot strip in half lengthwise and encase cut edge of seam. Stretch strip slightly as you sew, and it will naturally fold over cut edge. Stitch with straight stitch or medium-width zigzag.

Overlock Seams

Overlock machines sew narrow seams with thread-bound edges. As the machine stitches, the knives automatically trim standard ⅝" (1.5 cm) seam allowances to ⅛" to ⅜" (3 mm to 1 cm), depending on the stitch width selected. Overlock seams are pressed to one side. An exception is a flatlock seam, a decorative overlock seam stitched on the right side of a garment. The trimmed raw edges of the flatlocked seam lie underneath the stitching line.

You can sew a garment completely on an overlock machine or use a combination of overlock and conventional seams within a garment. In either case, be certain of fit before you sew. After overlocking, there is little seam allowance left for adjustments if the garment is too tight.

Overlock machines feed fabrics evenly without shifting the layers, so you can usually sew without pins, basting, or other time-consuming preparation. Simply hold the layers in position and sew. If seams have shaped or eased areas, use small snips or a marking pen on the raw edges to indicate where layers must be matched. Sew from one set of marks to the next, holding the layers together in front of the presser foot as you sew.

If it is necessary to secure the fabric layers more firmly, use basting tape or glue stick. Apply tape or glue stick to the outer edges of garment sections cut with standard ⅝" (1.5 cm) seam allowances. The taped or glued area will be trimmed off as you sew. Avoid using pins, because they will damage the overlock knives.

Overlock seams work well on a wide range of fabrics, but you may prefer the security of wider seam allowances on loose weaves and other fragile fabrics. You may also prefer a standard seam for a crisp finish on tailored garments. In these cases, stitch seams on a conventional machine. Also stitch a conventional seam to preserve full seam allowances for a zipper insertion.

How to Sew a Decorative Flatlock Seam

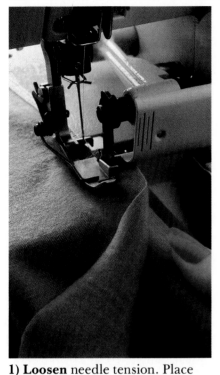

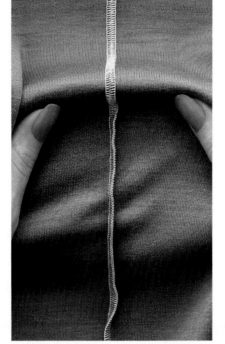

1) Loosen needle tension. Place fabric layers with *wrong* sides together. Stitch with needle on seamline so seam allowance is trimmed away.

2) Pull fabric layers apart to flatten seam. Raw edges of seam lie flat underneath looped threads. Seam is smooth and flat on right side.

3) Press, if desired. Trellis of stitch loops shows on right side. Ladder of horizontal stitches shows on wrong side.

Special Uses for Flatlock Seams

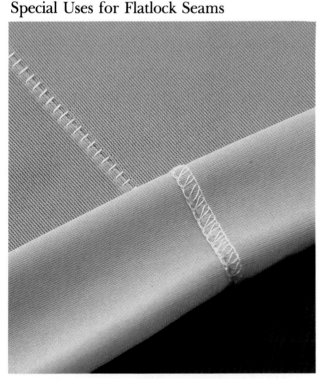

Tricot is sewn with a 2-thread or 3-thread flatlock seam, with *right* sides together so ladder shows on right side of garment. This flat finish prevents lingerie seams from showing through as ridges on outer garments.

Sweater knit is sewn with a 2-thread or 3-thread flatlock seam, with *right* sides together so ladder shows on right side of garment. Ladder sinks into knit texture and makes seam almost invisible. Trellis on wrong side helps to secure yarn floats on patterned sweater knits.

Overlock Edge Finishes

Overlock machines make fast, neat raw edge finishes for pressed-open seams and machine or hand-sewn hems. Convert a 4/2-thread overlock machine for edge finishing by removing the left-hand needle and the lower looper thread; the machine will form a 2-thread overedge stitch without chainstitching. Convert a 4/3-thread overlock machine by removing one of the needles; overlocking with three threads instead of four creates a less bulky edge finish and economizes on thread use. A 3-thread overlock machine can be used to finish raw edges without conversion. A 3/2-thread machine may be used as a 3-thread overedge or converted to 2-thread stitching.

Finish raw edges on an overlock machine either before or after sewing seams. Overlock after sewing

Four Ways to Use Overlock Raw Edge Finishes

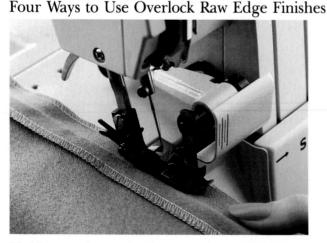

Finish seams by overlocking raw edges. Align raw edge of seam allowance with overlock knives to avoid trimming off too much seam allowance. Finish each seam allowance separately.

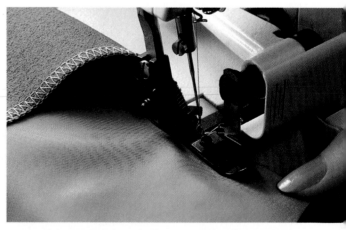

Underline garment section by edge-finishing before you sew. Place garment section and underlining with wrong sides together; finish raw edges of both layers in one step on overlock machine.

if cutting extra-wide seams for fitting purposes. You can use the trimming feature of the overlock machine to make all seams uniform. Overlock before sewing if working with a ravel-prone fabric, such as linen or a loose weave. You will not lose any of the seam allowance even if the fabric is handled extensively as you sew. Also overlock before sewing if underlining a garment section. Omit the time-consuming step of

basting the layers together, and finish raw edges on both fabric layers at once.

Use a wide, long overlock stitch to avoid loading the raw edge with a concentration of thread. If you overdo it, the stitches can show through as ridges on the right side of the garment when you press.

Prevent raveling by edge-finishing loose weaves and bulky knits before you sew. Overedge each garment section immediately after layout and cutting to minimize seam allowance loss during construction.

Prepare hems for stitching by overlocking raw edge. On shirttails (**a**) or other curved hems, overlock stitches automatically cup edge to ease in fullness. For shirts and blouses worn tucked in (**b**), overlock edge and omit hem for flat, smooth finish.

Darts

A dart is used to shape a flat piece of fabric to fit bust, waist, hip or elbow curves. There are two types of darts. A *single-pointed dart* is wide at one end and pointed at the other. A *shaped dart* has points at both ends. It is usually used at the waistline, with the points extending to the bust and hips. Besides providing a closer fit, darts are also used to create special designer touches and unique styles.

Perfect darts are straight and smooth, not puckered at the ends. The darts on the right and left sides of the garment should have the same placement and length.

How to Sew a Dart

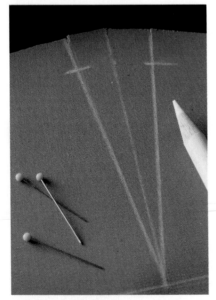

1) Mark dart using appropriate marking method for fabric. Mark point of dart with horizontal line.

2) Fold dart on center line, matching stitching lines and markings at the wide end, the point and in between. Pin in place, with heads of pins toward folded edge for easy removal as you stitch.

3) Stitch from wide end to point of dart. Backstitch at beginning of stitching line, then continue stitching toward point, removing pins as you come to them.

Dart Techniques

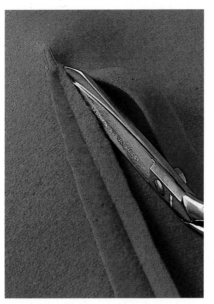

Shaped darts are stitched in two steps, beginning at the waistline and stitching toward each point. Overlap stitching at waist about 1" (2.5 cm). Clip dart fold at waistline and midway along points, to within ⅛" to ¼" (3 to 6 mm) of stitching to relieve strain and allow dart to curve smoothly.

Wide darts and darts in bulky fabrics should be slashed open on the fold line and trimmed to ⅝" (1.5 cm) or less. Slash to within ½" (1.3 cm) of point. Press dart open and press point flat.

Press darts over the curve of a tailor's ham to maintain the built-in curve. Vertical darts are usually pressed toward the center front or center back. Horizontal darts are usually pressed downward.

4) Taper to point of dart. When ½" (1.3 cm) remains, shorten stitch length to 12 to 16 stitches per inch (2.5 cm). Take last two to three stitches directly on fold. Do not backstitch at the point, because this may cause puckering. Continue stitching off edge of fabric.

5) Raise presser foot and pull dart toward front. About 1" (2.5 cm) back from point of dart, lower presser foot and secure thread by stitching several times in fold of the dart with stitch length set at 0. Clip threads close to knot.

6) Press folded edge of dart flat, being careful not to crease fabric beyond the point. Then place dart over curve of tailor's ham and press in proper direction (above). For a neat, flat finish, press darts before they are stitched into a seam.

Gathers

A soft, feminine garment line is often shaped with gathers. They may be found at waistlines, cuffs, yokes, necklines or sleeve caps. Soft and sheer fabrics produce a draped look when gathered; crisp fabrics create a billowy effect.

Gathers start with two stitching lines on a long piece of fabric. The stitching lines are then pulled at each end to draw up the fabric. Finally, the gathered piece is sewn to a shorter length of fabric.

The stitch length for gathering is longer than for ordinary sewing. Use a stitch length of 6 to 8 stitches per inch (2.5 cm) for mediumweight fabrics. For soft or sheer fabrics, use 8 to 10 stitches per inch. Experiment with the fabric to see which stitch length gathers best. A longer stitch makes it easier to draw up the fabric, but a shorter stitch gives more control when adjusting gathers.

Before you stitch, loosen the upper thread tension. The bobbin stitching is pulled to draw up the gathers, and a looser tension makes this easier.

If the fabric is heavy or stiff, use heavy-duty thread in the bobbin. A contrasting color in the bobbin also helps distinguish it from the upper thread.

How to Sew Basic Gathers

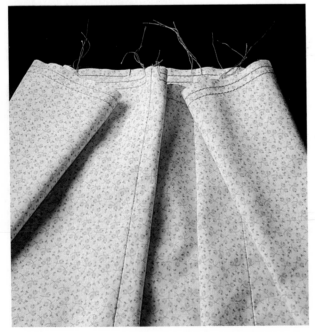

1) Stitch a scant ⅝" (1.5 cm) from raw edge on right side of fabric, starting and ending at seamline. Loosen upper tension and lengthen stitches appropriate to fabric. Stitch a second row in seam allowance, ¼" (6 mm) away from first row. This double row of stitching gives better control in gathering than a single row.

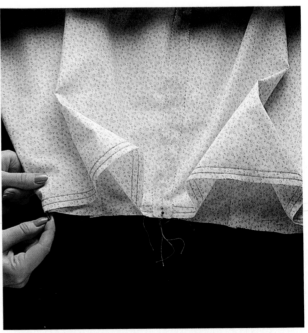

2) Pin stitched edge to corresponding garment section, right sides together. Match seams, notches, center lines and other markings. Fabric will droop between the pinned areas. If there are no markings to guide you, fold straight edge and gathered edge into quarters. Mark fold lines with pins. Pin edges together, matching marking pins.

3) Pull both bobbin threads from one end, sliding fabric along thread to gather. When half the gathered section fits the straight edge, secure bobbin threads by twisting in a figure-8 around pin. Pull bobbin threads from other end to gather remaining half.

4) Pin gathers in place at frequent intervals. Distribute gathers evenly between pins. Reset stitch length and tension for regular sewing.

5) Stitch, gathered side up, just outside gathering lines. Adjust gathers between pins as you stitch. Hold gathers taut with fingers on both sides of needle. Keep gathers even, so folds of fabric do not form as you stitch.

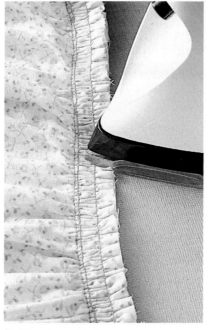

6) Trim seam allowances of any seams that have been sewn into the stitching line, trimming off corners at a diagonal.

7) Press seam allowance on wrong side, using tip of iron. Then open out garment and press seam in the direction it will lie in the finished garment. Press seam toward gathers for puffy look, toward garment for smoother look.

8) Press into gathers with point of iron on right side of garment, lifting iron as you reach seam. Do not press across gathers; this will flatten them.

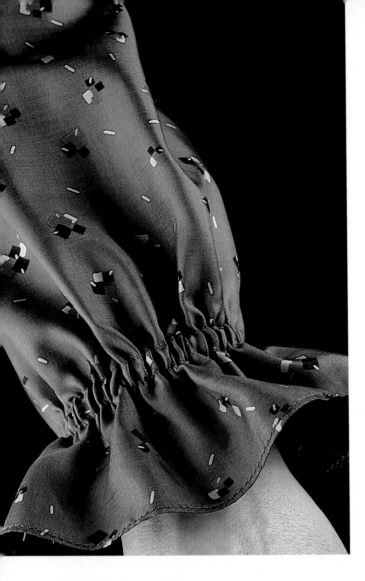

Gathering with Elastic

Gathers formed with elastic offer comfortable and easy fit in knits and active sportswear. This technique ensures uniform gathers and creates shape that is relaxed and not as close to the body as other shapebuilders.

Elastic can be stitched directly to the garment or inserted in a casing. A casing is a tunnel for elastic, created with a turned-under edge or with bias tape stitched to the fabric. Choose an elastic that is suitable to the sewing technique and area of the garment where it is used (page 36).

Elastic in a casing can be any width. Use a firm braided or nonroll elastic. Braided elastic has lengthwise ribs, and narrows when stretched.

Stitched elastic calls for woven or knitted elastics, which are soft, strong, and comfortable to wear next to the skin. On short areas such as sleeve or leg edges, it is easiest to apply the elastic while the garment section is flat, before side seams are stitched. When using stitched elastic at a waistline, overlap the ends of the elastic and stitch to form a circle before pinning to the garment.

Cut elastic the length recommended by the pattern. This length includes a seam allowance. To add elastic when the pattern does not call for it, cut the elastic slightly shorter than the body measurement plus seam allowance. Allow 1" (2.5 cm) extra for a stitched elastic seam, ½" (1.3 cm) extra for overlapping elastic in a casing.

How to Sew Elastic in Casing (waistline seam)

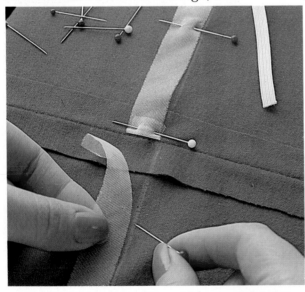

1) Pin sheer bias tricot strip or bias tape that is ¼" (6 mm) wider than the elastic to inside of garment along marked casing lines, beginning and ending at one side seam. Turn under ¼" (6 mm) at each end of bias tape and pin to seamline. For easy application, work on ironing board with garment wrong side out.

2) Stitch tape close to edges, leaving opening at seam to insert elastic. Do not backstitch at ends of stitching, because this stitching shows on the right side of the garment. Instead, pull all four ends to inside and knot.

How to Sew Stitched Elastic

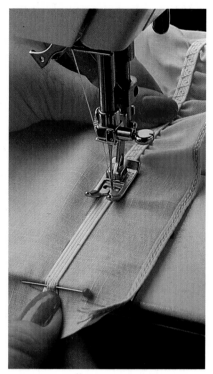

1) Fold elastic and fabric into fourths. Mark fold lines of elastic and garment with pins.

2) Pin elastic to wrong side of garment, matching marking pins. Leave ½" (1.3 cm) seam allowance at each end of elastic.

3) Stitch elastic to fabric, elastic side up, stretching elastic between pins, with one hand behind needle and other hand at next pin. Apply with a zigzag, multi-stitch zigzag or two rows of straight stitching, one along each edge of elastic.

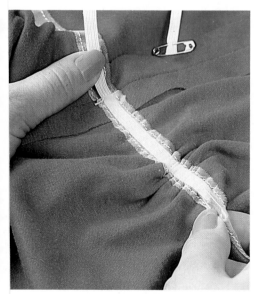

3) Insert elastic through casing using a bodkin or safety pin, taking care not to twist elastic. Place a large safety pin across free end of elastic to prevent it from pulling through.

4) Lap ends of elastic ½" (1.3 cm) and sew together with straight or zigzag stitches, stitching forward, backstitching, and forward again. Clip thread ends. Ease elastic back into casing.

5) Slipstitch ends of casing together. Distribute gathers evenly along the elastic.

Collars, Waistbands & Cuffs

Collars are important details worthy of careful sewing. A well-made collar circles your neck without rippling or pulling and keeps its neat appearance through repeated cleanings. Pointed tips should match. Edges should be smooth and flat.

Interfacing, usually cut from the collar pattern piece, adds shape, support, and stability. Most collar styles benefit from the slightly firm finish provided by fusible interfacings. Select the special crisp type of fusible interfacing suitable for men's shirts if you are working with classic shirting fabrics such as oxford cloth or broadcloth. If your fabric is soft or delicate, like challis or crepe de chine, choose a lightweight fusible that bonds at low iron temperatures.

Convertible collar looks similar to the notched collar and lapels on a tailored blazer. The front facings fold back to form the lapels. This collar can be worn open or closed. The top button is usually omitted on casual wear.

Shirt collar with a stand comes from menswear traditions. There are two separate sections: the collar, and the *stand* between collar and neckline. In some patterns the stand is an extension of the collar section. This eliminates one seam and is faster to sew, but the sewing methods for both versions are similar. For a professional look, topstitch collar edges and stand seams close to the edge.

Standing collar may be shaped or cut double depth and folded along its length to form a self-facing.

Tips for Sewing Collars

Trim outer edges of undercollar a scant ⅛" (3 mm) so the seam rolls toward the underside of the collar when stitched and turned. Pin right sides of collar and undercollar together with outer edges even.

Press collar seam open on a point presser; turn collar right side out. Gently push collar points out with a point turner. Press collar flat, allowing the seam to roll slightly toward the undercollar.

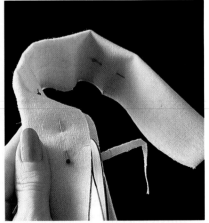

Roll collar into its finished position and pin. If necessary, trim raw edge of undercollar so it is even with upper collar edge. This makes the collar roll properly when it is sewn in place.

How to Sew a Pointed Collar (nonfusible interfacing)

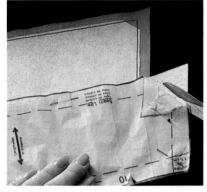

1) Trim corners of interfacing diagonally just inside seamline. Machine-baste interfacing to wrong side of upper collar, ½" (1.3 cm) from edge. Trim interfacing close to stitching.

2) Trim a scant ⅛" (3 mm) from outer edges of undercollar. This keeps undercollar from rolling to right side after collar is stitched to the neckline. Pin right sides of collar and undercollar together with outer edges even.

3) Stitch on seamline, taking one or two short stitches diagonally across each corner instead of making a sharp pivot. This makes a neater point when the collar is turned.

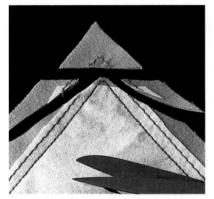

4) Trim corners, first across the point, close to stitching, then at an angle to the seam on each side of the point.

5) Grade seam allowances by trimming undercollar seam allowance to ⅛" (3 mm) and collar to ¼" (6 mm).

6) Press seam open on a point presser. Turn collar right side out.

7) Push points out gently with a point turner.

8) Press collar flat, rolling seam slightly to the underside so it will not show on finished collar.

How to Attach a Convertible Collar

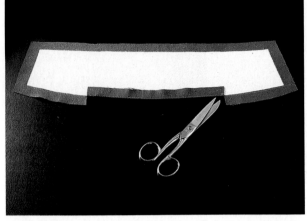

1) Staystitch upper collar neck seam before stitching to undercollar. Clip collar seam allowance to staystitching at shoulder marks. Press seam allowance to wrong side between clips.

2) Interface front facings up to foldline, finishing facing edges with a finish appropriate to the fabric. Turn under facing seam allowances at shoulder seams; press.

3) Stitch shoulder seams. Staystitch garment neck edge on seamline. Clip seam allowance at frequent intervals, stopping short of staystitching. Stitch upper and undercollars. Turn right side out, and press.

4) Pin undercollar only to garment between shoulder seams. Keep collar neck edge free. Pin upper collar and undercollar to front neck edge, matching markings.

5) Fold front facings over collar. Pin through all layers. Stitch neckline seam, right side of garment up; do not catch folded edge of collar in stitching. Trim across corners, and grade seam; turn facings right side out.

6) Bring folded edge of upper collar over neck seam, and edgestitch or slipstitch in place. Slipstitch facings to shoulder seam allowances.

How to Sew a Waistband with Nonroll Woven Waistbanding

1) Cut woven waistband stiffener the length of garment waistband, minus seam allowances at waistband ends. Cut waistband with ⅜" (1 cm) seam allowance on one long edge.

2) Finish one long edge of waistband with zigzag. Stitch waistband to garment, right sides together.

3) Lap stiffener over waistline seam allowances; edgestitch, lining up edge of stiffener with waist seamline. At ends of waistband, stiffener stops at seamlines, not at raw edges.

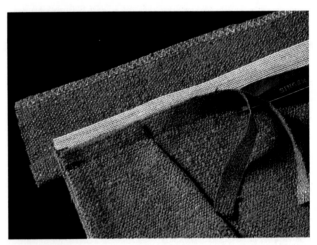

4) Grade waistband seam. Trim garment seam allowance close to edgestitching. Trim waistband seam allowance to ¼" (6 mm). Press waistband up.

5) Fold waistband along its length, right sides together. Top of waistband should extend slightly beyond stiffener. Stitch across ends. Trim seams.

6) Turn band right side out. Press waistband over stiffener. Pin, baste, or glue in place. From right side, stitch in the ditch, catching finished edge.

How to Attach a Cuff

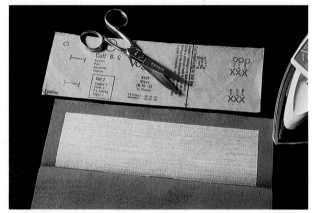

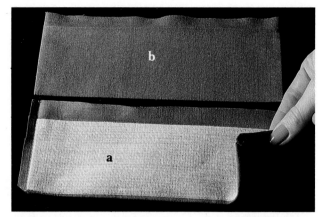

1) Fold cuff pattern in half and cut fusible interfacing from folded pattern, eliminating seam allowances. Fuse interfacing to upper cuff.

2) Press under seam allowance on interfaced edge. Fold cuff in half lengthwise, right sides together; stitch ends, opening out pressed seam allowance. Trim and grade seams. Press seams open **(a)**. Turn cuff right side out **(b)**.

3) Pin and stitch wrong side of sleeve to non-interfaced side of cuff, matching markings. Be sure ends of cuff are even with finished placket edges. Do not trim seam allowances.

4) Wrap free cuff section around placket opening to front of sleeve as far as it will go. The right side of cuff is on right side of sleeve. Pin about 1" (2.5 cm) from placket opening.

5) Stitch pinned area at each end of cuff exactly on first stitching so first row will not show on outside. Trim seam close to stitching to eliminate bulk.

6) Turn cuff right side out; press. Right side of cuff edge is stitched to sleeve for about 1" (2.5 cm) next to placket opening.

7) Edgestitch folded edge of cuff over seam. Topstitch ¼" (6 mm) from edge of cuff. For a cuff that is not topstitched, attach to right side of sleeve, turn to inside, and slipstitch in place.

136

Closures

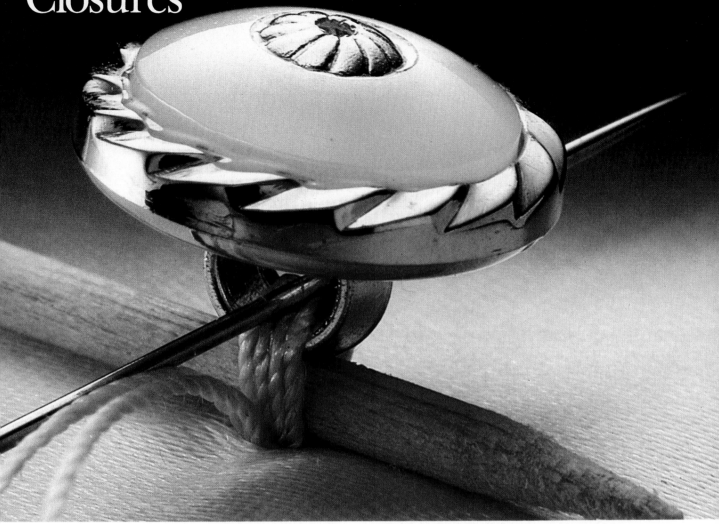

Zippers, buttons, snaps, and hooks and eyes are usually meant to be as inconspicuous as possible, but are sometimes used as decorative details. A stylish button, colorful separating zipper, or pearlized gripper snap can make a definite fashion statement.

Select the closure according to the style of garment and amount of strain that will be put on the opening. For example, a heavy-duty hook and eye closure (page 138) can better withstand the strain on a pants waistband than ordinary hooks and eyes. The back of the pattern envelope specifies the type and size of closures to purchase.

Because closures are under strain, it is important to reinforce the garment area where they are placed. Seam allowances or facings provide light reinforcement. Other closure areas should be reinforced with interfacing.

For sewing on buttons, snaps, and hooks and eyes, use an all-purpose thread, and sharps or crewel needles. For heavyweight fabrics or for closures that are under considerable strain, use heavy-duty, or topstitching and buttonhole twist thread.

Hooks & Eyes

Hooks and eyes are strong closures and come in several types. Regular, general-purpose hooks and eyes are available in sizes 0 (fine) to 3 (heavy), in black or nickel finishes. They have either straight or round eyes. Straight eyes are used where garment edges overlap, such as on a waistband. Round eyes are used where two edges meet, such as at the neckline above a centered zipper. Thread loops (page 138) can be used in place of round metal eyes on delicate fabrics or in locations where metal eyes would be too conspicuous. Button loops and belt carriers are made using the same technique, starting with longer foundation stitches.

Heavy-duty hooks and eyes are stronger than regular hooks and eyes, to withstand greater strain. Available in black or nickel finishes, they are used only for lapped areas. Large, plain, or covered hooks and eyes are available for coats and jackets. These are attractive enough to be visible and strong enough to hold heavy fabric.

How to Attach Waistband Hooks and Eyes

1) Position heavy-duty hook on underside of waistband overlap, about ⅛" (3 mm) from inside edge. Tack hook in place with three or four stitches through each hole. Do not stitch through to right side of garment.

2) Lap hook side over underlap to mark position of eye. Insert straight pins through holes to mark position. Tack in place with three or four stitches in each hole.

Round hook and eye is used for waistbands which do not overlap. Position hook as for heavy-duty hook. Tack through both holes and at end of hook. Position eye so it extends slightly over inside edge of fabric (garment's edges should butt together). Tack in place.

How to Make Thread Eyes

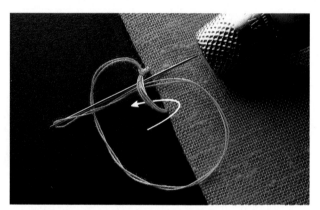

1) Insert needle with double strand of thread at edge of fabric. Take two foundation stitches the desired length of the eye. These are the anchor on which blanket stitch is worked.

2) Work blanket stitch by bringing eye of needle under foundation stitches and through the loop.

3) Bring needle through loop, pulling loop tight against foundation stitches. Work blanket stitch along entire length of foundation stitches.

4) Secure stitching by taking two small backstitches. Trim threads.

Snaps

Snaps are available as regular sew-on snaps, gripper-type snaps, or snap tape.

Sew-on snaps are suitable for areas where there is little strain, such as at the neckline or waistline to hold the facing edge flat when buttons are used, at the waistline of blouses, or at the pointed end of a waistband fastened with hooks and eyes. Sew-on snaps consist of two parts: a ball and a socket. Select a size that is strong enough to be secure, but not too heavy for the fabric.

Gripper-type snaps are attached with a special plier tool or a hammer. They have more holding power than a sew-in snap and will show on the right side of the garment. Gripper snaps can replace button and buttonhole closures in sportswear.

Snap tape consists of snaps attached to pieces of tape. The tape is stitched to the garment with a zipper foot. Snap tape is used in sportswear, home decorating, and for the inside seam of infants' and toddlers' pants.

How to Attach Sew-on Snaps

1) Position ball half of snap on wrong side of overlap section, 1/8" to 1/4" (3 to 6 mm) from the edge so it will not show on the right side. Stitch in place through each hole, using single strand of thread. Stitch through facing and interfacing only, not through to right side of garment. Secure thread with two tiny stitches.

2) Mark position of socket half of snap on right side of underlap section. Use one of the following methods: If there is a hole in center of ball half, insert pin from right side through hole and into underlap section. If there is no hole in ball, rub tailor's chalk on ball and press firmly against underlap.

3) Position center of socket half over marking. Stitch in place in same manner as ball half, except stitch through all layers of fabric.

Buttons

More than any other closure, buttons allow you to individualize your garment. Buttons can be decorative as well as functional. There are two basic kinds of buttons, *sew-through* and *shank* buttons, but the variations on these two types are endless.

Sew-through buttons are usually flat, with two or four holes. When they are merely decorative, they can be sewn so they lie directly against the garment. On all other applications, sew-through buttons need a thread shank. A *shank* raises the button from the garment surface, allowing space for the layers of fabric to fit smoothly when it is buttoned.

Shank buttons have their own shanks on the underside. Choose shank buttons for heavier fabrics, as well as when using button loops or thread loops.

When selecting buttons, consider color, style, weight and care.

Color. The color of buttons is usually matched to the fabric, but interesting fashion looks can be achieved with coordinating or contrasting colors. If you are unable to find an appropriate color match, make your own fabric-covered buttons with a kit.

Style. Select small, delicate buttons for feminine garments; clean, classic styles for tailored clothes; novelty buttons for children's clothes. Rhinestone buttons add sparkle to a velvet garment. Try leather or metal buttons with corduroy and wool tweeds.

Weight. Match lightweight buttons to lightweight fabrics. Heavy buttons will pull and distort lightweight fabrics. Heavyweight fabrics need buttons that are bigger or look weightier.

Care. Choose buttons that can be cared for in the same manner as the garment, either washable or dry-cleanable.

The back of the pattern envelope tells you how many and what size buttons to purchase. Try not to go more than ⅛" (3 mm) smaller or larger than the pattern specifies. Buttons that are too small or too large may not be in proper proportion to the edge of the garment. Button sizes are listed in inches, millimeters and *lines*. For example, a ½" button is also listed as 13 mm and line 20; a ¾" button, as 19 mm and line 30.

When shopping for buttons, bring a swatch of fabric with you to assure a good match. Cut a small slit in the fabric so a button on the card can be slipped through, giving you a better idea of how it will look when finished.

Sew on buttons with doubled all-purpose thread for lightweight fabrics, and heavy-duty or buttonhole twist for heavier fabrics. When attaching several buttons, double the sewing thread so you are sewing with four strands at once. This way, two stitches will secure the button.

How to Mark Button Location

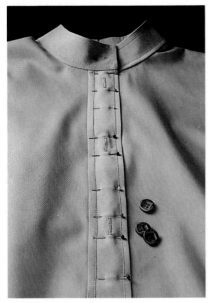

1) Mark button placement by lapping the buttonhole side of garment over the button side, matching center lines. Pin garment closed between buttonholes.

2) Insert pin straight through buttonhole and into bottom layer of fabric. For vertical buttonholes, insert pin in center of buttonhole. For horizontal buttonholes, insert pin at edge closest to outer edge of garment.

3) Carefully lift buttonhole over pin. Insert threaded needle at point of pin to sew on button. Mark and sew buttons one at a time, buttoning previous buttons for accurate marking.

How to Sew On a Shank Button

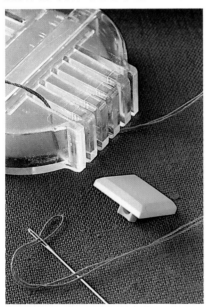

1) Cut a length of thread 30" (76 cm) long and run it through beeswax to strengthen it. Fold thread in half. Thread folded end through a crewel needle. Knot cut ends of thread. Position button at pin mark on the garment center line, placing shank hole parallel to the buttonhole.

2) Secure thread on right side with small stitch under button. Bring needle through shank hole. Insert needle down into fabric and pull through. Repeat, taking four to six stitches through the shank.

3) Secure thread in fabric under button by making a knot or taking several small stitches. Clip thread ends. If a shank button is used on a heavy fabric, it may also need a thread shank. Follow instructions for making a thread shank on a sew-through button (page 142).

Machine-made Buttonholes

Machine-made buttonholes are appropriate for most garments, especially those that are casual or tailored. There are four types: *built-in* (usually two or four-step), *overedge, one-step,* and *universal attachment.* Always make a test buttonhole with appropriate interfacing before making the buttonholes on your garment. The test buttonhole also reminds you at which point your machine begins the buttonhole stitching, so you can position fabric correctly.

1) Built-in buttonholes are made with a combination of zigzag stitching and bar tacks. Most zigzag machines have a built-in mechanism that stitches this type of buttonhole in two or four steps. The four steps are: zigzag forward, bar tack, zigzag in reverse, bar tack. A two-step buttonhole combines a forward or backward motion with a bar tack. Consult your machine manual for specific directions, because each machine varies. The advantage of this buttonhole is that it allows you to adjust the density of the zigzag to suit the fabric and size of the buttonhole. Use spaced zigzag stitches on bulky or loosely woven fabrics, closer stitches on sheer or delicate fabrics.

2) Overedge buttonholes are an adaptation of the built-in or one-step buttonhole. This buttonhole is stitched with a narrow zigzag, cut open, and then stitched a second time, so the cut edge is overedged with zigzag stitches. The overedge buttonhole looks like a hand-worked buttonhole. It is a good choice when the interfacing is not a close color match to the fashion fabric.

3) One-step buttonholes are stitched all in one step, using a special foot and a built-in stitch available on some machines. They can be stitched with a standard-width zigzag, or a narrow zigzag for lightweight fabrics. The button is positioned in a carrier in back of the attachment and guides the stitching, so the buttonhole fits the button perfectly. A lever near the needle is pulled down and stops the forward motion of the machine when the buttonhole reaches the correct length. All buttonholes are of uniform length, so placement is the only marking necessary.

4) Universal attachment buttonholes are made with an attachment that will fit any machine, including a straight-stitch machine. The attachment has a *template* which determines the size of the buttonhole. This method also offers the advantage of uniform buttonhole length and adjustable zigzag width. The *keyhole* buttonhole, used on tailored garments or heavy fabrics, can be made using this attachment. The keyhole at one end of the buttonhole provides space for the shank.

If buttonholes do not have to be respaced because of pattern alterations, make the buttonholes after attaching and finishing the facings but before joining to another garment section. This way there is less bulk and weight to handle at the machine.

How to Determine Buttonhole Length

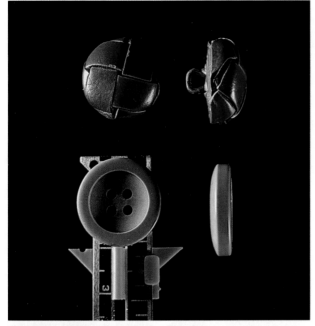

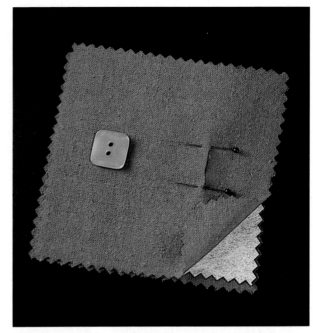

Measure width and height of button to be used. The sum of these measurements plus ⅛" (3 mm) for finishing the ends of the buttonhole is the correct length for a machine-worked buttonhole. The buttonhole must be large enough to button easily, yet snug enough so the garment stays closed.

Test proposed buttonhole. First, make a slash in a scrap of fabric the length of the buttonhole minus the extra ⅛" (3 mm). If button passes through easily, length is correct. Next, make a practice buttonhole with garment, facing and interfacing. Check length, stitch width, density of stitching and buttonhole cutting space.

How to Mark Buttonholes

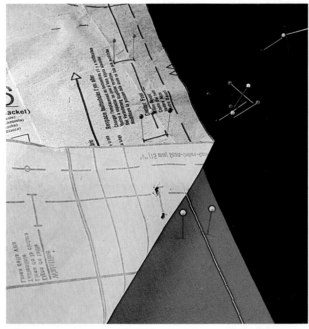

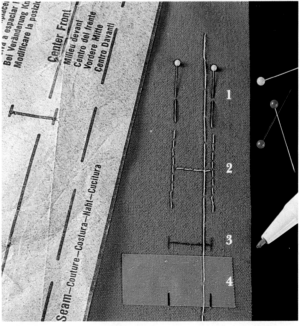

Place pattern tissue on top of garment, aligning pattern seamline with garment opening edge. Insert pins straight down through tissue and fabric at both ends of each buttonhole marking. Remove pattern carefully, pulling tissue over heads of pins.

Mark buttonholes using one of the following methods: **(1)** Secure pins. **(2)** Machine or hand-baste between pins and along ends. **(3)** Use a water-soluble marking pen. **(4)** Place a piece of tape above the pins and mark buttonhole length with a pencil; test fabric first to be sure tape does not mar it.

How to Insert a Lapped Zipper

1) Stitch seam, leaving opening for zipper. Press under ⅝" (1.5 cm) seam allowances.

2) Open zipper. Place face down on back seam allowance, with zipper teeth on pressed seamline. Using zipper foot, stitch zipper to seam allowance. Close zipper, and fold seam allowance back.

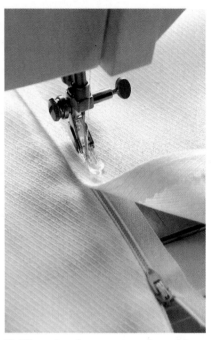

3) Place basting tape on free side of zipper tape. Position pressed seam allowance on zipper so fold laps over zipper teeth. Topstitch across bottom of zipper and up basted side.

How to Insert a Lapped Zipper with Machine Blindstitching

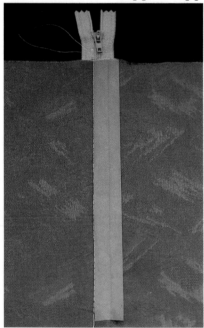

1) Use zipper that is 1" (2.5 cm) longer than the zipper opening. Prepare zipper as for lapped zipper, steps 1 to 3, above, except machine-baste lapping side of seam allowance instead of topstitching.

2) Fold lapped side of zipper on wrong side so seam allowance extends on right-hand side. Set machine for blindstitch. Using zipper foot, stitch along edge of zipper tape so periodic zigzag stitches pierce fold on lap.

3) Remove basting. Open zipper, and make bar tack across coils at top of garment. Cut off excess zipper tape. Press. From right side of garment, zipper looks similar to hand-picked zipper insertion.

Hems

Unless a hem is decorative, it should be virtually invisible from the right side. Use thread the same shade as, or slightly darker than, your fabric.

When hemming by hand, pick up only one or two threads from the outer fabric in each stitch. Do not pull the thread too tight during stitching. This causes the hem to look puckered or lumpy. Press carefully; overpressing creates a ridge along the edge of the hem.

The width of the hem is determined by the fabric and garment style. A hem allowance of up to 3" (7.5 cm) may be given for a straight garment; 1½" to 2" (3.8 to 5 cm) for a flared one. Sheer fabrics, no matter what the style, are usually finished with a narrow, rolled hem. A narrow hem on soft knits helps keep them from sagging. Machine-stitched and topstitched hems are fast and permanent.

Before hemming, let the garment hang for 24 hours, especially if it has a bias or circular hem. Try the garment on over the undergarments you will wear with it. Check to be sure it fits and hangs correctly. Wear shoes, and a belt if the garment is to be belted.

Hemlines are usually marked with the help of a second person using a pin marker or yardstick. Mark the hemline with pins or chalk all around the garment, making sure the distance from the floor to the hemline remains equal. Stand in a normal position and have the helper move around the hem. Pin hem up, and try on the garment in front of a full-length mirror to double check that it is parallel to the floor.

Pants hems cannot be marked from the floor up, as skirts and dresses are. For standard-length pants, the bottom of the pants leg should rest on the shoe in front and slope down slightly toward the back. Pin up the hem on both legs, and try pants on in front of a mirror to check the length.

Before stitching, finish the raw edges of the hem to keep the fabric from raveling and to provide an anchor for the hemming stitch. Select the hem finish (page 150) and stitch that is appropriate to the fabric and the garment.

Blindstitching by machine makes a fast, sturdy hem on woven and knit fabrics. Many sewing machines have this built-in stitch. A special foot or stitching guide makes blindstitching easy.

Seam binding or lace (above) provide a finish suitable for fabrics that ravel, such as wool, tweed, or linen. Lap seam binding ¼" (6 mm) over the hem edge on the right side of the fabric. Edgestitch the binding in place, overlappig ends at a seamline. Use woven seam binding for straight hems, stretch lace for curved hems and knits. Hem light to mediumweight fabrics with the catchstitch, bulky fabrics with the blindstitch.

Tailoring

Tailoring differs from dressmaking in a number of ways. The term *tailored* applies to fashions styled like menswear, such as a suit jacket. It also describes certain methods of construction and pattern design. The undercollar and collar on a tailored jacket, for example, are cut from two different pattern pieces to shape the collar. In dressmaking, both collar layers are usually cut from the same pattern piece. Details such as a welt pocket, notched collar, and full lining are typical in patterns for tailored fashions.

Tailoring also calls for extensive use of interfacings for building in shape. Entire garment sections, not just the details, are backed with interfacing when tailored. Two layers of interfacing may be used for shaping the roll line on jacket lapels. Because different kinds of interfacings have distinctive effects, a single tailored jacket may require several types of interfacing.

Fusible interfacings have eliminated most of the time-consuming handwork that was once the trademark of tailoring. With fusibles you can tailor expertly with just a little practice. However, it's important to choose the right fashion fabric and interfacing for the tailoring task at hand.

Using Fusible Interfacings

Four types of fusible interfacings may be used for tailoring; often all four are used in one garment. *Fusible tricot,* a knitted interfacing, adds body and support to the fabric without causing stiffness. Use it to stabilize garment sections such as sleeves, hems, front facings, and the upper collar. *Fusible hair canvas,* a woven interfacing, is firm and resilient. Use it for the jacket front and undercollar when the fabric needs strong support. *Weft insertion fusible* is a knitted interfacing with extra yarns inserted crosswise. In a medium weight, it is a softer alternative to hair canvas and is used to stabilize fashion details, such as vents on jacket hems and the roll lines of lapels and undercollars. In a lighter weight, it is an alternative to fusible tricot. *Crisp,*

nonwoven fusible interfacing is used to keep small details, such as pocket flaps, firm and smooth.

Test fusible interfacings by making a sample when tailoring. Because entire sections of the garment will be interfaced, the sample should be large enough to drape over your hand, at least 6" (15 cm) square (larger if you can spare the fabric). The ideal method for testing fusible interfacings is to fuse 6" (15 cm) squares of different types of interfacing on a long panel, leaving plain fabric in between. The contrast in feeling between interfaced and non-interfaced areas clearly shows the effect of each interfacing.

Choosing Tailoring Fabrics

When tailoring with fusible interfacings, you'll be more satisfied if you begin with a durable fabric of good quality. Natural fiber fabrics, such as wool, cotton, silk, and linen, respond well to fusing. Many fabrics made from synthetic fibers and blends, such as polyester and rayon, fuse nicely, too. However, some synthetics and metallic fibers are too heat sensitive for fusible interfacings.

Textured fabrics, such as tweeds and linen weaves, tailor well; their surfaces give the fusible adhesive something to grip for a strong bond. On the other hand, some fabrics with tight weaves and smooth surfaces, such as fine polyester gabardines, resist smooth fusing and should be used with sew-in interfacing.

Preshrink tailoring fabrics to prepare them for the extra steam used when fusing interfacings and to prevent shrinkage of the garment. Thorough steam-pressing preshrinks fabric effectively without sacrificing the fresh, new look. Steam-press fabric at home, or have a drycleaner do it for you. A faster and easier preshrinking method is tossing the fabric into a clothes dryer with a few damp towels. Tumble for 7 to 10 minutes at a medium-high heat. Remove immediately; lay flat to dry. Steam-press if necessary.

Sequence for Tailoring a Jacket

The first step in tailoring a jacket is to fuse interfacing onto the major sections. Make pockets next. Then sew the jacket together and make a notched or shawl collar. Finish the sleeves, including the sleeve hems, and set them in. Shape the shoulders with shoulder pads and sleeve heads. Hem the jacket, and sew the lining as the final step.

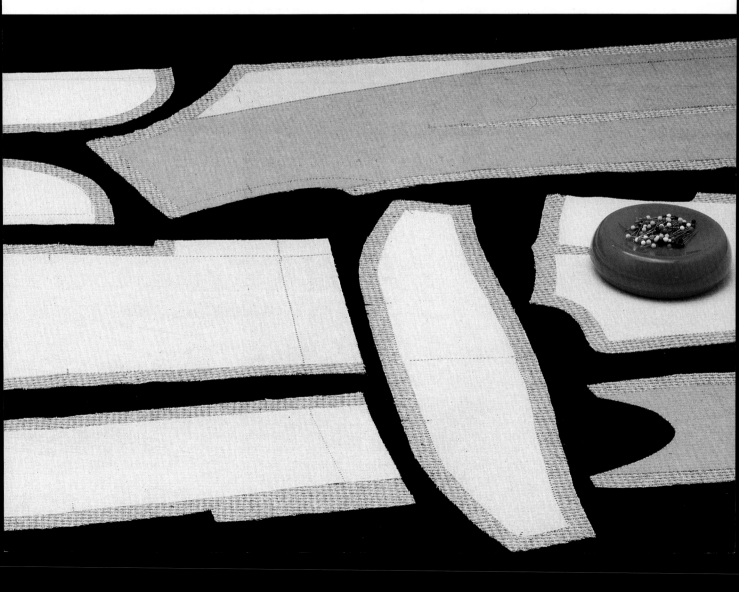

Interfacing the Jacket Sections

In one session, fuse interfacing to the jacket front, facing, back, collar, undercollar, and sleeves. Grouping the work is an efficient way to prepare major jacket sections for the steps that follow. After fusing, let the sections cool and dry on a flat surface. Wait overnight before handling medium to heavyweight woolens and textured tweeds. Wait one or two hours for fabrics of lighter weight.

Fusible interfacing is cut on the seamline rather than the cutting line in all places except at the armhole. Stitch interfacing in the seam at the armhole to support the sleeve. For lightweight fabrics, use the cutting line at the hem instead of the hem foldline.

How to Interface a Jacket Front and Facing

1) Trace seamlines of jacket front and side front pattern pieces on fusible weft insertion or hair canvas. Transfer all pattern markings to interfacing, including lapel roll line and dart stitching lines; it is unnecessary to mark fashion fabric.

2) Cut out any darts on dart stitching lines to eliminate bulk. Dart in fashion fabric will be stitched along cut edge of interfacing.

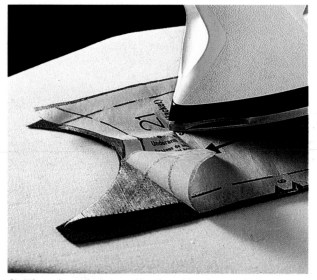

3) Place interfacing, adhesive side down, on wrong side of jacket sections. Place pattern on top to position darts and edges of interfacing at seamlines. Using dry iron, tack interfacing in place to prepare for permanent fusing. Set pattern piece aside.

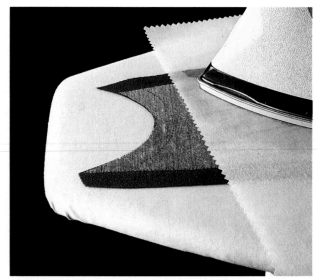

4) Place press cloth on interfacing. Begin at center of section, then fuse each end. To avoid disturbing fused sections, fuse remaining areas by alternating from one side to the other. Never slide iron, which could cause layers to shift.

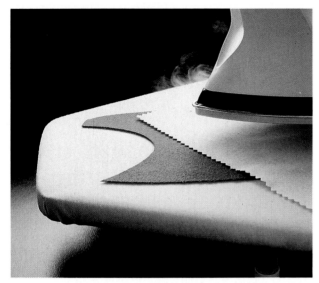

5) Turn jacket section over to right side. Using dry press cloth to protect right side of fabric, press thoroughly with steam iron. Lay flat to allow fused sections to cool and dry completely.

6) Fuse tricot knit interfacing or lightweight nonwoven interfacing to front facings after trimming seam allowances at front of facings. Interfacing extends to outer edge of facing.

Shaping Lapels

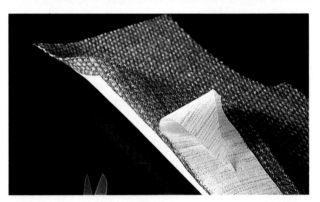

Layer. Add second layer of interfacing to lapel area only. Use weft insertion fusible interfacing, and cut it to fit from roll line to seamline of lapel; roll line should be placed on straight grain of interfacing to stabilize bias grain of jacket at roll line.

Hinge. When using fusible hair canvas, use a hinged roll line for a sharper edge on bulky or heavyweight fabrics. To make a hinge, cut interfacing on lapel roll line before fusing interfacing to jacket front.

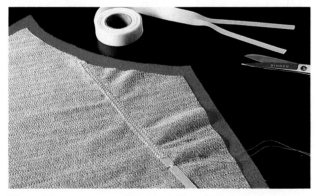

Tape. Use narrow twill tape ¼" to ½" (6 mm to 1.3 cm) shorter than lapel roll line to contour roll line; shorten tape ½" (1.3 cm) for full bust. Place one edge of tape next to roll line; zigzag both tape edges to jacket, easing interfacing to fit tape.

Fold fused lapel on roll line, and press a crease. Do not press crease at lower 2" (5 cm) of lapel roll line; gently steam this area instead. Lay lapel over tailor's ham for pressing. Leave lapel on ham until lapel is completely cool and dry.

How to Interface a Jacket Back with Fusible Interfacing

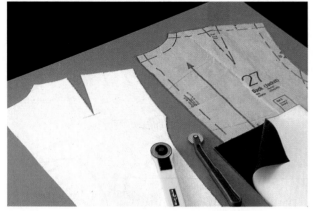

1) Cut interfacing for jacket back from same interfacing used for jacket front, or use lighter weight interfacing. Cut and mark as for jacket front interfacing, page 154, steps 1 and 2.

2) Fuse interfacing to jacket back, using same technique as for interfacing jacket front, pages 154 and 155, steps 3 to 5. Fuse interfacing to both jacket back sections before stitching center back seam.

How to Interface a Jacket Back and Hem

1) Cut partial jacket back interfacing from lightweight woven fabric when garment does not need a fused interfacing for the entire back. Stitch darts separately in interfacing and garment. Press interfacing darts toward armhole and garment darts toward center back.

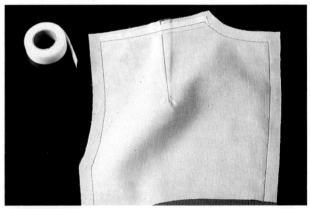

2) Staystitch interfacing to jacket back, ½" (1.3 cm) from raw edges. Include narrow twill tape stay in staystitching at shoulders to prevent bias shoulder seam from stretching.

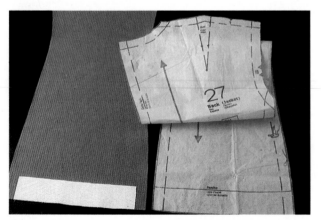

Hem without vent. Cut fusible knit or nonwoven interfacing crosswise to fit shape of hem from hem fold to raw edge; cut fusible weft insertion on the bias. Fuse as for jacket front interfacing, pages 154 and 155, steps 3 to 6.

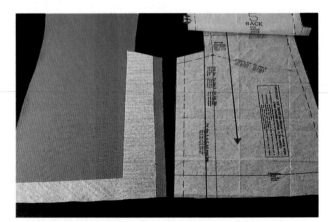

Hem with vent. Cut interfacing to stabilize vent underlap and overlap. Place straight grain of interfacing on lap foldlines.

How to Interface and Shape a Jacket Undercollar

1) Cut undercollar from fusible weft insertion or hair canvas on bias grain. To cut collar stand interfacing, trace undercollar pattern from roll line to neckline seam; place center back seam on straight grain fold.

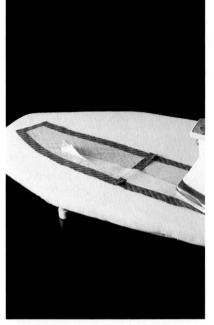

2) Transfer all pattern markings to both layers of interfacing. Fuse interfacing to undercollar; stitch center back seam. Fuse stand after stitching seam.

3) Fold undercollar on roll line, and press a sharp crease. Pin as pressed around tailor's ham, and steam. Leave in place on ham until completely cool and dry.

How to Interface Sleeves

1) Use lightweight fusible interfacing for comfort and appearance. Cut interfacing on seamlines of sleeve pattern. At sleeve hem, use cutting line instead of seamline. Transfer all pattern markings to sleeve interfacing.

2) Fuse interfacing to sleeve sections before sewing seams.

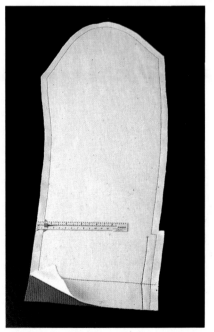

Alternative method: Back the jacket sleeves with batiste. Transfer pattern markings to batiste. Staystitch batiste to sleeve, ½" (1.3 cm) from raw edges. Machine-baste along hem and vent foldlines.

Tailoring a Notched Collar

A notched collar takes its name from the angle of the jacket collar where it joins the jacket lapels. The seams that meet there form a *notch*, or V-shaped cutout, on each side of the neckline. The seam is the *gorge* line. A crisp, flat, even notch is a hallmark of fine tailoring. The key to this detail is an artful combination of stitching and pressing, plus careful trimming of enclosed seam allowances to reduce bulk.

Several pattern pieces are needed to make a notched collar. The undercollar, interfaced and shaped, is the first section to be sewn to the jacket. Next, sew the upper collar to the facing; a portion of this facing becomes the outside of the lapels when the collar is finished. After sewing the final seam, which attaches the collar/facing section to the jacket, press and edgestitch or topstitch, using techniques on page 161 to shape and stitch the notches.

How to Sew a Notched Collar

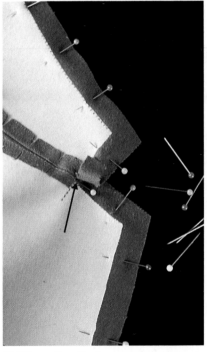

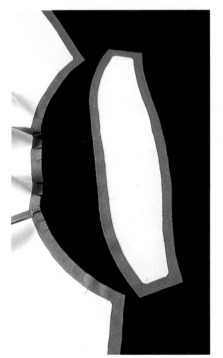

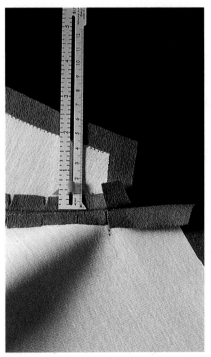

1) Staystitch jacket ½" (1.3 cm) from neckline raw edge. Clip to staystitching. This releases curved neckline seam allowance so it lies flat for easier sewing.

2) Match pattern markings to line up undercollar and jacket neckline edge. Stitch undercollar to jacket neckline up to pattern markings on lapels (arrow); clip to marking.

3) Press seam open over tailor's ham. Trim seam allowances to ¼" (6 mm) to reduce bulk.

4) Staystitch facing ½" (1.3 cm) from neckline edge. Clip to staystitching. Stitch collar to facing neckline up to pattern markings on lapels; clip to marking.

5) Press seam open over tailor's ham. Trim seam allowances to ⅜" (1 cm), slightly wider than undercollar to reduce bulk.

6) Pin collar/facing section to undercollar/jacket section, pinning through seams at collar notches (arrow) to be sure the seams line up precisely.

(Continued on next page)

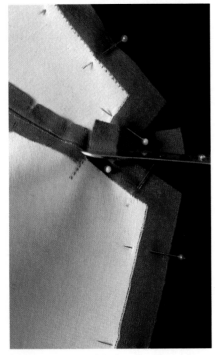

7) Trim excess fabric of collar seam allowance to stitching line on upper and undercollar.

8) Stitch seam, starting at bottom of one jacket edge. Shorten stitches 1" (2.5 cm) from lapel. Take one or two short stitches diagonally across lapel point. (Lapel removed from machine to show stitching.)

9) Stitch from lapel point to collar point, holding seam straight to ensure that notches match on both sides of jacket collar. Finish stitching seam, using same technique on other side.

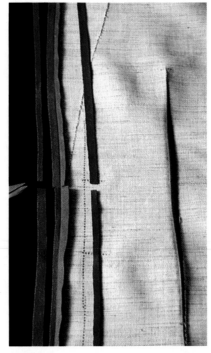

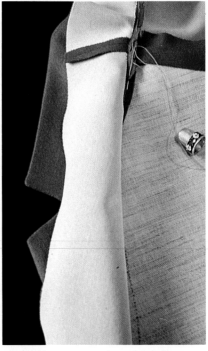

10) Press seam open, using point presser at lapel and collar points. Diagonally trim corners close to stitching. Grade seam allowance on undercollar/lapel to ¼" (6 mm), and on collar/facing to ⅜" (1 cm). Continue grading to lapel roll line.

11) Clip seam at ends of lapel roll line. Below clips, grade jacket front seam allowance to ⅜" (1 cm) and facing to ¼" (6 mm). Press seam open, turn right side out.

12) Tack upper and undercollar seams together with loose running stitch. If seams do not line up exactly because of bulk of fabric, tack the seams where they meet.

Tips for Pressing a Tailored Collar

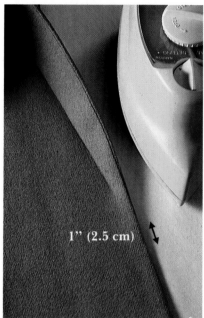

1) Press collar and lapels from underside. Roll seam toward underside of collar and lapels, stopping about 1" (2.5 cm) from end of lapel roll line. Press, using tailor's clapper to force steam out of fabric; this creates crisp edge.

2) Press lower 1" (2.5 cm) of lapel roll line so seam is at edge. Work from underside of lapels.

3) Press jacket front below lapel roll line from inside. Press so seam rolls toward jacket facing.

How to Topstitch a Tailored Collar

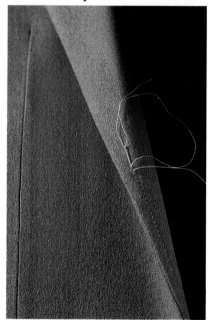

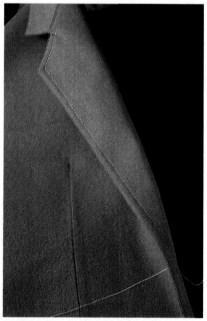

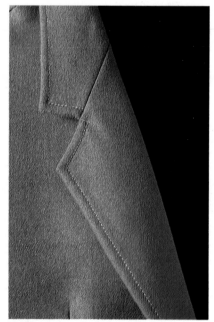

1) Topstitch on right side of jacket, beginning at one lower edge. When using topstitching thread in the needle, stop at bottom of lapel roll line. Clip threads. Pull threads through to facing side; bury ends between facing and garment.

2) Continue topstitching from right side of lapel. Start at exact point where stitching ended, or overlap 2 stitches. At collar notch, pivot and stitch up to notch edge. (The garment is off the machine only to show detail. Do not remove from machine.)

3) Shorten stitch length, pivot, and stitch in the ditch to topstitching line of collar. Pivot, and stitch around collar to other notch. Repeat at second notch. Break topstitching at end of lapel roll line as described in step 1.

Shaping the Shoulders

Jackets need inside support for firm, smooth shape at the shoulders. In tailoring, the two important shaping aids are shoulder pads and sleeve heads.

Shoulder pads can be custom-made to fit the jacket armhole, using the jacket pattern pieces. To fit your figure, adjust the size and thickness of the shoulder pad. If one shoulder is higher than the other one, the pad can be made thicker to compensate for the difference. If your shoulders are sloping, use a thicker pad than the pattern suggests. For square shoulders, use a thinner shoulder pad.

On tailored garments such as jackets and coats, the front of the shoulder pad is wider than the back to fill in the hollow area below the shoulder and to create a smooth line. The back is narrower than the front to fit around the shoulder blades. For a full bust, make the shoulder pad slightly shorter in front. Whenever you try on the jacket or coat for fitting, slip the shoulder pads in place. The shape

and size of the shoulder pads can make a big difference in the way the shoulder and sleeve fit.

To build the pads to the desired thickness, cut graduated layers of a thin filler, such as polyester fleece or cotton/polyester quilt batting. These fillers add lift without being too soft. For the upper layer of a shoulder pad, use fusible hair canvas. The goat's hair fibers in the canvas grip the jacket fabric, helping to secure the pad to the garment. Also, the strong, resilient canvas makes the shoulder pads firm and wrinkle free.

Sleeve heads are strips of filler that support the sleeve caps on a tailored jacket to boost the caps and smooth out any wrinkles where the sleeve was eased to fit the armhole. Sleeve heads also improve the way the jacket sleeves drape. The same filler used for shoulder pads (fleece or quilt batting) can be used to make sleeve heads. Necktie interfacing cut on the true bias grain can also be used.

How to Make a Custom Shoulder Pad

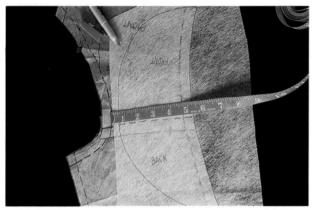

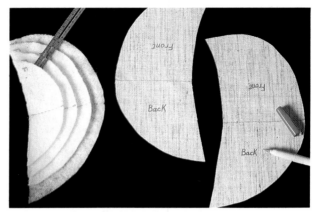

1) Lap jacket front and back patterns at shoulder seam. Trace armhole between front and back notches. End shoulder pad pattern ½" (1.3 cm) from neck seam edge, about 5" (12.5 cm) from armhole. Mark shoulder seam on pad pattern. Label armhole front and armhole back.

2) Cut pattern from fusible hair canvas. Transfer shoulder seam markings. Mark front and back of armhole on canvas. Also cut four layers of filler, gradually reducing layers by about ¾" (2 cm) in size, to make ½" (1.3 cm) thick pad. Adjust sizes and numbers of layers to make pad desired thickness.

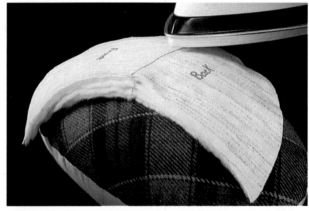

3) Stitch around armhole edge and across shoulder marking with running stitches to hold filler layers together. Add more rows of stitches about 1" (2.5 cm) apart, fanning rows out from armhole edge.

4) Fuse hair canvas to widest layer of fleece, placing pad over tailor's ham to press pad to shape of shoulder. Tack pad to jacket by hand, placing canvas layer next to jacket.

How to Make a Sleeve Head

1) Cut strip of filler 1⅞" (4.7 cm) deep and the length of jacket sleeve cap. Sleeve cap is eased area of set-in sleeve, between pattern markings. Match one long edge of sleeve head to raw edge of armhole seam allowance.

2) Stitch sleeve head to seamline around sleeve cap, using running stitches. When sleeve is turned right side out, sleeve head folds into two layers. Top layer extends beyond bottom layer to prevent ridge on outside of jacket.

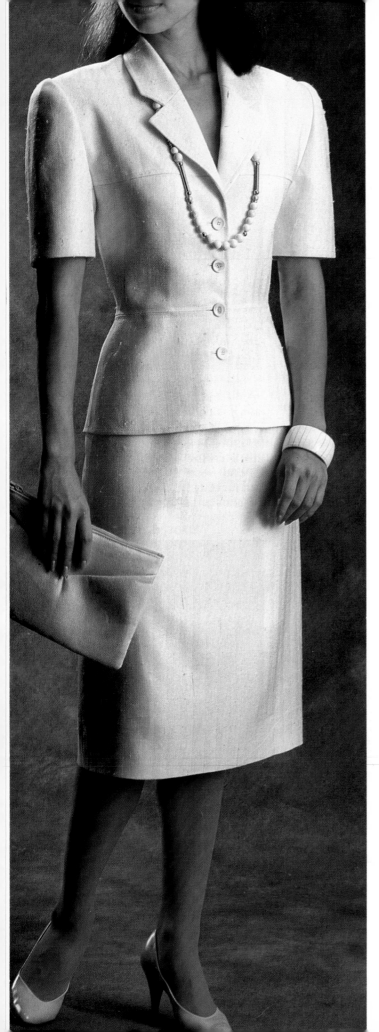

Lining a Skirt

Few patterns provide linings for skirts and pants, but adding a lining makes garments hang better and is easy to accomplish. The method given here is for a slip lining, which is free-hanging and attached at the waistline; the skirt or pants and the lining are hemmed separately. An advantage of a slip lining is that the garment is easy to press because you can lift the whole lining out.

Unlike jacket and coat linings, skirt and pants linings are usually worn next to your skin. In warm or humid climates, fabrics made from rayon, cotton, or cotton blends may feel more comfortable than those made from polyester and similar synthetic fibers.

Tips for Lining Skirts & Pants

Cut the lining from the major front and back pattern pieces. Omit small pattern pieces such as the waistband, facings, and pockets. For a gathered skirt in a lightweight fabric, the skirt and lining may be treated as one layer of fabric. For a heavier weight gathered skirt, cut the lining from a pattern for a simple A-line skirt, or make small pleats or released tucks instead of gathers in the lining. Or pleat out the fullness from the tissue pattern before cutting the lining, allowing some ease for movement. Any of these methods eliminates bulk at the waistline.

Omit any seam extensions for in-seam pockets when you cut out a lining. Straighten the cutting lines on the front and back pattern pieces to change the pocket openings to plain seams. If the garment has slanted pockets, lap the front pattern pieces to cut the lining without pockets.

Shorten the pattern pieces so the lining will be 1" (2.5 cm) shorter than the skirt or pants after hemming. If you plan to make a 1" (2.5 cm) hem in the lining, cut the lower edge of the lining at the hemline of the skirt or pants.

Transfer pattern markings at the zipper opening and the waist to the lining sections after cutting. These markings will help you position the lining inside the skirt or pants.

Assemble the skirt or pants, including the zipper and pockets, before attaching the lining. All stitching on the garment should be completed except for the waistband and the hem. Press seams open. Unless the fabric ravels easily, it is not necessary to finish the seams.

How to Line a Skirt

1) Stitch lining seams, leaving seam open at zipper; press open. Slip lining over skirt, wrong sides together, matching seams. Machine-baste together on waist seamline, folding lining under at zipper edge.

2) Fold lining edges under to expose zipper coil and allow easy opening and closing of zipper. Pin and slipstitch lining to zipper tape.

3) Apply waistband. Hem lining so it is 1" (2.5 cm) shorter than skirt. Sew lining hem by hand or machine, as desired.

Darts, Ease, or Pleats in Linings

Darts. Pin tucks in the skirt or pants lining, matching the dart markings. Darts in skirt or pants are pressed toward center front and back. Press tucks in lining in opposite direction to reduce bulk.

Eased or slightly gathered area. Slip lining over skirt, wrong sides together. Machine-baste at waistline seam. Gather lining and skirt as if they were one layer of fabric, pulling up ease to fit waistband.

Pleat-front skirts or pants. Machine-baste pleats separately in lining and garment. Press lining pleats flat in opposite direction of skirt pleats. Slip lining over skirt, wrong sides together. Machine-baste at waistline.

Sewing Activewear

Rugby shirts, running shorts, T-shirts, and warm-up suits are designed for active sports comfort but have also become fashion items. One of the reasons for their popularity is their comfort. These garments are usually made of soft knit fabrics and have snug-fitting ribbed, drawstring, or elasticized edges for even greater comfort. See pages 59 and 60 for the selection of fabric and the use of a knit gauge to determine the correct amount of stretch in a fabric.

Pullover sweatshirts and pull-on pants are easy to sew because there are few pattern pieces, all the sewing is done by machine, and the construction can be simplified by the use of flat methods (pages 178 and 179). Fitting for active sportswear is minimal. Patterns usually come in small, medium, large, and extra-large sizes rather than the more specific numbered sizes necessary for other garments.

Fabric Preparation

Preshrink fabrics, tapes, and trims. Preshrink notions to prevent edges and detail areas from rippling in the finished garment. Use the washing and drying methods recommended by the fabric's manufacturer. Do not preshrink ribbings. This distorts ribbing and makes accurate layout and cutting difficult.

Preshrinking the fabric restores the original shape of knits such as sweatshirt fleece and velour, preventing twisted seams in the finished garment. Washing also removes chemical finishes and excess dyes from knits and makes the fabrics easier to sew.

After preshrinking, knits may ripple or look uneven along the selvage edges. To prepare the fabric for pattern layout, fold it along a lengthwise rib and smooth out any wrinkles. It is important to align the pattern sections on the straight grain of the fabric. If sections are cut off-grain, the finished garment will twist instead of draping properly.

Ribbings

Ribbing has lengthwise ridges with great crosswise stretch and recovery, enabling the ribbing to return

to its original size and shape. Because of its stretch and recovery qualities, ribbing may be used instead of a hem to finish necklines, wrists, ankles, armholes, and waistlines. Ribbed edges provide a snug but comfortable fit for pullover and pull-on garments.

Purchasing Ribbings

Most ribbings are sold by the inch (centimeter) in tubular form. A typical ribbing is 22" (56 cm) wide. Polyester/cotton ribbings (1) are a suitable choice for sweatshirt fleece, lightweight jersey, and T-shirt knits. For outerwear, nylon/spandex ribbing (2) provides a firmer, stronger edge. These tubular ribbings are cut to the correct length for the garment. Because the ribbing is folded crosswise to finish the outer edge, it is cut twice the finished width.

For casual knit shirts, use a ribbing set (3) for the collar and the sleeve edges; the set, which is usually striped in one or two additional colors, has finished outer edges. For dressier knit garments, finished edge ribbing (4) is sold by the yard (meter). It is a single layer of ribbing to be cut to size for the specific garment. Ready-made cuffs (5) in doubled tubular form eliminate the need to fit the ribbing to the garment. The fold forms the finished edge.

Because the color selection of ribbings may be limited, a contrasting ribbing is often a more attractive choice than striving for a perfect match. You could also substitute other fabrics, such as two-way stretch spandex knit, for ribbing, as long as the fabric has good stretch and recovery qualities. Also, you can cut self-fabric strips crosswise if working with a knit that stretches at least 25 percent in this direction.

Cutting Ribbings

Ribbings vary in their amount of stretch, so it is best to estimate the length of ribbing required either by pin-fitting it on your body or by measuring the garment edge. The finished width should be in proportion to the size of the garment edge. For example, waistline ribbings are cut wider than ribbings for necklines and sleeveless armholes.

Cut ribbing from a single thickness, or fold it crosswise and cut it doubled as it will be applied to the garment. Lightweight ribbings are easier to handle if folded and pressed lightly before cutting; be careful not to stretch the ribbing while pressing. The chart on page 172 provides measurements for cutting folded and unfolded ribbings.

How to Apply Lapped Ribbing to a V-Neckline

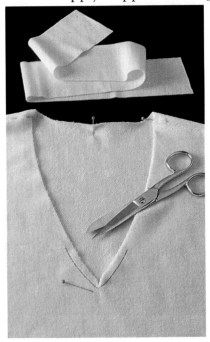

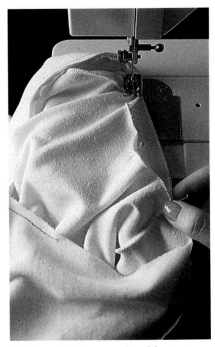

1) Cut ribbing slightly longer than the cut edge of neckline. With short stitches, staystitch on the seamline 2" (5 cm) on either side of the V. Clip carefully to the V. Fold ribbing in half lengthwise.

2) Pin ribbing to right-hand side of neckline in ¼" (6 mm) seam; leave 1" (2.5 cm) for lapping. With garment on top, begin stitching at center front. Stretch ribbing slightly as you sew.

3) Stop stitching at shoulder seam. Measure back neckline between shoulder seams. Mark ribbing with pin at point equal to two-thirds the measured length. Match pin mark to shoulder seam.

4) Stitch ribbing to garment across back neckline and down left-hand side of neckline, stretching ribbing slightly. Stop stitching before reaching point of V, leaving an opening equal to width of ribbing. Remove garment from machine.

5) Turn ribbing seam to inside. Lay garment out flat. Tuck the extensions inside the seam opening with right-hand side overlapping left. Pin ribbing at center front in lapped position.

6) Fold front of garment out of the way. From wrong side, stitch opening closed; pivot at point of V, and stitch free end of ribbing to right-hand seam allowance. Trim extensions close to stitches.

Waistline Finishes

Sweatpants or warm-up pants are simple to sew because they have only two major pattern pieces and the fit at the waistband is adjustable. There are several ways to finish pants at the waistline. None of the techniques is difficult, but they may require adapting the pattern by marking new cutting lines above the waistline.

Elastic in a casing is a simple and easy waistline finish. Elastic 1" or ¾" (2.5 or 2 cm) wide is normally used in the casing.

Ribbing waistband with a drawstring or elastic is less bulky and more comfortable than a casing. Ribbing of a contrasting color is decorative as well as practical.

Elastic with built-in drawstring is 1½" (3.8 cm) elastic knitted with a flat cord running through its center. It is generally sold on rolls in fabric stores.

Casing with multiple rows of elastic does not twist or roll. Three rows of ½" (1.3 cm) elastic create a waistband slightly wider than most elasticized casings. For a narrower waistband, use two rows of elastic instead of three.

Elasticized waistband with several rows of stitching is a comfortable, non-roll finish for knit sweatpants or nylon warm-ups. Elastic applied with this method will not twist or shift. Use elastic with good stretch and recovery qualities so the waistband retains its fit. As an option, you can add a drawstring.

175

How to Sew Pants with Elastic in the Casing

1) Mark casing on pattern, above waistline. Allow twice the width of elastic, plus ½" (1.3 cm). For example, mark 2½" (6.5 cm) casing for 1" (2.5 cm) wide elastic. Cut elastic to fit waist comfortably, plus ½" (1.3 cm) seam allowance.

2) Stitch leg seams on pants, right sides together. Use conventional straight stitch or narrow zigzag stitch, and trim seam allowances to ¼" (6 mm). Or serge seams.

3) Slip one leg inside the other, right sides together. Stitch crotch seam on pants, using a reinforcing stretch stitch or double-stitched narrow seam. Zigzag or overedge upper edge of pants.

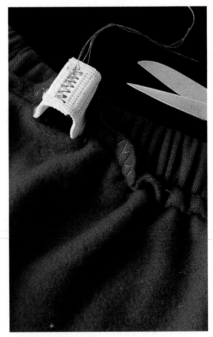

4) Form casing by folding over waist edge an amount equal to width of elastic plus ½" (1.3 cm). Stitch casing so distance between fold and stitches equals width of elastic plus ⅛" (3 mm). Leave 2" (5 cm) opening to insert elastic.

5) Thread elastic through casing, using safety pin or bodkin. Lap ends of elastic ½" (1.3 cm), and stitch securely with closely spaced zigzag stitch.

6) Slip lapped seam of elastic into opening in casing. Stitch opening closed, stretching elastic as you sew. Finish leg edges with ribbing, hem, or elastic in casing.

How to Sew a Ribbing Waistband with Drawstring

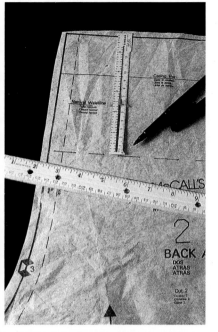

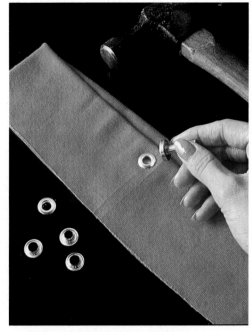

1) Mark cutting line on pattern below waistline a distance equal to the finished depth of ribbing, minus ¼" (6 mm) seam allowance. Mark cutting line 2¼" (5.7 cm) below waistline for 2½" (6.5 cm) ribbing waistband.

2) Cut ribbing 5½" (14 cm) deep (twice finished depth plus seam allowances). Cut ribbing to equal two-thirds measurement at cut edge of waistline; add ½" (1.3 cm) for seam allowances. Stitch ribbing ends in ¼" (6 mm) seam, and finger press seam open.

3) Fold ribbing in half lengthwise. Lightly press fold. Insert grommet or make small buttonhole through single layer of ribbing at center front, below fold. Grommet or buttonhole will be used for drawstring insertion.

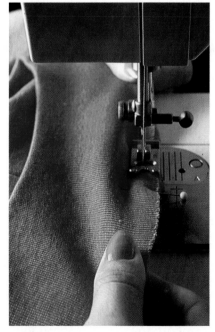

4) Divide ribbing and waist edge into fourths, and mark with pins. For larger waist, divide ribbing and garment into eighths.

5) Pin ribbing to pants, right sides together, matching markers and placing grommet opening or buttonhole at center front on right side of pants. Stitch, using straight stitch, narrow zigzag, or overlock; stretch ribbing as you sew.

6) Insert drawstring with bodkin or safety pin. To reinforce, topstitch ribbing seam. If using twin needle, straddle seam so one line of topstitching falls on each side of seam.

Sweatsuits & Warm-ups

Sweatsuits and warm-ups consist of a sweatshirt or jacket and pull-on pants. Sweatsuits for sports activities are usually made of cotton or cotton/polyester knit fleece. Warm-ups are worn for warming up during the first few minutes of sports activity and for keeping warm after the activity or exercise. Design features of sweatsuits and warm-ups also make them popular for casualwear.

How to Sew a Sweatshirt (flat method)

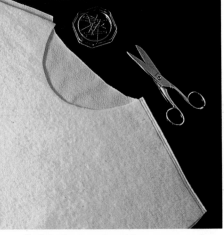

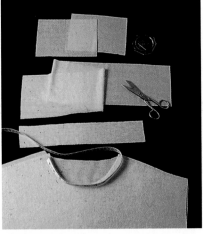

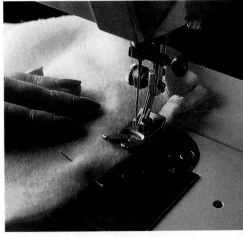

1) Stitch one shoulder seam, using double-stitched seam or overedge stitch. Or serge the seam on an overlock machine.

2) Cut neck ribbing two-thirds the distance around neckline, plus ½" (1.3 cm) for seam allowances. Cut ribbing for waist and wrists to fit body comfortably, plus ½" (1.3 cm) for seam allowances.

3) Apply neck ribbing, using flat method (page 173). Stitch other shoulder seam, beginning stitching at neckline edge; backstitch or secure ends of thread.

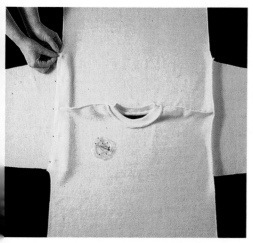

4) Pin sleeves to shirt, matching pattern symbols at shoulder seams. Stitch sleeve seams. Leave underarm seams unstitched.

5) Apply wrist ribbings, using flat method (page 173). Stitch one underarm seam, right sides together. Leave one side open.

6) Apply waist ribbing, using flat method (page 173). Stitch remaining underarm seam.

Leotards & Swimsuits

Use two-way stretch knit fabrics for fitted actionwear such as swimsuits, leotards, tights, and unitards (one-piece body suits that combine leotard and tights). Select styles that are practical for the sport and flattering to your figure. Princess seams are slenderizing. So are patterns with a center panel of a contrasting color; to minimize hips, use a dark color for the side panels. High-cut legs on swimsuits and leotards give the appearance of longer legs and a slimmer torso. For a full-busted figure, choose a pattern with a bustline shaped by darts or seams.

To fill out a slender figure, use a pattern with shirring, draping, or ruffles. Or take advantage of the fact that camouflaging is not necessary, and use patterns with high-cut legs or bold cutouts. A simple pattern style sewn in a splashy print is also a way to enhance a slender figure.

One of the benefits of sewing actionwear is making garments to suit your taste and meet your needs, down to the smallest details. You can add a full-front lining to a swimsuit. Build in minimum support at the bust by adding a bandeau lining. A bandeau, an alternative to lining the front, is a straight elasticized lining in the bust area only. For firmer support, purchased bra cups can be added to the bandeau. White or light colors and lightweight knits should be lined because they will become translucent when wet.

Measure from the indentation at the breast bone in front; bring the tape measure between your legs to the prominent bone at the top of your neck in back. Keep the tape measure snug to duplicate the fit of the finished garment.

Fitting & Pattern Adjustments

To keep alterations to a minimum, buy a pattern to fit the bust or high bust measurement. This way you will avoid extensive fitting adjustments; the two-way fabric stretches to fit many different figure shapes. Make length and hip adjustments before cutting.

If you are different sizes in the bust and hip areas, choose a multi-sized pattern, following the cutting lines for the appropriate sizes and blending them at the waistline. For one-piece garments such as swimsuits and leotards, measure your torso length (as shown on opposite page) and compare it to the torso lengths given on the chart at right. Ask someone to help; this is difficult to do by yourself.

If your measurements fall within the range given for your bust size, no pattern adjustment is necessary before you cut. Do not measure the pattern pieces for this comparison because they will measure less than actual body measurements.

If the measurement indicates that you should lengthen or shorten the torso, make the adjustment on the pattern adjustment line on the front and back pattern pieces. If two pattern adjustment lines are indicated on the pattern (above and below the waistline), adjust one-fourth the amount at each adjustment line. Lining will limit the stretch of the knit, so when lining the front of a swimsuit, add 1" (2.5 cm) in overall length; add ½" (1.3 cm) in front and back.

To adjust a leotard or swimsuit pattern for a higher leg cut, draw a new cutting line above the original on the front and back pattern pieces. Begin at the side seam and taper smoothly into the crotch area. Make sure the front and back side seams still match in length. Do not change the width of the pattern in the crotch area. For a lower leg cut, make a similar adjustment on the pattern but draw a new cutting line *beneath* the original.

Comparison of Bust Size with Torso Length

Bust Size	Torso Length
30" (76 cm)	52" to 54" (132 to 137 cm)
32" (81.5 cm)	53" to 55" (134.5 to 139.5 cm)
34" (86.5 cm)	54" to 56" (137 to 142 cm)
36" (91.5 cm)	55" to 57" (139.5 to 145 cm)
38" (96.5 cm)	56" to 58" (142 to 147.5 cm)
40" (102 cm)	57" to 59" (145 to 150 cm)
42" (107 cm)	58" to 60" (147.5 to 152.5 cm)
44" (112 cm)	59" to 61" (150 to 155 cm)

How to Fit Your Torso Length

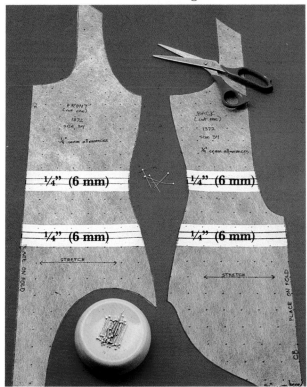

1) Adjust the pattern one-half the needed amount. Example shows adjusting for 2" (5 cm) difference by spreading pattern ¼" (6 mm) on two adjustment lines; to remove length, fold pattern into ⅛" (3 mm) tucks. If pattern has only one adjustment line, make one-fourth of adjustment on front and back.

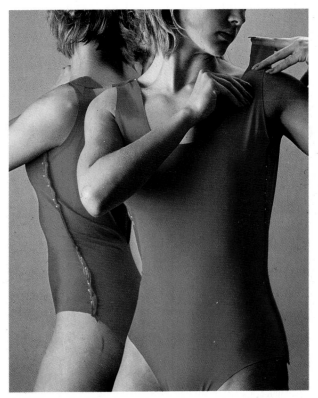

2) Fit garment after basting side seams and before sewing on elastic. Leave shoulder seams open so they can be adjusted for a snug fit. Adjust leg cut at a length that is flattering to your legs.

Finishing Edges

To stabilize edges and to ensure a snug fit on two-way stretch knit garments, use elastic at necklines, armholes, waistlines, and leg openings. Elasticized edges also allow you to slip the garment on and off easily without adding a zipper or other closure, and they self-adjust to fit your figure. Do not depend on elasticized edges to solve fitting problems. Try on the garment before finishing the edges, and adjust the fit as needed. If a swimsuit is too long, shorten by stitching deeper shoulder seams. If leotard armholes are too small and feel binding, enlarge them by trimming the openings.

If you have not adjusted the neckline, armhole, or leg openings, cut elastic into the lengths specified by the pattern. If you have changed the size of the openings, follow the guidelines given in the chart below. Most patterns print cutting information for elastic on the guide sheet or furnish a cutting guide on the margins of the pattern tissue. If working with a multi-sized pattern, follow the cutting instructions for your size. If using a pattern with several views, be sure to cut the elastic for the style you have chosen; for example, a high-cut leg requires longer elastic than a standard leg style.

Guidelines for Cutting Elastic

Type of Edge	Length to Cut Elastic
Leg opening	Measurement at cut edge of leg opening, minus 2" (5 cm) for adult sizes or 1" (2.5 cm) for children's sizes.
Waistline	Measurement at cut edge of waistline, minus 4" to 6" (10 to 15 cm) according to degree of snug fit desired. Check to see that elastic fits comfortably over hips.
Armhole	Measurement at cut edge of armhole.
Neckline	Measurement at cut edge of neckline. For a snug fit in low, scooped, or V-shaped necklines, use elastic 1" to 3" (2.5 to 7.5 cm) shorter.

How to Apply Elastic

1) Butt ends of elastic, and zigzag or 3-step zigzag to stitch securely. To avoid jamming machine, hold thread ends behind presser foot and make first stitch on length of elastic rather than on cut edge. Backstitch to secure.

2) Divide elastic into fourths, and mark with pins. Place one pin next to ends of elastic. Divide garment edge into fourths, and mark with pins; for neckline or waistline, place one pin at center back and one at center front. Shoulder seams and side seams are not necessarily halfway between centers.

3) Relax elastic when pinning front of leg; then stretch elastic to fit the back. To shape garment to figure contours, stretch elastic as you sew the back of the leg opening.

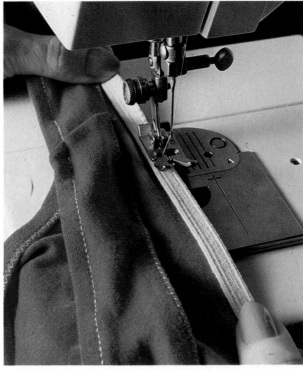

4) Stitch outer edge of elastic to garment, using narrow zigzag stitch. On 3-thread overlock machine, stitch with cutting blades positioned so they will not cut into the elastic.

5) Fold elastic over, toward inside of garment. Elastic is now covered with garment fabric.

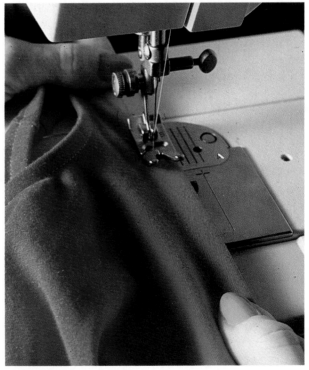

6) Lengthen stitches and loosen tension slightly to straight-stitch or narrow zigzag through all layers ¼" (6 mm) from edge; stretch as you sew. Or topstitch with twin-needle straight-stitching, using woolly nylon thread on bobbin.

Sewing for Children

Sewing children's clothes can be quite economical and need not be time-consuming. Because children's garments require less fabric than garments for adults, the fabric cost is usually minimal. You may be able to use fabric from other sewing projects to construct a garment, or part of a garment, for a young child.

Most children's clothing designs follow simple lines, have few pieces, and are easy to sew. They are a good starting point for a beginning sewer or for a sewer whose skills need updating.

Planning for Safety

Build safety into children's garments. Avoid loose strings or excess fabric that may get tangled, especially for infants. Beware of long skirts or gowns that may cause a child to trip, or very full sleeves that may catch on objects. Limit tie belts and drawstrings to short lengths, and securely fasten buttons and trims. Use fire-retardant fabrics for sleepwear.

Customizing Clothes for Children

Creative touches can make a garment special to a child. Use a child's crayon drawing as a guide to colors and shapes for a machine-embroidered design. Or let children color or paint fabric before you cut out the pattern. Some children may enjoy designing their

clothes by drawing the garment they would like and then having you match the color and general style. Simple, original appliqués can reflect a favorite hobby or special toy.

Involve the child in selecting patterns, fabrics, and notions. For young children learning to identify colors, primary colors of red, yellow, and blue are popular. Look at colors of a favorite toy and the colors a child often chooses for painting or drawing. Consider the coloring of the child's hair, eyes, and skin; select colors that compliment them.

Features for Self-dressing

To encourage self-dressing, choose garments with loose-fitting necklines and waistlines and with manageable fasteners. Make closures easy to see and reach on the front or side of a garment. Hook and loop tape can be used for closures on most types of garments. Young children can easily unfasten simple, large, round buttons and snaps, but may have difficulty closing them with small hands. They also enjoy smooth-running zippers with large teeth and zipper pulls. Pull-on pants that have elastic waists are easier for young children to pull on and off. Children can be frustrated by trying to fasten hooks and eyes, tiny buttons, and ties.

Tips for Planning Garments for Growth and Comfort

Add ribbing cuffs to lower edges of sleeves or pants legs so you can turn up built-in room for growth.

Choose pants patterns in a style that can be cut off for shorts when outgrown in length.

Use elastic waists on generously sized pants or skirts for comfort during growth spurts.

Allow extra crotch and body length in one-piece garments to prevent them from becoming uncomfortable as the child grows.

Add elastic suspenders with adjustable closures.

Choose dress and jumper patterns with dropped waist or no waist for comfort and maximum length of wear.

Use knit fabrics for easier sewing and maximum stretch for growth and comfort.

Consider patterns with pleats, gathers, and wide shapes that allow for growth without riding up.

Select patterns with raglan, dolman, and dropped sleeves to offer room for growth and less restriction of movement.

Select oversized styles for comfort.

Receiving Blankets & Hooded Towels

Receiving blankets and hooded towels can be made large enough to accommodate the growth of the child. Choose soft, warm, and absorbent woven or knit fabrics. Select from flannel, interlock, jersey, thermal knit, terry cloth and stretch terry. Two layers of lightweight fabric can be used with wrong sides together. Round all corners for easy edge application.

Cut a 36" (91.5 cm) square blanket or towel from 1 yd. (.95 m) of 45" or 60" (115 or 152.5 cm) wide fabric. When using 45" (115 cm) wide fabric, the mock binding and hood require an additional ¼ yd. (.25 m). Cut a 1½" (3.8 cm) wide binding strip on the lengthwise or crosswise grain, 2" (5 cm) longer than the distance around the item; piece, as necessary. Press binding in half, with wrong sides together.

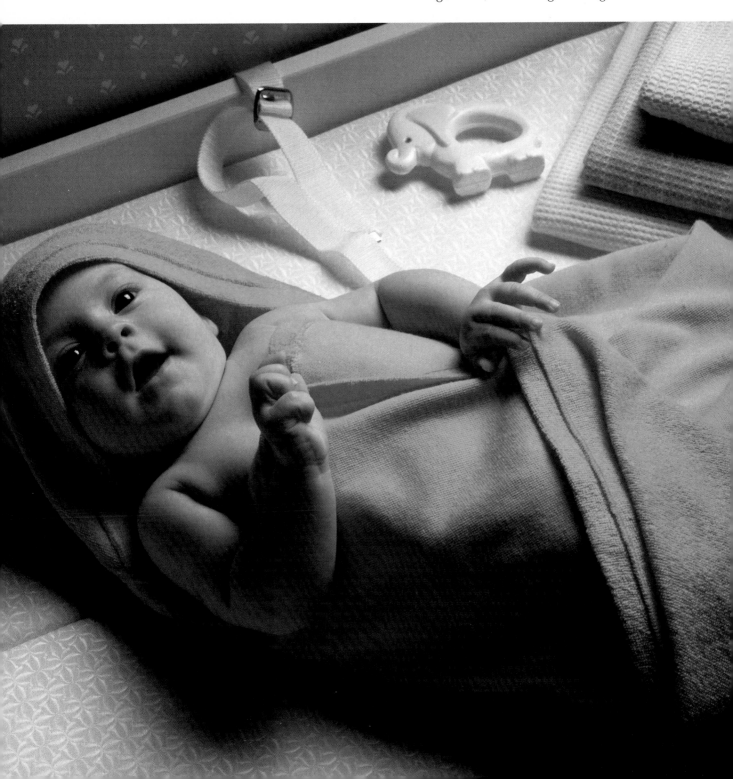

How to Finish Edges with a Mock Binding

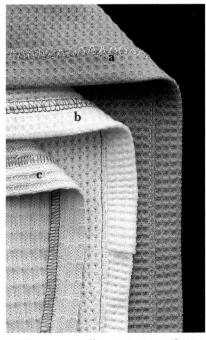

1) Use overedge stitch or serge binding to right side of fabric, starting 1½" (3.8 cm) from end of binding. Stitch to within 2" (5 cm) of start of binding, stretching fabric slightly at corners; do not stretch binding. (If flatlock stitch on serger is used, stitch *wrong* sides together.)

2) Fold 1" (2.5 cm) of binding to inside; lap around first end of binding. Continue stitching binding to fabric, stitching over previous stitches for 1" (2.5 cm) to secure the ends.

3) Turn seam allowance toward blanket or towel; topstitch through all layers of overedged **(a)** or serged **(b)** seam, to hold seam allowances flat. If flatlock **(c)** stitch is used, pull binding and fabric flat.

How to Sew a Hooded Towel

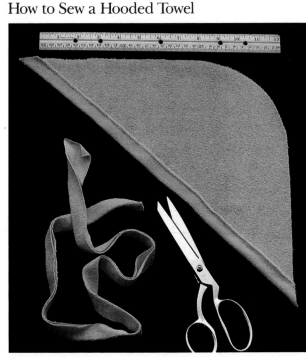

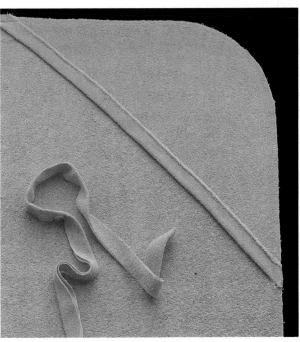

1) Cut a right triangle with two 12" (30.5 cm) sides from matching or contrasting fabric. Round right angle corner, and finish diagonal edge with mock binding, above.

2) Position wrong side of the hood to right side of the towel. Stitch triangle to one rounded corner of towel, ¼" (6 mm) from matched edges. Finish outside edges, above.

Bibs

Infant bibs are quick and easy to make. Create durable bibs from terry cloth or knit fabric or from fingertip towels, and customize the bibs with simple appliqué techniques and bias tape. Increase absorbency by using a double layer of fabric. Back a fabric bib with soft, pliable plastic to protect clothing; finish edges with wide double-fold bias tape. Or use a fingertip towel with prefinished edges.

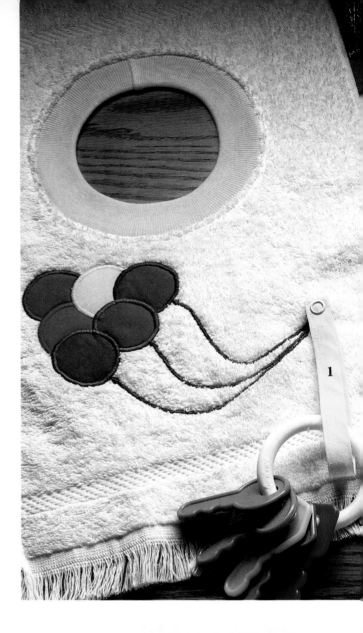

Custom Bibs

Attach a toy or pacifier to a bib with a snap-on strip **(1)**. Stitch together the edges of a 12" (30.5 cm) strip of wide double-fold bias tape, and fold under the ends of the strip. Attach one end to the bib with the ball half of a gripper snap. Attach the socket half of the gripper snap to the other end of the tape. Slip the toy or pacifier onto the tape; snap securely to the bib.

A purchased squeaker can be inserted between the appliqué and bib **(2)** before you stitch the appliqué (page 197).

A fingertip towel makes an absorbent, washable bib. Fold the towel for double absorbency under the chin **(3)**, and attach double-fold bias tape around the neck edge.

How to Make a Pullover Bib

1) Use fingertip towel. Cut 5" (12.5 cm) circle with center of circle one-third the distance from one end of towel. Cut 3" (7.5 cm) wide ribbing, with length two-thirds the circumference. Stitch short ends to form circle, using ¼" (6 mm) seam allowance.

2) Fold ribbing in half, with wrong sides together. Divide ribbing and neck edge into fourths; pin-mark. Matching pins, and with seam at center back, pin ribbing to neck edge, with raw edges even. Stitch ¼" (6 mm) seam, stretching ribbing to fit neckline.

3) Fold seam allowance toward bib. Edgestitch to bib through all layers.

How to Make a Tie-on Bib

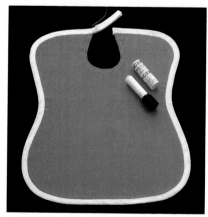

1) Press wide double-fold bias tape to follow curve of outer edge of bib. Glue-baste tape over raw edge of bib, positioning the wider tape edge on the wrong side; edgestitch in place.

2) Cut bias tape 30" (76 cm) longer than neck curve. Center bias tape over the neck edge; glue-baste. Edgestitch from one end of tie around neckline to other end. Bar tack bias tape at edge of bib (arrow) by zigzagging in place; tie knot at each end.

Alternative. Cut fingertip towel as for pullover bib, opposite. Fold so neck opening forms a half circle. Zigzag raw edges together with wide stitch. Apply bias tape for ties and neck finish, step 2, left.

Adding Durability

Build in durability as you construct children's garments. Seams and knees are subject to the most stress during dressing and active play, but both areas can be strengthened easily as you sew the garment.

Seams are most vulnerable at the crotch, shoulder, neck, and armhole. Strengthen the crotch and armhole seams with double-stitched, mock flat-fell, or edgestitched seams. Reinforce shoulder and neckline seams with decorative twin-needle seam finish (page 192), stitching before crossing with another seam. Machine-stitch hems for added strength in activewear.

The knee area wears out faster than any other part of a child's garment and is difficult to reach for repairs. Flat construction techniques allow you to reinforce knee areas as you construct the garment.

Patches

Tightly woven fabrics make the most durable patches. Interface, pad, or quilt patches for extra durability and protection at the knee, especially for crawling toddlers. Fuse the patch to the garment to make the application easier and to strengthen the patch.

Double-knee and decorative patches are cut according to the child's size. For infants, cut the patch 3½" × 4" (9 × 10 cm); for toddlers, 3¾" × 5" (9.5 × 12.5 cm); for children, 4½" × 6" (11.5 × 15 cm).

Round the corners of decorative patches to simplify application and to eliminate sharp corners that could catch and tear.

Double Knees. Apply double-knee patches to the right side or the wrong side of the garment. The double layer of fabric adds strength to the knee area. You may also pad the area with polyester fleece, and machine-quilt, for extra durability.

Extended Pockets. An extended pocket serves as both pocket and double knee, and is applied to right side of garment.

Decorative Knee Patches. For a decorative knee patch, use pinking shears to cut shapes from soft, nonraveling double-faced polyester bunting. Glue-baste in position, and topstitch to garment. Coordinate the color of the patch with ribbing or other trim. For a piped patch (page 193), select two coordinating fabrics for patch and piping. Quilt the patch fabric, if desired, before applying piping. Patches can be repeated on the elbows.

How to Reinforce Seams Using a Twin Needle

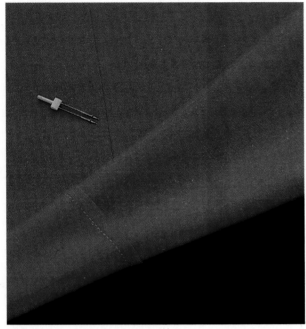

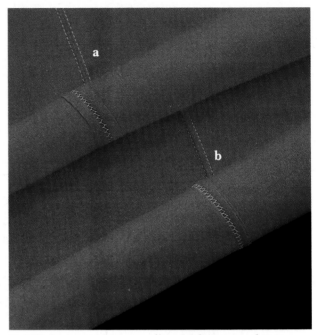

1) Stitch a plain seam. Press seam allowances to one side or open; trim to ¼" (6 mm). Insert twin needle in conventional sewing machine.

2) Stitch, centering seamline **(a)** between the two rows of stitching. For seam allowances pressed to one side **(b)**, you may prefer to stitch in the ditch with one needle as other needle stitches through garment and seam allowances.

How to Add Double-knee Patches

1) Cut two patches 6½" (16.3 cm) long and width of pattern at knee; press under ¼" (6 mm) on long edges. Mark placement lines on front of pants leg 3" (7.5 cm) above and below center of knee.

2) Cut polyester fleece to finished patch size; place on wrong side of patch, under ¼" (6 mm) seam allowances. Glue-baste patch in position over placement lines. Edgestitch long edges.

3) Machine-quilt patch to garment by topstitching through all layers, to provide extra strength. Construct garment according to pattern directions.

How to Add Decorative Knee Patches

1) Cut two patches to size (page 190); round corners. Iron paper-backed fusible web to back of patches. Cut two strips of fabric for piping 1" × 24" (2.5 × 61 cm); cut on bias for woven fabrics or crosswise grain for knits.

2) Press strips in half lengthwise, wrong sides together. Stitch to right side of each patch, raw edges even, with ¼" (6 mm) seam allowance.

3) Curve ends of piping into seam allowance, so folded ends overlap and taper to raw edge. Trim piping even with raw edge of patch.

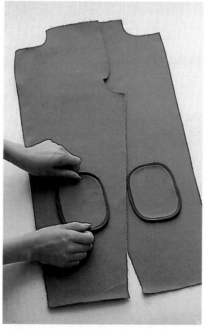

4) Trim seam allowance to ⅛" (3 mm). Press seam allowance to wrong side of patch, pulling piping out from patch. Remove paper backing from fusible web.

5) Fuse one patch to front of pants leg, parallel to hemline with center of patch slightly below center of knee. On the other pants leg, align second patch with first; fuse.

6) Stitch patch to garment, stitching in the ditch. Finish pants according to pattern directions.

Adding Grow Room

Build in grow room when you construct children's clothing, to get the maximum amount of wear from the garments. Without this extra room, a child going through a rapid growth spurt may be unable to wear a garment that is well liked and in good condition. The easiest place to add grow room is at the lower edge or sleeve hem. Rolled-up lined cuffs can be gradually lowered as the child grows. To add a coordinated look, select a lining fabric to match a shirt or other part of the ensemble. Cut lining on the straight grain or bias; add interest with a plaid or stripe. When sewing a garment that has straps, add extra length to the straps, and use overall buckles for easy length adjustment.

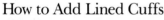

Ribbing. Make ribbing twice the recommended finished width. Fold the ribbing up, and gradually unroll it to add length as the child grows. Add ribbing to outgrown sleeves or pants legs by opening the hem and using the hemline for the new stitching line.

Inserts and trims. Planning carefully for balanced finished proportions, cut off the lower edge of the garment. Cut an insert of coordinating fabric, lace, or eyelet 1" (2.5 cm) wider than desired length, to allow for ¼" (6 mm) seam allowances on insert and garment. Stitch upper edge of insert to garment, then stitch lower section of garment to insert. Trims with finished edges can be stitched to the right or wrong side of a garment at the hemline for added length.

How to Add Lined Cuffs

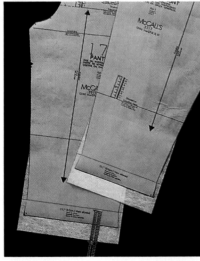

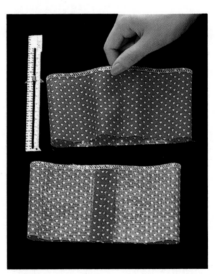

1) Adjust pattern at hem; lengthen hem allowance to 2½" (6.5 cm). Straighten side seams above original hemline for 4" (10 cm) to eliminate taper. Cut out garment; assemble according to pattern directions, but do not hem.

2) Cut two cuffs 3½" (9 cm) wide, and 1" (2.5 cm) longer than the circumference of finished sleeve or pants leg. Stitch short ends of cuff, right sides together, using ½" (1.3 cm) seam; press open. Serge upper edge, or turn under ¼" (6 mm), and press.

3) Stitch cuff to garment, with right sides together and raw edges even, using ¼" (6 mm) seam; match cuff seam to inseam. Turn cuff at stitching line, and press to wrong side of garment; topstitch at lower and upper edges. Fold cuff to right side.

Appliqués

Appliqués are a traditional method for decorating children's garments. Select from three basic types of appliqués; purchase iron-on or sew-on appliqués, or design your own. For a fast and easy decorative touch, fuse purchased iron-on appliqués to a garment, following the manufacturer's directions. Purchased sew-on appliqués may be fused to the garment using fusible web. You may wish to topstitch to secure the appliqué through many launderings.

You may want to design your own custom-made appliqués. Look at magazines, ready-to-wear garments, or coloring books for ideas. Fruit, animals, numbers, toys, hearts, and rainbows are all popular shapes for children's appliqués. Consider cutting motifs from printed fabrics.

Before assembling the appliqué, plan the work sequence. Smaller pieces may need to be positioned on and stitched to larger pieces before applying appliqué to the garment, and some pieces may overlap other pieces.

Embellish the appliqués with bows, buttons, ribbons, pom-poms, fabric paint, or cord. Cut ends of cord may be placed under appliqué pieces before fusing. Trims may be stitched or glued in place, using permanent fabric glue.

Tips for Appliqués

Practice stitching an appliqué on a test piece before working with the garment piece.

Select a colorfast fabric for an appliqué that is compatible with garment fabric in weight and care requirements; preshrink all fabrics.

Remember that it is easiest to stitch around large, simple shapes with few corners.

Leave a fabric margin in a geometric shape around intricate motifs cut from printed fabrics.

Apply paper-backed fusible web to the wrong side of the appliqué fabric before cutting out the shape.

Add durability to a garment by applying an appliqué with fusible web at knees or elbows.

Add ½" (1.3 cm) to sides of appliqué pieces that will go under another piece; trim to reduce bulk when final placement is determined.

Remember that shapes drawn on paper backing of fusible web will be reversed on the garment; draw mirror images of letters or numbers.

Apply tear-away stabilizer to the wrong side of a garment for smooth satin stitching at the edge of an appliqué.

Use a special-purpose presser foot with a wide channel to prevent buildup of satin stitches.

Apply an appliqué to garment before joining seams. It is easier to apply an appliqué while fabric is flat.

How to Make and Apply an Appliqué

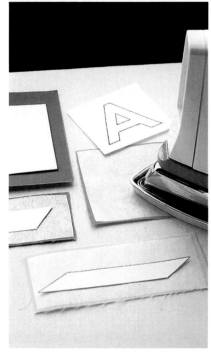

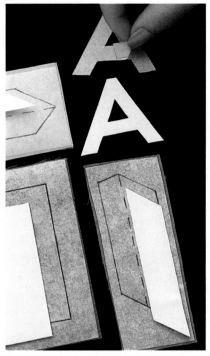

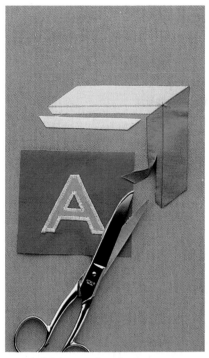

1) Apply paper-backed fusible web to wrong side of appliqué fabric, following manufacturer's directions. Allow fabric to cool.

2) Draw design on fabric or paper backing; add ½" (1.3 cm) to sides of appliqué pieces that go under another piece. Cut out design and remove paper backing.

3) Position appliqué pieces on the garment fabric. Trim appliqué pieces under other pieces to reduce bulk; leave scant ¼" (6 mm). Fuse appliqué pieces to garment.

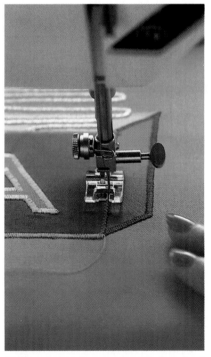

4) Cut tear-away stabilizer 1" (2.5 cm) larger than appliqué. Glue-baste to the wrong side of garment, under appliqué. Zigzag stitch around appliqué, using short, narrow stitches.

5) Decrease the upper tension, and adjust stitches for short, wide zigzag; satin stitch around appliqué edges to cover all raw edges. Remove tear-away stabilizer.

Appliqué with squeaker. Apply fusible interfacing to wrong side of appliqué. Place squeaker under appliqué; glue appliqué in place at edges. Complete appliqué as in steps 4 and 5, left.

Appliqué Techniques

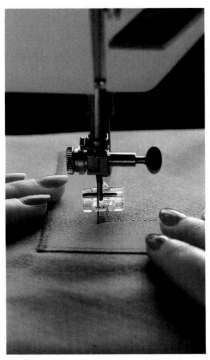

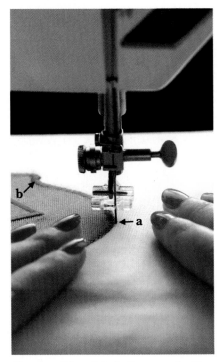

Outside corners. Stitch past the edge of the appliqué one stitch. Raise presser foot, pivot fabric, and continue stitching.

Inside corners. Stitch past corner a distance equal to width of satin stitch. Raise presser foot, pivot fabric, and continue stitching.

Curves. Pivot fabric frequently. For outside curves, pivot with needle on outer edge of stitching (**a**); for inside curves, pivot with needle at inner edge of stitching (**b**).

Appliqués from printed fabric. Cut designs from fabric to use as appliqués. For an intricate design, cut a fabric margin in a simple shape.

Decorated appliqués. Decorate an appliqué with buttons, bows, bells, ribbons, or pom-poms. Attach the decorations with permanent fabric glue, or stitch securely.

No-sew appliqués. Place purchased appliqué face down on paper; apply slightly larger piece of paper-backed fusible web to appliqué. Remove paper backing and excess web at edges. Fuse; topstitch if desired.

Trapunto Appliqués

Trapunto is a method for padding an appliqué to give it a three-dimensional look. Traditional trapunto techniques consist of applying the appliqué to the right side of the fabric, slashing the backing fabric, stuffing with fiberfill, and closing the slash, using hand stitches.

To achieve the same three-dimensional look, use the easy alternate method that follows. Experiment with the amount of fiberfill; small amounts work best. After stitching, fuse the appliqué to the fiberfill to stabilize the padding through laundering and wear.

How to Sew a Trapunto Appliqué

1) Prepare fabric as for appliqué, steps 1 and 2, page 197. Do not fuse appliqué to garment.

2) Glue-baste stabilizer to wrong side of garment. Zigzag appliqué to the garment with short, narrow stitches; use a screwdriver to lightly fill appliqué with fiberfill just before stitching is completed.

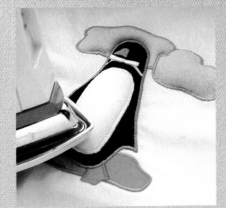

3) Satin stitch as for appliqué, step 5, page 197. Pierce appliqué with a pin; distribute fiberfill evenly. Remove stabilizer. Lightly press appliqué to fuse fiberfill to the web; do not press flat.

Especially for Boys

Boys' clothing usually ranges from traditional classic to well-worn sports clothes. However, some occasions call for special attire. Accessorize a boy's suit with suspenders, a bow tie, or a reversible vest.

Suspenders are quick and easy to make, using belting, or decorative elastic. Suspenders should be ⅛" (3 mm) narrower than the hardware.

There are two styles of suspenders: crisscross and cross-brace. Both styles require clips to fasten to the pants waistband and adjusters for easy length alterations as the child grows.

To prevent suspenders from slipping off the shoulders, you may use a slide for crisscross suspenders or make a cross-brace to hold suspenders together in front.

To determine the finished length of crisscross suspenders, measure the child diagonally across the shoulder. For cross-brace suspenders, measure straight over the shoulder.

How to Make Crisscross Suspenders

1) Cut two straps 10" (25.5 cm) longer than finished suspender length. Apply liquid fray preventer to cut ends. Insert one end through adjuster (**a**), then through clip (**b**), then back to adjuster; insert, and close tab (**c**).

2) Insert free ends through slide by bringing both ends of straps through side openings and out lower end of slide. Straps cross on back of slide.

3) Thread free end through back clips; turn 1" (2.5 cm) to wrong side. Double-stitch through both thicknesses of strap. Position back slide and front adjusters for comfortable fit.

How to Make Cross-brace Suspenders

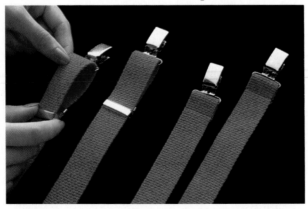

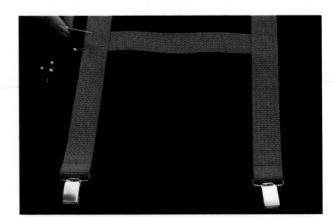

1) Cut two straps 10" (25.5 cm) longer than finished suspender length. Apply liquid fray preventer to cut ends. Attach adjusters and clips, as in steps 1 and 3, above.

2) Try on suspenders with adjusters in back; position adjusters for comfortable fit. Cut cross-brace to fit at mid-chest between outer edges of straps. Apply liquid fray preventer to cut ends. Place cross-brace under straps; stitch as shown.

How to Make a Reversible Vest

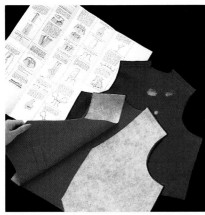

1) Cut two fronts and one back from fabric; repeat, using coordinating fabric. Follow pattern directions to attach pockets to interfaced vest front. Stitch all shoulder seams; press open.

2) Stitch vests together at front, neck, and armhole edges, right sides together, matching shoulder seams. Trim seam allowances to ¼" (6 mm); clip curves to stitching. Press seams open.

3) Turn vest right side out by pulling front through shoulder to back, one side at a time. Press, positioning seamline exactly on the edge.

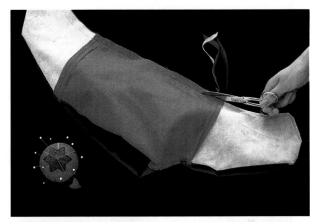

4) Stitch side seams of both layers in one continuous step, matching armhole seams. Press seams open. Trim seam allowances to ⅜" (1 cm).

5) Stitch lower raw edges, with right sides together and side seams matching; leave 3" (7.5 cm) opening for turning. Trim seam allowances to ¼" (6 mm); trim corners.

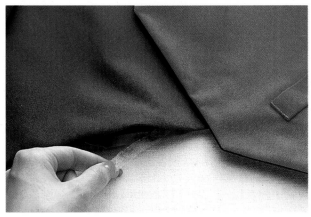

6) Turn vest right side out through opening at lower edge. Press lower edge, positioning seamline exactly on the edge. At opening, turn in raw edges, and fuse. Topstitch vest ¼" (6 mm) from edges, if desired.

7) Mark snap positions on both sides of each vest front. Apply snaps according to package directions, using decorative caps on both parts of snaps.

Heirloom Strips

Fabric strips for machine heirloom sewing may be embellished with machine embroidery and pin tucks, or gathered for puffing strips.

Machine embroidery is the easiest technique to use. Experiment with wing needles, decorative stitches, and machine embroidery thread.

Make pin tucks, using a pin-tuck presser foot and a twin needle. Twin needles are sized according to the distance between needles and the thickness of the needles. Use a 1.8 (70) or 2 (80) needle for fine fabrics. The fabric strip should be wider than the finished width to allow for the fabric that forms the tucks. Make an uneven number of tucks, with the middle tuck at the center.

Create puffing strips by gathering both sides of a fabric strip before joining it to entredeux. Cut fabric to the desired width plus ½" (1.3 cm) for two seam allowances, and one and a half times the finished length. Set the zigzag stitch length (page 203); set the stitch width to zigzag over ⅛" (3 mm) of the edge of the fabric. Press, but do not starch, the fabric strip before gathering; do not press after gathering.

How to Machine-embroider Using a Wing Needle

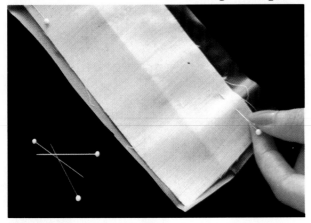

1) Cut fabric to desired width plus ½" (1.3 cm) for two seam allowances. Apply spray starch to fabric strip; press. Fold strip lengthwise; lightly finger press fold to mark stitching line. Pin a strip of water-soluble stabilizer to back of fabric.

2) Stitch one or more rows, using a decorative stitch and a wing needle. Remove stabilizer according to manufacturer's directions; press fabric strip.

How to Roll, Whip, and Gather a Puffing Strip

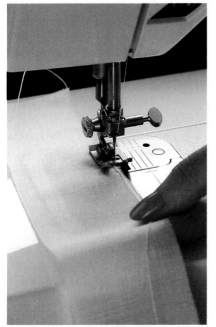

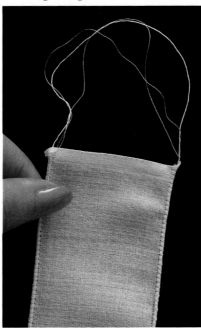

1) Cut fabric and set stitch length and width, opposite. Place a thread along edge on right side of fabric, leaving a 3" (7.5 cm) thread tail. Zigzag stitch over thread; fabric will roll over thread.

2) Zigzag stitch one edge of fabric. Turn fabric, and leave a 4" (10 cm) loop of thread before stitching down other side. Leave 3" (7.5 cm) thread tail at end.

3) Pull encased threads from each end to evenly gather both sides of puffing strip. Gather to desired length; distribute gathers. Knot gathering threads at each end.

How to Sew Pin Tucks

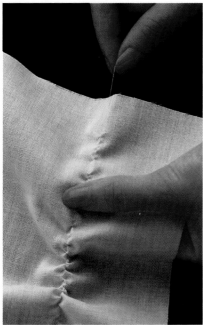

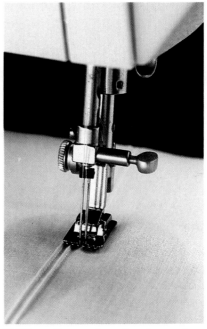

1) Cut fabric strip about 2" (5 cm) wider than finished width. Pull thread lengthwise on strip to mark position for center tuck. Tighten upper thread tension slightly; set stitch length to 12 to 14 stitches per inch (2.5 cm).

2) Apply spray starch to fabric strip; press. Using pin-tuck presser foot and twin needle, stitch over pulled-thread mark; hold the fabric taut. Bobbin thread draws two needle threads together, creating pin tuck.

3) Place first tuck under channel of pin-tuck presser foot; determine distance from first tuck by channel selection. Stitch additional tucks. Trim equal amounts on each side of strip, allowing for ¼" (6 mm) seam allowance on each side.

Joining Heirloom Strips

Join fabric strips, laces, and trims for heirloom sewing with a narrow seam that is neat and durable. Machine methods closely duplicate traditional hand stitches but are much faster to do and easier to master. For additional strength, use entredeux between fabrics and laces or trims. Use spray starch on all strips except puffing strips. Press all strips before stitching.

Several techniques are used for joining strips. One of the joining techniques used in heirloom sewing is rolling and whipping. This technique rolls a tiny amount of fabric around the adjoining lace or trim, adding strength to the seam. When applying flat lace to a hem edge, press the seam allowance toward the fabric. You may also want to edgestitch through all layers. A rolled seam sewn on the serger produces the same result as rolling and whipping.

The narrow zigzag stitch on a conventional sewing machine or the flatlock stitch on a serger may be used to join two laces with finished edges. Use a narrow zigzag stitch to join trimmed entredeux to lace with finished edges.

Gather laces before joining them to trimmed entredeux. Pull a heavy thread in the lace heading to create gathers or, if the lace lacks a heavy thread, machine-stitch a gathering line. Trim the remaining seam allowance on the entredeux and use entredeux with gathered lace to highlight a yoke seam or a neck edge.

Selecting Joining Techniques

Edges to Be Joined	Conventional Machine	Serger
Entredeux to puffing strip	Rolled and whipped seam	—
Fabric to entredeux	Rolled and whipped seam	Rolled seam
Fabric to flat lace	Rolled and whipped seam	Rolled seam
Lace to entredeux	Zigzag seam	—
Lace to lace	Zigzag seam	Flatlock seam

How to Gather Lace and Join to Entredeux

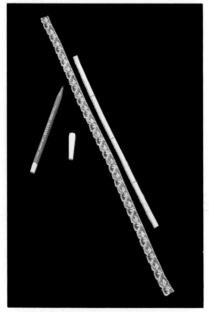

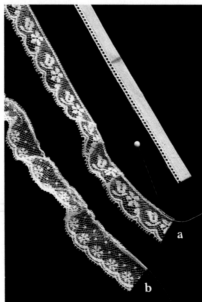

1) Cut entredeux 1" (2.5 cm) longer than needed; trim away one seam allowance. Cut flat lace 1½ times longer than entredeux. Divide lace and entredeux into fourths; mark.

2) Pull heavy thread in lace heading from both ends to gather lace (**a**). For laces without a heavy thread, stitch next to lace edge, using 14 to 16 stitches per inch (2.5 cm); pull bobbin thread to gather (**b**). Match marks on lace and entredeux.

3) Set zigzag stitch length (page 203). Butt trimmed entredeux edge to lace; zigzag 1" (2.5 cm) at a time, using a narrow stitch. Use a small screwdriver to hold gathers under presser foot. Continue to end; remove gathering thread.

How to Use the Rolled and Whipped and the Rolled Seam Joining Methods

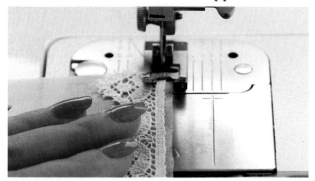

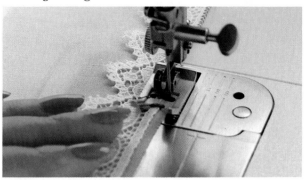

Roll and whip fabric to flat lace. 1) Set zigzag stitch length (page 203). Lay starched and pressed strips, right sides together, with bottom strip extending ⅛" to ³/₁₆" (3 to 4.5 mm) beyond top strip.

2) Set zigzag stitch width so left swing of stitch is ⅛" (3 mm) from edge of top strip and right swing of stitch extends over edge of bottom strip. As needle moves to the left, edge of bottom strip rolls over seam; upper thread tension may need to be loosened.

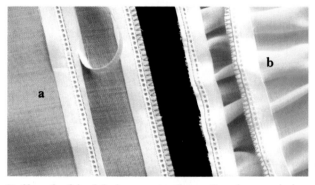

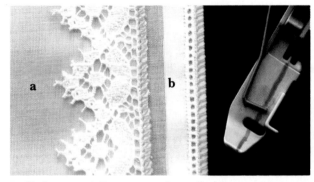

Roll and whip fabric to entredeux. Set zigzag stitch length (page 203). To join entredeux and flat fabric **(a),** place starched and pressed strips right sides together and raw edges even; stitch in the ditch next to the entredeux holes. Trim seam allowances to scant ⅛" (3 mm). To join entredeux to a puffing strip **(b),** trim entredeux seam allowance to scant ⅛" (3 mm); position strips, and stitch in the ditch. Remove the gathering thread. Finish both seams as in step 2, above.

Rolled seam. Adjust serger for rolled hem setting, following manufacturer's directions; set stitch length at 2 to 3 mm. Stitch lace to fabric **(a),** with right sides of strips together and raw edges even. To stitch entredeux to fabric **(b),** mark line from needle position to end of presser foot (arrow). Use line as a guide to stitch in the ditch next to holes of entredeux.

How to Use the Zigzag and Flatlock Joining Methods

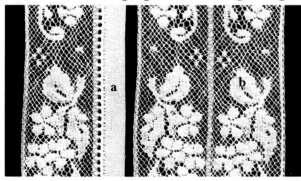

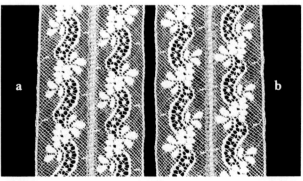

Zigzag seam. Set zigzag stitch length (page 203); set width for narrow stitch. For entredeux **(a),** trim one seam allowance and butt trimmed edge to lace; stitch. For laces **(b),** place right side up and butt edges; stitch.

Flatlock seam. Adjust serger for flatlock stitch following manufacturer's directions. Stitch; pull laces flat. Ladder of stitches **(a)** shows on right side when laces are stitched with right sides together. Trellis of stitches **(b)** shows on right side when laces are stitched with wrong sides together.

Home Decorating Projects

Planning a Project

You are the decorator when you sew for your home. The prospect can be as overwhelming as planning and coordinating the window treatments, pillows, and accessories for an entire new home, or it can be as simple as selecting a fabric for a kitchen curtain. Often, however, the single sewing project becomes only a beginning for a project to refresh or update a whole area of the house.

Start by looking at your decorating needs and sewing projects room by room. A home generally looks larger and more pleasing when colors and patterns flow easily from one room to the next. Colors and patterns should relate, but they may branch off into different color schemes and moods. Devise a plan for your sewing project as a whole, but then work at it step by step. Any project will look smaller when broken into smaller pieces.

Where to Start

Most designers start planning the color scheme and direction for a home with the first rooms that are seen. The entry and the living room are usually these focal points. If the dining room is connected to the living room, look at the entry, living room, and dining room as one unit when considering colors and moods.

From the dining room you may move into the second area, the kitchen and family room, and sometimes the utility room and a related bathroom. A separate look or mood may coordinate these rooms, but the colors and fabrics you select should be compatible with the colors you have selected for the living and dining rooms. If the kitchen joins these first two areas of the home, it should be compatible, too.

The third area, the master bedroom and bath, is another distinct area that has a special mood. Bedrooms are personal areas that are more apt to have fabrics and colors that reflect your personality, tastes, and interests. The remaining bedrooms and baths for children or guests may have another color and fabric direction. A guest bedroom may do double-duty as a sewing room, home office, or den.

Record Keeping

An important part of the sewing plan is a notebook with pocket folders so you have a place to collect samples and swatches. Organize your notebook into the four general areas of the home. Leave plenty of pages between sections for all the information you

will collect for each room. Clip pictures and fill your notebook with ideas. Look for a mix in fabrics and colors, and interesting uses of texture and trimmings. The more ideas you collect for each room, the better.

Keep window measurements, room plans, pictures, and snapshots for each room in this notebook, along with phone numbers of important resources. A sturdy tote bag can be used for carrying heavy, bulky samples.

Sources of Ideas

For inspiration, save magazine pictures of rooms that you like. Some classic styles remain stable year after year. It is often the detailing of trims, colors, and fabrics that can update home furnishings.

Many designers keep design magazines and trade publications that will also give you ideas. Furniture stores, model rooms, and catalogs have photos of window treatments, pillows, and accessories that you can sew. Most major cities have model homes and showcase houses that show the newest in decorating trends. Wallcovering books are also inspirational sources of decorating ideas; they show ideas for mixing fabric prints and using borders and stripes.

Creating an Atmosphere

List five words that you and your family would use to describe the results you wish to achieve from your decorating. These words will evoke different feelings about color, fabric patterns, and texture as well as furniture design and shape. For a family room or kitchen you may think of sunny, bright, clean, crisp, and cheery — or rich, warm, mellow, cozy, and traditional.

Elegant, comfortable, or traditional might be appropriate for the living-dining area. Strong, masculine, and rustic might be words for a library, den, or bath. Contemporary, clean, spacious, and

dramatic might be words for a bedroom. For someone else the mood for a bedroom might be romantic, soft, plush, feminine, and comfortable.

In the photo above, beige, gold, and pink tones suggest elegance. Fabrics with subtle sheen accent the mitered stripes on pillows, the softly shirred Austrian valances, and the fabric rosette. Simply changing a color or fabric can change the feeling in the room and create a different overall effect of the decorating. Use the chart on the opposite page to get you started with your own decorating ideas.

Guidelines for Decorating

Overall Effect	Suggested Colors	Fabrics & Textures	Items to Sew
Elegant, special, or refined	Refined colors: mauve, taupe, gold, metallic, ecru	Shiny fabrics or fabrics with sheen: silks, fine cottons, antique satins, moirés, rayon trims	Mitered pillows (page 219), swags & jabots (page 268), Austrian valances (page 264)
Comfortable, casual	Autumn colors: rust, tan, gold	Smooth to lightly textured finishes, no scratchy finishes: polished cottons, chintzes, warp sateens, casements	Turkish floor cushions (page 219), cloud shades (page 251), balloon shades (page 254)
Cozy, restful	Soft to medium shades: blue, mauve, green	Softly padded or quilted fabrics, inviting prints: cotton sheetings, warp sateens, chintzes	Duvet covers (page 310); pillow shams, dust ruffles and bed skirts (pages 312, 315); mock box pillows (page 282); mock corded pillows (page 284)
Practical	Multi-colors, medium shades: red, blue, orange	Washable or stain-resistant fabrics, overall prints: sheetings, cotton blends	Tapered valances (page 266), knife-edge pillows or liners (page 278), square & rectangular tablecloths (page 300)
Conservative, clean & neat, tidy, crisp	Light colors, warm tones: white, mauve, peach, ecru, maize	Fabrics with woven designs, nubby textures, allover prints: sheer linens, cottons, casements	Pinch-pleated draperies (page 236), bound tiebacks (page 244), padded cornices (page 273), bound placemats (pages 302, 304)
Tailored, masculine	Earth tones, rich colors: rich rust & brown, intense blue & green	Geometrics, plaids, stripes: upholstery fabrics, tapestries	Mitered pillows (page 219), flanged shams (page 314), trimmed placemats (page 307), box pillows (page 285), Roman shades (page 247)
Cheerful	Bright, clear colors: pink, yellow, blue, green, orange	Bold florals & stripes, fabrics with contrasting colors: decorator cotton prints, warp sateens	Cloud shades (page 251), balloon shades (page 254), pillow shams (page 312), tab top curtains (page 232)
Romantic	Fresh colors: pastel pink, blue, green, peach, ivory	Fabrics that encourage touching: silks, polished cottons, sateens, florals, water-color prints, laces, eyelet borders	Pouf valances (pages 261), cloud valances (page 262), ruffled pillow shams (page 312) and dust ruffles (page 315), ruffled pillows (page 286), round tablecloths (page 298)
Contemporary	Neutral tones: beige, gray, ivory, cream	Textured or smooth fabrics: simple designs, solids, casements	Roman shades (page 247), padded cornices (page 273), mock corded pillows (page 284), mock box pillows (page 282), flange pillows (page 288)
Traditional, classic	Reliable colors: green, white, blue, burgundy	Timeless fabrics: antique satins, jacquards, matelassés, linens, velvets	Pinch-pleated draperies (page 236), swags & jabots (page 268), corded knife-edge pillows (page 280), tufted cushions (page 295)

Fabric Selection

It pays to use good quality fabrics for home decorating projects. A good quality decorator fabric usually lasts longer and results in a finer finished look. Some of the most popular home decorator fabrics are shown here and on the next pages to help you with your selection.

As a rule, the tighter the weave or higher the thread count (number of threads per inch), the stronger the fabric. Most decorator fabrics have a higher thread count than garment fabrics.

Many decorator fabrics have a stain-resistant finish. To test, drop a small amount of water on the sample. If the water beads up instead of soaking in, the fabric will repel stains. This is more of a concern for cushions, pillows, slipcovers, and upholstery than for window treatments. Also, make sure that the dyes do not rub off when the fabric is handled or rubbed between your fingers.

Consider the end use, and be sure that the fabric is appropriate to the function. A decorative top treatment for a curtain, for example, will receive little wear; if a simple style is selected, it can be changed easily to update a look. Fabric for such a project does not get the heavy use that a chair cushion does; nor is it used as long as the average drapery. Remember that the average drapery may hang in a room anywhere from eight to fifteen years.

When comparing costs for large amounts of fabric, consider that prints may cost more than solid fabrics because you will need more fabric to match the motifs. The larger the repeat, the more likely you are to waste fabric when matching.

Lightweight open weaves are often used for window treatments because they let in the sunlight yet offer more privacy than undraped windows. Casement fabrics (**1**) are loosely woven, with uneven yarns and open areas. The variation in the weave creates a design in the fabric. Polyester, cotton, or linen fibers may be used. Laces and eyelets (**2**) may look delicate and fragile, but are easy to sew and provide a light, airy look. Wide borders and finished edges eliminate hemming. Sheers (**3**) vary in fiber content but are usually polyester for a sheer, transparent look. Imported sheers can be up to 118" (295 cm) wide with embroidered or decorative hems.

Fiber Content

Cotton is a basic, strong, all-purpose fiber for home furnishing fabric. It dyes well for vibrant colors and has good wearability. It may be used as a blend with many other fibers.

Linen is strong, but it will wrinkle. If wrinkling is a concern, crush a handful of fabric tightly in your fist and release it to see if wrinkles are retained. Decorator fabrics usually do not have crease-resistant finishes.

Rayon and acetate are often used together or in blends for a rich, silky appearance. Acetate may stretch in draperies and may spot if it gets wet.

Polyester is used alone or combined with other fibers to add stability. With all synthetics, use a low iron temperature when pressing.

Decorator Fabric vs. Garment Fabric

Decorator fabrics can be more expensive than garment fabrics, but garment fabrics may not have all the features you need. Normally, garment fabrics are not treated with stain-resistant finishes, and they usually have a lower thread count so they are not as durable. Use garment fabrics if the item will get little or no wear and your goal is simply to create an effect. Some garment fabrics are not heavy enough for a drapery, but may be acceptable as a curtain, valance, or dust ruffle.

If using garment fabric, preshrink it. If repeated washing will be necessary for an item, do not sew it with materials that cannot be washed, such as buckram or linings.

Mediumweight basics are versatile multipurpose fabrics used for window treatments, cushions, cornices, and fabric screens. Chintz (**1**) is a glazed, plain-weave cotton or cotton-blend fabric. This tightly woven fabric is available in solid colors or prints that are often large, traditional florals. Warp sateen (**2**) is a cotton or cotton blend that has a softer hand than chintz but feels heavier. Warp threads float on the surface to create a smooth surface. This fabric is multipurpose for draperies, bedspreads, cushions, and slipcovers. Antique satin (**3**) varies in fiber content and quality. It is a very drapable, mediumweight solid fabric, which has slubs and a sheen.

Mixing & Matching Fabrics

Using a number of complementary patterns and colors helps to connect areas in rooms and give your home continuity.

Geometric prints, stripes, patterns and solids can work together to give a room style and interest. Fabric manufacturers make it easy to coordinate fabrics by designing groups of complementary patterns, prints and solids which you can use in any combination.

If you coordinate fabrics on your own, unroll the bolts and compare them side-by-side in natural light. Examine the fabrics from several angles to judge the compatibility of print and color.

Bolts often come from different dye lots. To avoid problems of slight color variations or differences in pattern printing, buy fabrics for large projects from only one bolt. Check patterned fabrics to be sure they are printed on the straight grain. Also remember that wider fabrics generally mean fewer seams, especially in curtains.

Consider where the fabric will be used and how it relates to other fabrics in the room. Most stores have display cuts or swatch books of their decorator fabrics available. They may permit you to take swatches home. This gives you a chance to see the fabric next to other fabrics and lets you see it in your home lighting which may be very different from store lighting. If swatches are not available, ask for a sample from the bolt or buy a small piece before you invest in a large cut.

Choosing Colors

Keep these points in mind as you shop for fabrics.

• What colors already exist in the room? Take paint chips, carpet swatches or small cushions with you when you compare fabric.

• What wood tones are in your room? Fabric colors can enhance the natural tones and richness of wood.

• Color affects your mood. Pastels, neutrals and cooler shades, such as blues and some greens, are soothing. Bright shades and warmer colors like reds and yellows tend to stimulate. Dark colors create a cozy feeling.

• Color alters perceptions. Colors appear darker against light backgrounds, lighter against dark surfaces. Warm colors make objects seem larger, while cool colors make them recede. In general, avoid using bold contrasting colors in small rooms.

• Keep the room's exposure in mind. You may want to warm a northern exposure with warm tones, or cool down a hot sunny room with pale blues.

• Light colors show soil more readily than dark colors.

• At windows, pale colors diffuse light while dark colors block it. Hold up a length of fabric in direct sunlight to see if it creates the effect you want.

• Finally, consider your own preferences. Use these guidelines and your own taste to choose colors and patterns that beautify your home and reflect your personal style.

Borders, Stripes & Wide Fabrics

Fabrics with borders or wide stripes have many possibilities for coordinating color and design within a room. By removing a border from one fabric and applying it to another, or applying it in an unusual way, you can create an entirely new fabric. You can also manipulate striped fabrics to change their appearance by using them diagonally, mitering to the center, or cutting them apart to create a border on a coordinating fabric.

Estimate the amount of border that it will take for the project or decorative effect. It is possible to get several yards of border from a few yards of striped fabric cut into strips. Doing this is usually more economical than buying a bordered fabric. When cutting the stripes, allow ½" (1.3 cm) seam allowance on each side of the stripe for application.

Railroading Wide Fabrics

To eliminate seams, *railroad* a fabric. To railroad a fabric, turn the fabric on its side so that the normal width of the fabric becomes the length. This technique can often be used on valances, cornices, and dust ruffles, but is particularly practical for short curtains and seamless sheer draperies when fabric is extra wide.

The advantage of making draperies without seams is that there is no unevenness or puckering where widths of fabric are joined. In sheer fabrics, having no seams has the additional advantage of eliminating shadows at the seams. Railroading may require less fabric, and it saves time because there are no seams to sew.

Coordinate bedroom accessories with bordered sheets and pillowcases. Miter the border from a sheet for a flange edge on pillow shams. Also use the border to trim a neckroll pillow.

Use a border or a stripe as a boxing strip or insert on Turkish cushions.

Miter stripes to meet at the center of a pillow.

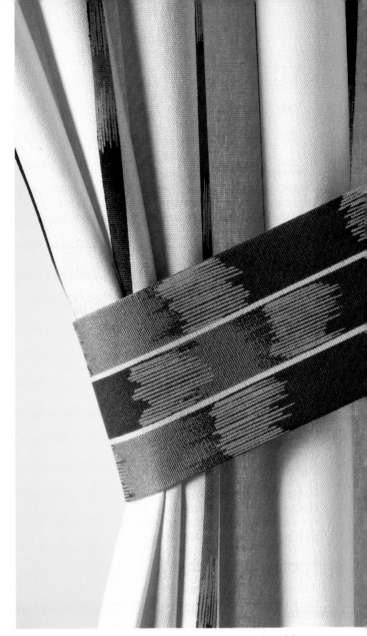

Use a border or a stripe to coordinate tiebacks with draperies.

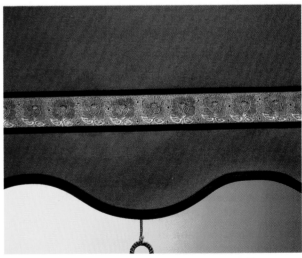

Appliqué a border on a solid fabric for banding on edges of shades.

Matching Prints

Prints require careful planning. To avoid wasting fabric or making costly errors, cut, match, and stitch carefully. Prints must be positioned to please the eye, and they must be sewn to match at every seam. Start matching a print at eye level so if the match does become imperfect, it will be off at the top or bottom of the panel, where it is less noticeable.

Start a full print at the bottom of a curtain or panel. If the print is behind a sofa or piece of furniture, position a full print at the top of the furniture line.

Match motifs across drapery or curtain panels. Be sure that motifs on all curtain panels match at eye level when there are several windows in the same room or area.

Because most decorator fabrics have a stabilizing finish applied to the surface, it is not advantageous to pull a thread to straighten a crosswise end. Cut decorator fabrics at right angle to the selvages, or follow a printed motif.

Two Ways to Cut Crosswise Ends

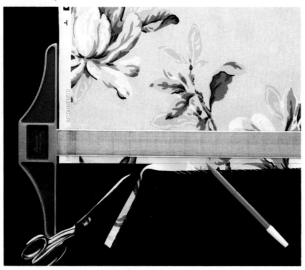

Use T-square or right angle to straighten crosswise ends. Place the T-square or right angle parallel to selvage. Mark cutting line; cut on marked line with shears or rotary cutter.

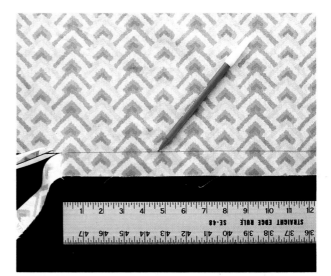

Follow a design line that runs across fabric on crosswise grain. Cut along design with shears or rotary cutter.

How to Match Prints Traditionally

1) Match motifs from wrong side by placing point of pin through matching designs. Pin at close intervals to prevent shifting.

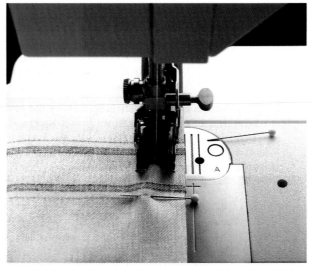

2) Stitch, using Even Feed™ foot to keep seam aligned. Remove pins as you come to them.

How to Match Prints As You Sew

1) Position panels with right sides together, matching the selvages.

2) Fold selvage back at top of panel until pattern matches on both panels.

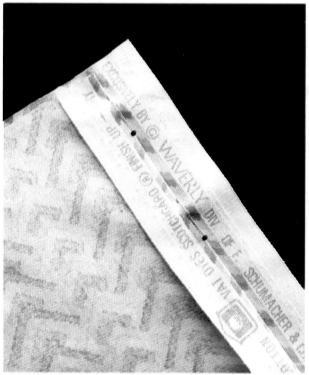

3) Pin next to the fold at point where the design matches; turn fabric over to the right side to check matching. No other pins are necessary.

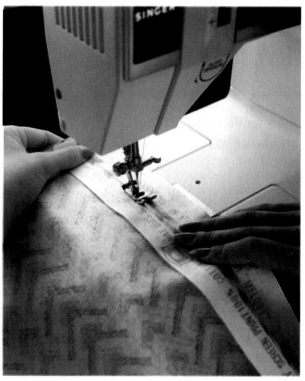

4) Stitch from right side as close to the fold as possible. Keep fabric taut while lining up motif as pinned. Continue sewing without additional pins, matching the motifs as you stitch. Trim off selvages.

CURTAINS & DRAPERIES

Curtains are flat, nonpleated panels, so they are easier to clean and press than many other window treatments. Draperies have permanent pleats. Curtains are often made of lightweight or sheer fabrics. Heavier fabrics such as linen, chintz, or polished cotton look best for formal, floor-length curtains. Lighter, crisper fabrics work well for casual, sill-length, and cafe curtains. Sheer curtains are usually two and one-half to three times the fullness of the finished width; heavier fabrics require only double fullness.

Curtain Casings & Headings

A casing or *rod pocket* is the hem along the upper edge of the curtain or valance. The curtain rod is inserted through the casing so that the fullness of the curtain falls into soft gathers. Before cutting the curtains, decide on the casing style and depth of heading (optional). A simple casing places the curtain rod at the uppermost edge of the curtain.

For simple casings, add to the cut length an amount equal to the diameter of the rod plus ½" (1.3 cm) to

turn under and ¼" to 1" (6 mm to 2.5 cm) ease. The amount of ease depends on the size of the rod and thickness of the fabric. Wide casings are used on the flat *Continental® rod* or *cornice rod*. These rods are 4½" (11.5 cm) wide.

A heading is a gathered edge above the casing. It finishes the curtain decoratively and does not require cornices or valances.

For casings with headings, use the formula for a simple casing, adding to it an amount twice the depth of the heading. Headings may be from 1" to 5" (2.5 to 12.5 cm) deep, and the depth should be appropriate for the length of the curtain: in general, the longer the curtain, the deeper the heading.

Wooden, brass, or plastic poles may be covered with a *shirred pole cover*. The exposed pole between the curtain panels is covered with a casing made from a tube of matching fabric (above). The casing may be plain or have a heading the same height as the curtain heading.

Finish lower and side hems of curtains before sewing casings and headings.

How to Sew a Simple Casing

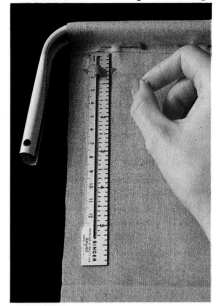

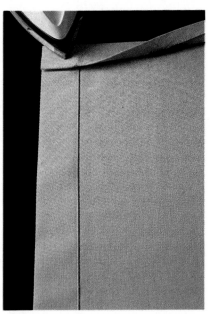

1) Determine casing depth by loosely pinning a curtain fabric strip around the rod. Remove rod and measure the distance from the top of the strip to the pin. Add ½" (1.3 cm) to be turned under.

2) Press under ½" (1.3 cm) along upper cut edge of curtain panel. Fold over again and press to form a hem equal to amount measured in step 1.

3) Stitch close to folded hem edge to form casing, backstitching at both ends. If desired, stitch again close to the upper edge to create a sharp crease appropriate for flat or oval curtain rods.

How to Sew a Casing with a Heading

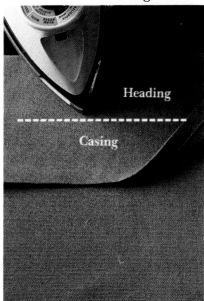

1) Determine the depth of the casing as directed in step 1, above. Determine the depth of heading, opposite. Press under ½" (1.3 cm) along upper cut edge of the curtain panel. Fold and press again to form hem equal to casing plus heading depth.

2) Stitch close to folded edge, backstitching at both ends. Mark heading depth with a pin at each end of panel. Stitch again at marked depth. To aid straight stitching, apply a strip of masking tape to the bed of the machine at heading depth, or use seam guide.

3) Insert rod through casing and gather curtain evenly onto rod. Adjust heading by pulling up the folded edge so the seam is exactly on the lower edge of the rod. A wide heading may be made to look puffy and more rounded by pulling the fabric out on each side.

How to Sew a Continental™ or Cornice Rod Casing with a Heading

1) Measure window after rod has been installed to determine total length. Add 15½" (39.3 cm): 5½" (14 cm) for the casing and seam allowance, 8" (20.5 cm) for the double-fold hem, and 2" (5 cm) for 1" (2.5 cm) heading. For a deeper heading, add twice the desired heading depth.

2) Turn under ½" (1.3 cm) on upper edge of curtain and press. Fold over again 6" (15 cm) for casing and heading. Stitch 1" (2.5 cm) from upper folded edge to form heading. Stitch close to folded edge to form casing.

3) Insert rod through casing and gather curtain evenly onto rod. Hang on installed brackets. For a wide heading, use two Continental or cornice rods, installed one above the other. Add 10" (25.5 cm) for second casing.

How to Make a Shirred Pole Cover

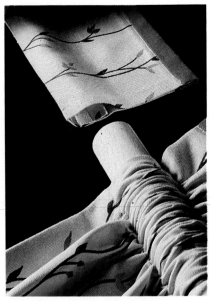

1) Cut fabric two and one-half times the length of pole area to be covered; cut width equal to circumference of pole plus 1½" (3.8 cm). For pole cover with a heading, add amount equal to twice the heading depth.

2) Stitch ½" (1.3 cm) hems on short ends. Fold strip in half lengthwise, right sides together, and pin long edges together. Stitch ½" (1.3 cm) seam. Press seam open. Turn cover right side out.

3) Press cover so that seam is at back of pole. To form heading, stitch again at appropriate distance from upper folded edge. If desired, add narrow binding to upper edge, opposite. Gather pole cover onto rod between two curtain panels.

Lining Curtains

Linings add body and weight to curtains to help them hang better. A lining also adds opaqueness, prevents fading and sun damage to curtain fabric, and provides some insulation.

Curtains may be lined the traditional way or lined to the edge with coordinating fabric to create a custom look.

Select linings according to the weight of the curtain fabric. White or off-white sateen is the most often used lining fabric. Specially treated linings that resist staining and block out light are also available.

Cutting Directions

For a lined curtain with a casing, cut the curtain as directed on page 220. For lining with 2" (5 cm) double-fold hem, cut lining the finished length of curtain plus 2½" (6.5 cm); cut lining 6" (15 cm) narrower than cut width of curtain. Seam and press widths, aligning curtain and lining seams if possible.

For curtains lined to the edge, cut curtain and lining the finished length plus amount for double-fold hem and ½" (1.3 cm) for seam at upper edge. Cut panels the finished width plus 1" (2.5 cm) for side seams.

How to Line Curtains

1) Turn, press, and stitch 2" (5 cm) double-fold hem in lining. Turn and press double-fold hem in curtain. Tack weights inside fold of curtain hems at seams, and stitch curtain hems.

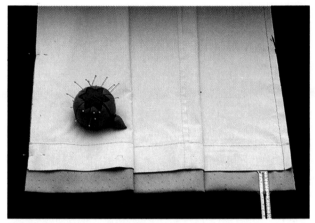

2) Place lining on curtain, right sides together, so lining is 1½" (3.8 cm) above curtain hem. Pin and stitch ½" (1.3 cm) seams on sides.

3) Turn curtain right side out. Center lining so side hems are equal width. Press side hem with seam allowance toward center. Continue to the top edge of the curtain.

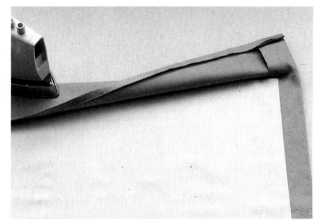

4) Press ½" (1.3 cm) seam allowance across upper edge of curtain. Fold upper edge of curtain down an amount equal to depth of casing and heading. Lining ends at foldline.

Tab Top Curtains

Fabric tabs are an attractive alternative to conventional casings or curtain rings. Tab top curtains used with a decorative curtain rod create a traditional country look, a contemporary tailored look or a casual cafe look. They are also ideal for stationary side panels. Tabs give top interest to a curtain, and can be made with contrasting fabric, decorative ribbon or trim.

Only one and one-half to two times the fullness is needed for tab top curtains. Allow ½" (1.3 cm) seam allowance at the upper edge of the curtain instead of the usual casing allowance. When determining the finished length, allow for the upper edge of the curtain to be 1½" to 2" (3.8 to 5 cm) below the rod. This determines the length of the tabs. Determine number of tabs needed by placing a tab at each edge of the curtain, and space the remaining tabs 6" to 8" (15 to 20.5 cm) apart.

How to Sew Tab Top Curtains

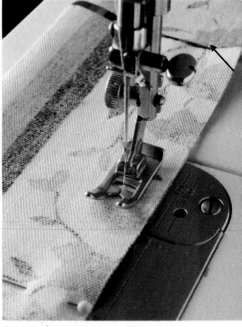

1) Cut a 3" (7.5 cm) facing strip equal in length to the width of the curtain panel. Press under ½" (1.3 cm) on one long side and each short end. Press double-fold lower and side hems of curtain. Stitch lower hem only.

2) Measure tab length by pinning a strip of fabric over the rod and marking the desired length with a pin. Add ½" (1.3 cm) for seam allowance. Cut tabs to measured length, and two times the desired width plus 1" (2.5 cm).

3) Fold each tab in half lengthwise, right sides together. Stitch ½" (1.3 cm) seam along cut edge; sew from one tab to the next, using continuous stitching (arrow). Turn tabs right side out. Center seam in back of each tab; press.

4) Fold each tab in half so raw edges are aligned. Pin or baste tabs in place on right side of curtain, aligning raw edges of tabs with upper edge of curtain. Place end tabs even with side hem foldline of curtain.

5) Pin facing to upper edge of curtain, right sides together, so raw edges are aligned and tabs are sandwiched between facing and curtain. Stitch ½" (1.3 cm) seam, with curtain side hems extended.

6) Press facing to wrong side of curtain so tabs extend upward. Fold curtain side hems under facing, covering seam allowance; grade. Stitch side hems. Slipstitch facing to curtain. Insert curtain rod through tabs.

Ruffled Curtains

Ruffled curtains add a charming, warm touch to any room of the house, and the weight of ruffles helps curtains hang better. The ruffle on a curtain usually extends along one side and across the bottom. In the directions that follow the curtain is hemmed after the ruffle is attached, and the ruffle extends into the casing and heading.

Ruffle fullness depends on fabric weight and ruffle width. Sheer fabrics usually need triple fullness; crisper fabrics need only two or two and one-half times fullness. Wide ruffles should be fuller than narrow ruffles. You will usually need to purchase less additional fabric when ruffles are cut on the crosswise grain. If ruffles are cut on the selvage, use the selvage edge in the seam. Hem the edge of the ruffle before gathering.

Single ruffles are one layer of gathered fabric with a hemmed edge. Narrow ruffles should have a hem no wider than ¼" (6 mm).

Double ruffles require a double width of fabric which is folded in half, wrong sides together. The folded edge eliminates the need for a hem. Because of the extra bulk created by two layers, it is best to make double ruffles from lightweight fabrics.

The zigzag stitch, the ruffler, and the narrow hemmer can speed up the task of making ruffles. Begin by cutting the fabric the appropriate width for a single or double ruffle. Then seam sections together at the short ends to make a continuous length, using plain seams for double ruffles and French seams for single ruffles. Hem one long edge of single ruffles, either by machine-stitching a double-fold ¼" (6 mm) hem, or by using a narrow hemmer.

Two Timesaving Ways to Make Ruffles

Zigzag over a strong, thin cord on wrong side of fabric to make long ruffles easier to adjust into even gathers. Use cord, crochet cotton, or dental floss, placed ⅜" (1 cm) from raw edge. Use wide zigzag stitch so cord does not get caught in the stitching.

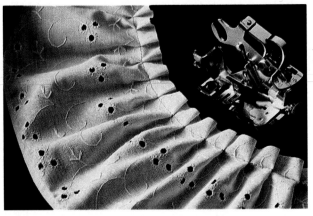

Use a ruffler attachment to tuck or gather as you sew. Make a test strip and adjust ruffler to desired fullness. Measure the test strip before and after stitching to determine length of fabric needed. Omit steps 1 through 3 (opposite) when using ruffler.

234

How to Attach Ruffles

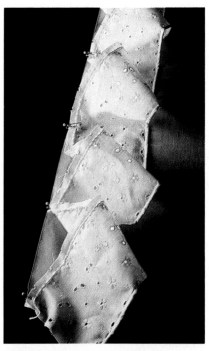

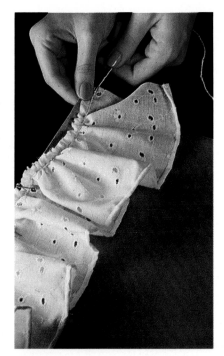

1) Divide curtain edge into equal segments; mark with pins. Divide ruffle strip into same number of segments. Allow extra fullness in segments to be placed at corner, so ruffle will lie flat in finished curtain.

2) Pin the ruffle strip to the unhemmed edge of the curtain, right sides together; match marking pins on the ruffle strip to marking pins on the curtain edge.

3) Pull up gathering cord until ruffle is same size as edge of curtain. At lower edge, release gathers the depth of hem. At upper edge, release gathers the depth of casing and heading.

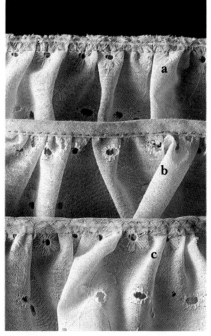

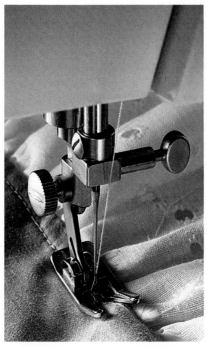

4) Pin in place as necessary to distribute gathers evenly. Stitch a ½" (1.3 cm) seam, gathered side up, controlling gathers with fingers on each side of the needle.

5) Trim seam allowances and overedge **(a)** using zigzag stitch, or encase seam with double-fold bias tape **(b)**, or encase seam with lightweight bias tricot strips **(c)**.

6) Press seam toward curtain. Topstitch on curtain side ¼" (6 mm) from seam so ruffle will lie smooth and even. Stitch hem and casing. Ruffle is gathered on right side, but flat on wrong side.

Pinch-pleated Draperies

Pinch-pleated draperies are a popular treatment for windows because draperies open to let in light, and close for privacy. The pleats are spaced at intervals to control the fullness of the drapery. The more fabric that is pleated into the drapery panels, the fuller the draperies become.

Although pleater tapes are a quick solution for some draperies, the fullness, spacing, and depth of the pleats are limited when you use these tapes. The only way to have total control over the fullness and position of the pleats is the traditional buckram heading used in drapery workrooms.

Before you can determine the size of the drapery panels, you must determine the hardware and the mounting. For conventional rods, measure from ½" (1.3 cm) above the top of the rod to the desired finished length. For draperies that are mounted on decorative rods, measure from the pin holes in the rod to the desired finished length.

Remember to include stackback when mounting the rods. This is the amount needed at the side of the windows for the drapery to clear the window when

the drapery is open to its fullest. Actual stacking space will vary with the weight of the fabric, the fullness, and whether or not the drapery is lined, but it can be estimated at one-third the window width measurement. For center-pull draperies, allow for half the stacking space on each side of the window.

✂ Cutting Directions

Measure the window, and follow the guidelines for curtains and draperies (pages 220 and 221). There are two basic measurements to consider: finished length and finished width. Estimate yardage and cut the lengths for drapery and lining, using the chart on the opposite page. These directions are for a pair of draperies.

YOU WILL NEED

Decorator fabric for draperies.

Lining fabric for lined draperies.

Conventional traverse rod, ringless decorator traverse rod, or wood pole set.

Buckram, 4" (10 cm) wide; length equal to width of panels before pleating.

Estimate Yardage

Drapery Length*	
1) Desired length as measured from rod	
2) 8" (20.5 cm) for heading	+
3) 8" (20.5 cm) for double hem	+
4) Cut drapery length	=
Drapery Width	
1) Rod width (from end bracket to end bracket on conventional rods; from end ring to end ring on decorative rods)	
2) Returns	+
3) Overlap [standard is 3½" (9 cm)]	+
4) Finished drapery width	=
Drapery Widths per Panel	
1) Finished width times 2, 2½, or 3 (fullness)	
2) Width of fabric	÷
3) Fabric widths needed: round up or down whole width	=
4) Divide widths by 2	÷
5) Number of widths per panel	=
Total Drapery Fabric Needed	
1) Cut drapery length (figured above)	
2) Fabric widths needed (figured above)	×
3) Total fabric length	=
4) Number of yd. (m) needed: total fabric length divided by 36" (100 cm)	yd. (m)

Lining Length	
1) Finished length of drapery (from top of heading to hem)	
2) 4" (10 cm) for double hems	+
3) Cut lining length	=
Lining Width	
1) Number of widths per panel (figure as for drapery widths per panel, above)	
2) Multiply widths by 2	×
3) Total fabric widths	=
Total Lining Fabric Needed	
1) Cut length (figured above)	
2) Fabric widths (figured above)	×
3) Total fabric length	=
4) Number of yd. (m) needed: total fabric length divided by 36" (100 cm)	yd. (m)

* For fabrics requiring pattern match, see page 26.

Drapery Pleats

Use the drapery pleat worksheet to determine the number and size of pleats and spaces per panel; this should be done after panels are sewn together and hemmed. The recommended amount of fabric required for each pleat is 4" to 6" (10 to 15 cm). The recommended space between pleats is 3½" to 4" (9 to 10 cm), approximately the same amount as the center overlap. If the worksheet calculation for the pleat size or the space between pleats is greater than the recommended amount, add one more pleat and space; if the calculation is smaller than the recommended amount, subtract one pleat and space.

Drapery Pleat Worksheet

Finished Panel Width	
1) Finished drapery width (figured left)	
2) divided by 2	÷
3) Finished panel width	=
Space between Pleats	
1) Number of widths per panel (figured left)	
2) Times number of pleats per width*	×
3) Number of pleats per panel	=
4) Number of spaces per panel (one less than pleats)	
5) Finished panel width (figured above)	
6) Overlap and returns (figured left)	−
7) Width to be pleated	=
8) Number of spaces per panel (figured above)	÷
9) Space between pleats	=
Pleat Allowance	
1) Flat width of hemmed panel	
2) Finished panel width (figured above)	−
3) Pleat allowance	=
Pleat Size	
1) Pleat allowance (figured above)	
2) Number of pleats in panel	÷
3) Pleat size	=

*Figure 5 pleats per width of 48" (122 cm) fabric, 6 pleats per width of 54" (140 cm) fabric. If you have a half width of fabric, figure 2 or 3 pleats in that half width. For example, for 48" (122 cm) fabric, 2½ widths per panel = 12 pleats.

How to Sew Lined Pinch-pleated Draperies

1) Stitch drapery fabric, following step 1, page 238. Sew lining widths as necessary, using plain or serged seams. (Remove selvages to prevent puckering.) Turn under and stitch a 2" (5 cm) double bottom hem.

2) Place drapery on table or large flat surface. Lay lining on top of drapery, with *wrong* sides together and hem of lining ¾" (2 cm) above the hem of the drapery.

3) Trim 3" (7.5 cm) from each outside edge of lining. Trim lining so it is 8" (20.5 cm) from top edge of drapery.

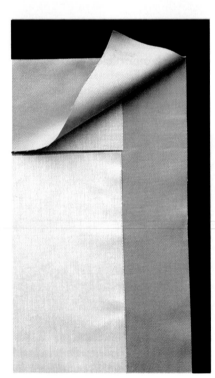

4) Follow step 2, page 238. Then fold heading over *twice,* folding buckram over lining at the top. Press; pin or hand-baste.

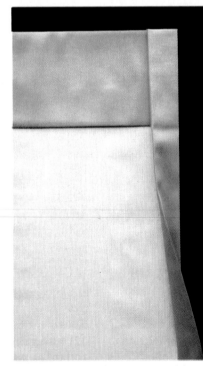

5) Fold double 1½" (3.8 cm) side hems over the lining.

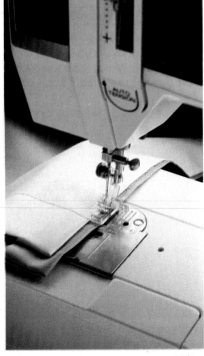

6) Blindstitch side hems (page 227). Finish draperies, following steps 5 to 12, pages 238 and 239.

Dressing Draperies

Window treatments need hand-dressing, or training, to keep them looking their best and most attractive. Before hanging draperies, press them with a warm, dry iron to remove any wrinkles. After draperies are hung, if wrinkles still exist, press with a warm, dry iron over a hand-held roll of paper towels.

If fabric is particularly hard to train into pleats, you may want to finger press. Place the front edge of the drapery between the thumb and index finger, and follow the front edge of the pleat all the way to the hemline. Finger pressing creates a light crease and helps train the drapery and tailor the pleat.

Roman shades may also need to be raised and then tied in position for a few days to set the folds. Then when the shade is raised again after being lowered, the pleats will naturally fold into the right position.

How to Dress Draperies

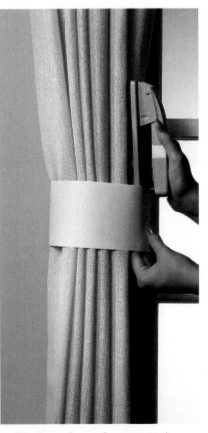

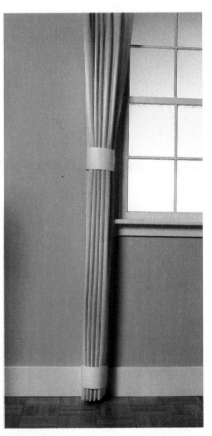

1) Draw draperies into the stacked position. Starting at top, guide pleats into soft folds. If lined, catch lining in folds. Make sure depth of folds is even. Use grain of fabric as guide to keep pleats perpendicular to floor.

2) Staple a piece of paper or tie a piece of muslin around the pleats halfway between top and hem to hold them in place. Do not fasten so tightly that wrinkles appear.

3) Staple second piece of paper at the hemline. The draperies should hang straight from the rod. Leave tied for 5 to 7 days. Humidity will encourage the setting process.

Tiebacks

Tiebacks are a decorative way to hold curtains open. Make them straight or shaped, ruffled or plain. Use matching or contrasting solids, coordinating prints or bordered fabrics. Interface all tiebacks to add stability.

An easy way to make tiebacks the proper length is to complete and hang the curtains before sewing the tiebacks. Cut a strip of fabric that is 2" to 4" (5 to 10 cm) wide; experiment by pinning it around the curtains to determine the best tieback length. Slide the strip up and down to find the best location for tiebacks. Mark the wall for positioning cup hooks, which will be used to fasten the tiebacks. Remove the strip and measure it to determine the finished size.

✂ Cutting Directions

For straight tiebacks, cut a piece of heavyweight fusible interfacing the finished length and two times the finished width. To cut fabric, add ½" (1.3 cm) on all sides for seams.

For shaped tiebacks, cut a strip of brown paper for pattern, 4" to 6" (10 to 15 cm) wide and slightly longer than the tieback. Pin the paper around the curtain and draw a curved shape around the edge of the paper. Experiment by pinning and trimming the paper to get the effect you want. Cut two pieces of fabric and heavyweight fusible interfacing for each tieback. Cut interfacing same size as pattern. To cut fabric, add ½" (1.3 cm) on all sides for seams.

YOU WILL NEED

Decorator fabric for tiebacks.

Heavyweight fusible interfacing.

Brown paper for pattern.

Fusible web strips, length of finished tieback width.

Two ⅝" (1.5 cm) brass or plastic rings for each tieback.

Two cup hooks.

How to Sew Straight Tiebacks

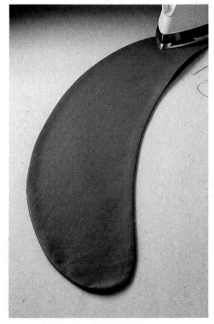

1) Center fusible interfacing on wrong side of tieback and fuse. Press the short ends under ½" (1.3 cm). Fold tieback in half lengthwise, right sides together. Stitch ½" (1.3 cm) seam, leaving short ends open. Press open.

2) Turn tieback right side out. Center seam down back and press. Turn pressed ends inside. Insert fusible web at each end and fuse. Or slipstitch closed.

3) Hand-tack ring on back seamline at each end of tieback, ¼" (6 mm) from edge **(a)**. Or press corners diagonally to inside to form a point; slipstitch or fuse corners in place. Attach ring **(b)**.

How to Sew Shaped Tiebacks

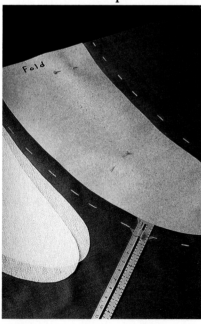

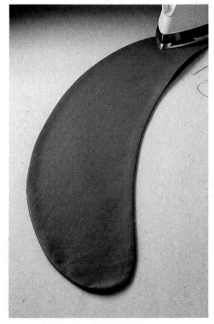

1) Position pattern on fold to cut fabric and interfacing. Center interfacing on wrong side of each tieback piece and fuse.

2) Pin tieback pieces, right sides together. Stitch ½" (1.3 cm) seam, leaving 4" (10 cm) opening on one long edge for turning. Grade seam allowances; notch or clip curves at regular intervals.

3) Turn tieback right side out; press. Insert fusible web at opening and fuse. Or slipstitch closed. Hand-tack rings at each end of tieback ¼" (6 mm) from the edge.

Bound Tiebacks

Binding emphasizes the graceful line of a curved tieback and allows you to pick up an accent color from the room decor or from the curtain fabric. Shaped tiebacks are easier to bind than straight tiebacks because the bias binding will ease around curves.

✂ Cutting Directions

Cut two pieces of fabric and two pieces of fusible interfacing from the pattern; do not add seam allowances to tieback. Make bias tape as on page 280. Cut the tape 1" (2.5 cm) longer than the distance around the tieback.

How to Bind Shaped Tiebacks

1) Position pattern on fold to cut fabric and interfacing. Fuse interfacing to wrong side of tieback. Pin wrong sides of tieback together.

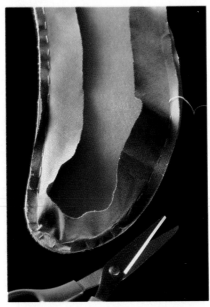

2) Press under ½" (1.3 cm) on one end of bias strip. Starting with pressed end, baste strip to tieback, right sides together, clipping to ease around curves. Stitch strip ½" (1.3 cm) from edge.

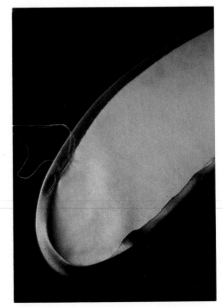

3) Press bias strip over edge of tieback. Turn under cut edge of bias strip to meet seamline; slipstitch. Hand-tack rings to ends of tieback.

Ruffled Tiebacks

Adding ruffled tiebacks changes the appearance of the curtains and the look of a window. Make ruffles from a matching or coordinating fabric in a width that suits the length of the curtain. Purchased pregathered lace or eyelet ruffles may be used to reduce sewing time.

✂ Cutting Directions

Cut ruffle the desired width plus 1" (2.5 cm) for seams, and two and one-half times the finished length.

Cut a straight tieback and interfacing (page 242). The tieback should be in proportion to the ruffle width, usually less than half as wide.

How to Sew Ruffled Tiebacks

1) Fuse interfacing to wrong side of tieback. Press under ½" (1.3 cm) on one long side and both ends of tieback. Stitch a ¼" (6 mm) hem on one long side and both ends of ruffle. Fold ruffle and tieback into fourths; mark folds with snips.

2) Zigzag over a cord (page 234). Pin wrong side of ruffle to right side of tieback, matching snips and raw edges. Pull up gathering cord until ruffle fits tieback. Distribute gathers evenly and pin. Stitch ruffle ½" (1.3 cm) from edge.

3) Fold tieback in half lengthwise, wrong sides together. Pin the folded edge over ruffle seam. Edgestitch across ends and along gathered seam. Hand-tack the rings to ends of tieback.

How to Make a Roman Shade

1) Sketch the shade to use as a guide for ring locations, page 249, step 7. Cut shade fabric; seam for width, if necessary. If fabric ravels, finish side edges with zigzag stitch or liquid fray preventer.

2) Place shade fabric wrong side up on work surface. Mark finished width. Press 1½" (3.8 cm) side hems.

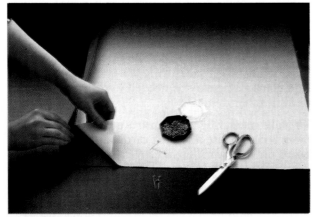

3) Place lining on shade fabric, wrong sides together. Slip lining under side hems. Smooth and press lining. Pin in place; slipstitch, if desired.

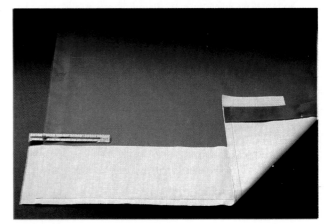

4) Center and pin facing strip on right side of shade, even with lower edge, with 1" (2.5 cm) extending at each side. Stitch ½" (1.3 cm) from lower edge. Press toward wrong side of shade.

5) Fold and press facing extensions to back of shade so they do not show on the right side. Fuse or stitch in place.

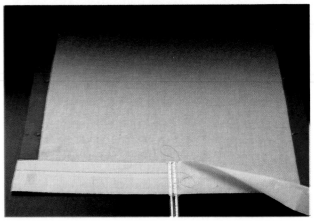

6) Turn under raw edge of facing 1½" (3.8 cm); turn under again 3" (7.5 cm). Stitch along folded edge. Stitch again, 1" (2.5 cm) from first stitching to form pocket for weight rod.

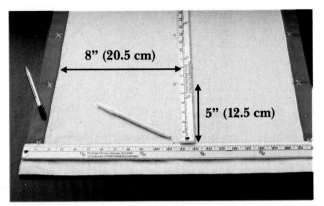

7) Mark locations for rings with horizontal and vertical rows of X's. First, mark outside vertical rows 1" (2.5 cm) from shade edges so rings hold side hems in place. Space vertical rows 8" to 12" (20.5 to 30.5 cm) apart across shade. Position bottom row just above the rod pocket. Space horizontal rows 5" to 8" (12.5 to 20.5 cm) apart.

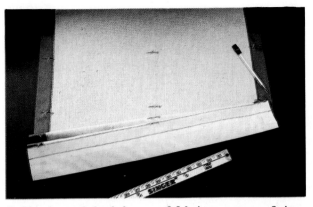

8) Pin through both layers of fabric at center of ring markings, with pins parallel to bottom of shade. Fold shade in accordion pleats at pins to position shade for machine or hand stitching of rings. If using ring tape, omit steps 9a and 9b.

9a) Attach rings by placing fold (pin in center) under presser foot with ring next to fold. Set stitch length at 0, and zigzag at widest setting. Secure ring with 8 to 10 stitches, catching small amount of fold in each stitch. Lock stitches by adjusting needle to penetrate the fabric in one place (width setting at 0) for 2 or 3 stitches.

9b) Tack rings by hand if zigzag stitch is not available. Use double thread. Secure with 4 or 5 stitches in one place, through both fabric layers. Reinforce all rings in bottom row with extra stitches; they hold the weight of the fabric.

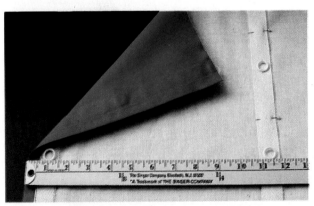

9c) Use ring tape instead of rings, if desired. Turn under ½" (1.3 cm) at bottom of tape and place at top of rod pocket. Pin tape to shade in vertical rows, lining up rings horizontally. Stitch both long edges and bottom of tape with zipper foot, stitching all tapes in same direction.

10) Staple or tack shade to top of mounting board. If shade is mounted outside of window frame, paint or wrap the board with lining fabric before attaching shade. This gives the shade a finished look.

(Continued on next page)

How to Make a Roman Shade (continued)

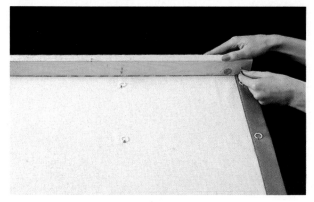

11) Insert screw eyes on mounting board to line up with vertical rows; place one screw eye above each row. On heavy or wide shades, use pulleys instead of screw eyes.

12) Tie a nonslip knot in bottom ring. Apply white glue to knot and ends of cord to prevent knot from slipping. Thread cord through the vertical row of rings.

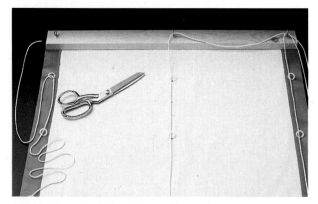

13) Cut lengths of cord, one for each row of rings. Each cord will be a different length; cords go up the shade, across the top and partway down one side. String cord through rings and screw eyes, with excess cord at one side for pulling.

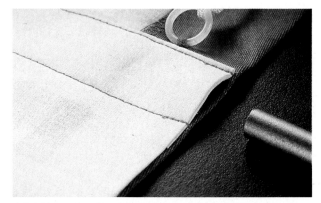

14) File ends of weight rod or cover ends with tape. Insert rod into rod pocket and slipstitch ends closed. A galvanized or iron rod, painted to resist rusting, can be used instead of a brass rod.

15) Mount shade (page 246). Adjust cords with shade lowered so the tension on each cord is equal. Tie cords in a knot just below screw eye. Braid cords and secure at bottom with a knot or drapery pull.

16) Center awning cleat on edge of window frame or on wall. Wind cord around cleat to secure shade position when the shade is raised.

Cloud Shade

The cloud shade is another easy-to-make variation of the Roman shade with a soft shirred heading. Because this shade has a light, airy look, lining is usually not necessary. Lightweight, soft, or sheer fabrics are suggested for cloud shades.

Cloud shades are generally mounted inside the window and may be used alone or under draperies. The shade's shirred heading has a finished look that makes a valance or cornice unnecessary. A short cloud shade may also be used as a valance over other window treatments.

Cloud shades made of lightweight fabrics may be shirred on a curtain rod or wooden pole, omitting the need for a mounting board. In this case, finish the upper edge of the shade with a simple casing (page 229) and insert screw eyes directly into the window frame.

Directions for making a cloud shade are given on pages 252 and 253. Read about Roman shades on pages 247 to 250 before beginning this project.

✂ Cutting Directions

Cut decorator fabric so width of shade is two to three times width of window and about 12" (30.5 cm) longer than window. Seam fabric together as necessary for desired width. Also cut facing strip 4" (10 cm) wide; the length equal to the width of the finished shade plus 1" (2.5 cm).

YOU WILL NEED

Decorator fabric for shade and facing strip.

Four-cord shirring tape, length equal to width of shade.

Notions: mounting board, plastic rings, screw eyes or pulleys, shade cord, weight rod, white glue, awning cleat, and staple gun, as for Roman shade.

How to Make a Cloud Shade

1) Seam fabric if necessary for width, using French seams. Turn under and press 1" (2.5 cm) double-fold side and lower hems. Straight-stitch or blindstitch hems.

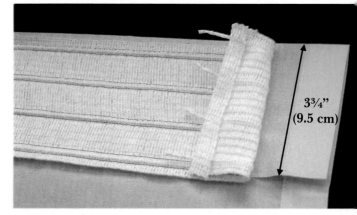

3¾" (9.5 cm)

2) Turn under 3¾" (9.5 cm) at upper edge. Pin shirring tape ¼" (6 mm) from fold. Pull out ½" (1.3 cm) of cord at each end; turn tape under to finish ends. Using zipper foot, stitch on each side of cord. (Contrasting thread is used to show detail.)

5) Pull other ends of cords until shade gathers up to width of mounting board. Knot, glue and trim pulled cord ends as in step 4, above.

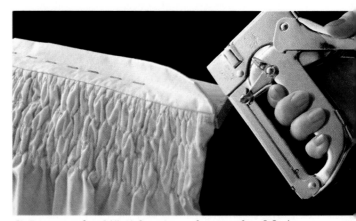

6) Press under ½" (1.3 cm) on short ends of facing strip. Fold strip in half lengthwise, wrong sides together. Pin raw edges of strip to right side of shade above shirring tape; stitch ½" (1.3 cm) from edge. Staple strip to top of mounting board.

How to Make a Balloon Shade

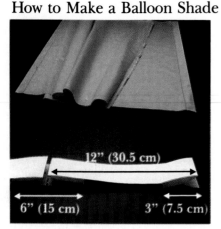

12" (30.5 cm)

6" (15 cm)   3" (7.5 cm)

1) Prepare fabric as in step 1, above, but do not hem lower edge. Fold pleats in pattern 9" to 12" (23 to 30.5 cm) apart and about 6" (15 cm) deep. Use even number of pleats with half pleat at each side.

Fold   Center   Fold
        of
      pleat

2) Place paper pattern on shade at lower edge. Place seams at back folds of pleats. Mark pleat fold lines with ¼" (6 mm) snips. Repeat this step along the upper edge of the shade.

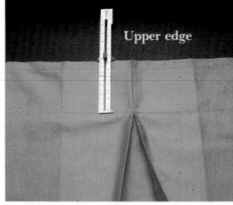

Upper edge

3) Fold, pin and press pleats the entire length of shade. Stitch ½" (1.3 cm) from upper and lower edges to secure pleats. Stitch again 3" (7.5 cm) from upper edge for mounting guideline.

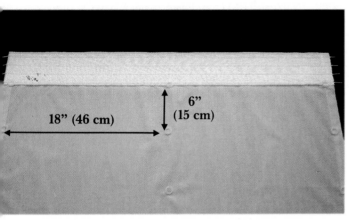

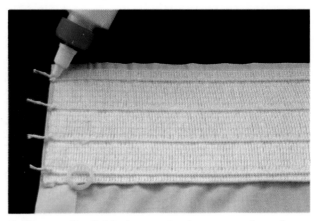

3) Mark positions for rings. Space horizontal rows about 6" (15 cm) apart. Space vertical rows 18" to 36" (46 to 91.5 cm) apart; rows will be half that distance apart when shirring tape is gathered. Attach rings, page 249, step 9a or 9b.

4) Knot ends of shirring cords along one edge of shade to keep the cords from pulling out. Apply white glue to knots so they stay in place. Trim ends.

7) Tie together bottom three rings of each vertical row. This creates a permanent pouf in the shade, even when it is completely lowered. String and mount as for Roman shades, page 250, steps 13, 15 and 16.

8) Cover the weight rod with matching fabric. Insert rod in lower hem. Gather fabric evenly on the rod to correspond to gathers on upper edge. Slipstitch ends of hem closed.

4) Press under ½" (1.3 cm) on short ends of facing strip; press in half lengthwise, wrong sides together. Pin strip to bottom of shade on right side. Stitch ½" (1.3 cm) from edge for rod pocket; finish seam.

5) Press strip to wrong side. Attach rings through one layer at center of pleats, with bottom rings on facing fold and top rings below guideline, page 249, step 9a or 9b. Vertical rows should be about 6" (15 cm) apart.

6) Staple upper edge of shade to mounting board, with mounting guideline at the upper edge of mounting board so stitching does not show. Finish as for cloud shade, steps 7 and 8, above.

Balloon Shade

The balloon shade is another variation of the Roman shade. A series of evenly placed box pleats gives this shade a fuller, softer effect than the more tailored Roman shade.

Made from soft, sheer, or unlined fabrics, balloon shades drape into gentle poufs or swags. With sturdier fabrics, the shade's softness remains but the fabric may require hand dressing to even out the fullness of the shade.

Linings are optional. Follow directions for a lined Roman shade (page 248) if opaqueness or additional body is required.

Directions for making a balloon shade are given on pages 252 and 253. Before beginning this project, read about a Roman shade on pages 247 to 250.

✂ Cutting Directions

Cut decorator fabric and seam, if necessary, so width of shade is two to two and one-half times width of window and about 12" (30.5 cm) longer than window. Also cut facing strip 1" (2.5 cm) longer than width of finished shade and 3" (7.5 cm) wide.

Make a paper pattern to help you position the pleats accurately on the shade. Make pattern by cutting a narrow strip of paper the same length as the unfinished width of the shade. (Adding machine paper works well.)

YOU WILL NEED

Decorator fabric for shade and facing strip.

Lining fabric for lining (optional).

Notions: mounting board, plastic rings, screw eyes or pulleys, nylon cable cord, weight rod, white glue, awning cleat, and staple gun as for Roman shade.

Shortcuts for Window Treatments

The timesaving way to sew decorative curtain, drapery, and valance headings is with self-styling tape. The tapes are simply stitched flat to hemmed panels and woven-in cords are pulled to create the heading. For best results, use these tapes on medium to lightweight or sheer fabrics.

To estimate the amount of fabric needed, measure the width of the rod, including rod returns, if any. Multiply by 2½ for fabric fullness for the pleating or the folding tape. Multiply by 2½ or 3 for fullness for the smocking or shirring tapes. Lightweight and sheer fabrics are more luxurious with more fullness. Add an allowance for double side hems to determine how wide to cut the fabric panels. Divide total by width of fabric for the number of widths needed.

Measure finished length of curtain and add 6" (15 cm) for double 3" (7.5 cm) bottom hem and 1" to 5" (2.5 to 12.5 cm) for the top hem, depending on style of tape or rod being used. Add another 2" (5 cm) for a double top hem on sheer fabrics.

Multiply length by the number of widths needed and divide by 36" (100 cm) for the number of yards (meters) required. Add 6" (15 cm) to finished width to determine how much tape to buy for each panel.

To hang the finished panels, use standard metal drapery pins or special hooks that fit into loops woven into the top of the shirring tape. As an option, on smocked or shirred headings you can make a rod pocket to hang curtain or valance on flat curtain rod or pole and omit hooks or pins.

Curtain and drapery headings are quick and easy to make with self-styling tapes. Pinch pleats, box pleats, shirring, and smocking are possible with the least amount of measuring and sewing.

Matching tiebacks for shirred or smocked window treatments are easy to make, using the same type of tape selected for the heading. Simply apply the tape to the wrong side of a fabric strip, and pull the cords to shirr or smock to size.

Self-styling Tapes for Curtain, Drapery, and Valance Headings

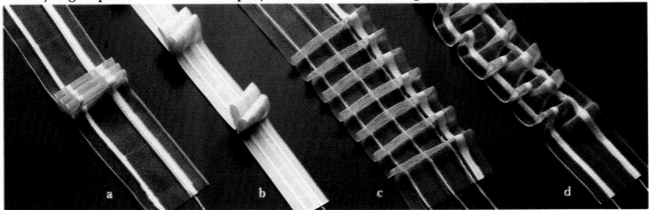

Self-styling cords and hook loops are woven into tapes for a variety of curtain, drapery, and valance headings. Use pleating tape **(a)** for soft pleated headings for draw draperies on sheers, laces, and lightweight fabrics. Folding tape **(b)** makes a two-pleat heading, appropriate to small windows, or a 3" (7.5 cm) box pleat for dust ruffles and valances. Shirring tape **(c)** draws curtain panels into narrow, evenly spaced pencil pleats. Smocking tape **(d)** creates soft alternating pleats for a smocked look.

Pleating tape is used for classic pinch pleats to hang on a traverse rod or a decorative pole rod with cafe rings. For decorative and cafe rods, press under 1½" (3.8 cm) on top edge. Stitch tape ½" (1.3 cm) from edge. For traverse rods, turn under 1" (2.5 cm) and stitch tape ¼" (6 mm) from edge. For draw draperies, arrange the pleating tape so pleats do not form at the ends of the panel. Also allow 4" to 5" (10 to 12.5 cm) at end of drapery panels for overlap at center of rod.

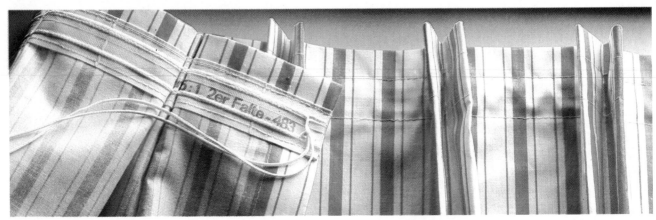

Folding tape is used for a tailored two-pleat heading or box pleats. Because the two-pleat heading stacks compactly, this heading is well-suited for recreational vehicles and boats as well as residential window treatments. Stitch and hang finished panels as for pinch pleats with pleating tape, above.

Box pleats are also made with folding tape. Stitch tape on *right* side of fabric ½" (1.3 cm) from upper edge. Pull cords to create pleats. From right side, flatten and press the pleats. For pleated valance, stitch mounting flap of lining or matching fabric below tape. Turn under and staple valance to a mounting board, or insert curtain hooks and hang on a flat curtain rod. For dust ruffle, stitch muslin deck to pleated panel.

Smocking tape creates a stationary window treatment with soft smocked folds. Hang finished panels on cafe rod, decorative pole rod with cafe rings, or flat curtain rod. To hang on a flat curtain rod, insert metal drapery hook every 3" (7.5 cm). Or, make panels with rod pocket, using method given for shirred heading on page 259. Two rows of smocking tape can be applied for extra-deep heading if desired.

Shirring tape is used to draw up fabric panels evenly into soft folds. Select this heading for stationary window treatments such as tieback draperies, curtains, and valances. Hang the finished panels on a decorative pole rod with glides, a cafe rod with rings, or a flat curtain rod. Smocked and shirred headings may be 2½ to 3 times fullness.

Austrian Valance

The Austrian valance is a shortened version of the elegant Austrian shade, characterized by vertical rows of shirring, horizontal gathers, and soft scallops at the lower edge. Sheer and soft fabrics work best for this treatment, which is often trimmed with fringe. The valance is unlined to gather and drape beautifully.

There can be any number of scallops across the lower edge, but they are usually about 8" to 12" (20.5 to 30.5 cm) apart. This measurement may vary for wider or narrower windows. To determine the finished width of each scallop, divide the width of the mounting board by the number of scallops desired.

The directions that follow are for a valance mounted inside the window frame.

✄ Cutting Directions

Cut fabric 1½ times the width of mounting board and 2½ times the finished length. Cut sheer fabric

3 times the length. If it is necessary to seam widths together, position seams at shirring lines.

YOU WILL NEED

Decorator fabric for valance and, if desired, for mounting board.

Two-cord shirring tape, the cut length of valance (plus extra for finishing) times number of scallops, plus one.

1" (2.5 cm) twill tape, width of finished valance plus 1" (2.5 cm).

Optional trim, the cut width of the valance, plus extra for finishing.

Mounting board, 1" × 2" (2.5 × 5 cm), heavy-duty stapler, staples; tacks or pushpins.

Two angle irons for mounting.

Wooden dowel for weight rod, the finished width of valance.

How to Sew an Austrian Valance

1) Seam fabric if necessary for width. Press under 1½" (3.8 cm) on each side. For trim at lower edge, press ½" (1.3 cm) at bottom of curtain to *right* side. Pin heading of trim over raw edge; stitch. For valance without trim, stitch double 1" (2.5 cm) hem.

2) Divide cut width by number of scallops. For example, if the hemmed width is 72" (183 cm) and there are four scallops, the width of each scallop before shirring is 18" (46 cm). Mark at upper and lower edges.

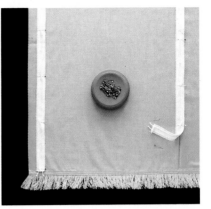

3) Pin 2-cord shirring tape from lower to upper edge on each mark. Place tape 1" (2.5 cm) from sides to cover raw edges. Stitch both edges of tape in same direction.

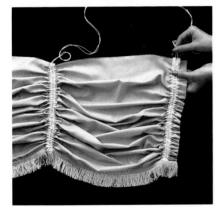

4) Tie cords at bottom so they will not pull out; pull shirring tape cords from top, gathering all cords to the same finished length. Secure ends of cord with knot.

5) Mark mounting board to match *finished* width of scallops. Valance is wider than mounting board. Match tape to marks, and tack. Divide excess fabric evenly on each side of markings; pleat and pin in place.

6) Remove valance from mounting board. Stitch twill tape over raw edge to finish upper edge and to use for mounting.

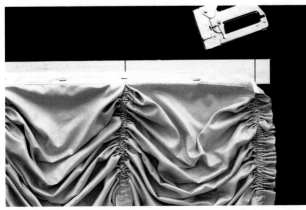

7) Staple or tack twill tape to top of mounting board. Place staples 6" (15 cm) apart.

8) Cover wooden dowel with matching fabric. Hand-tack to back of valance at shirring lines.

Tapered Valance

The graceful curve of a tapered valance frames a window in soft folds of fabric. This valance is often used over mini-blinds and pleated shades to soften severe lines, or with short cafe curtains for a comfortable, casual look.

Tapered valances are usually lined when print fabrics are used, because you see the wrong side of the fabric as it cascades down the side of the window. If the lower edge has a ruffled finish, however, it does not have to be lined because the fall of the ruffle hides the wrong side of the fabric. Lightweight or sheer fabrics are also good choices for a ruffled valance, and do not require a lining.

The side length can be to the sill or apron, but it should be no less than one-third the length of the window. To determine the finished length at center of valance, see Measuring for a Top Treatment, page 260. To check the curve, you may wish to make a paper pattern or mock-up with old sheets or lining fabric.

✂ Cutting Directions

Cut fabric and lining 2 times the width of the rod. To estimate length, measure at longest point and add amount for rod pocket and heading plus 1" (2.5 cm) for seam allowance and turn-under. To determine cut length at center of valance, add allowance for rod pocket and heading plus ½" (1.3 cm) for turn-under to desired finished length at center.

For unlined valance with ruffle, use 2½ times fullness for valance. Subtract width of ruffle from finished length. Cut ruffle 2 times the length of the curve and finished width plus 1" (2.5 cm); seam fabric as necessary. Measure the curve after cutting the valance; or make a test muslin, and measure.

YOU WILL NEED

Decorator fabric for valance.

Lining for valance.

Flat curtain rod or Continental® rod.

How to Sew a Tapered Valance

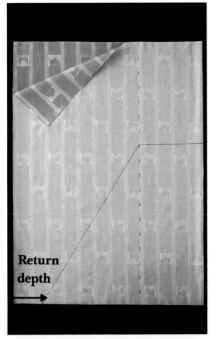

1) Seam fabric widths as necessary. Divide and mark fabric vertically into thirds. Fold in half. At center, mark cut length. At side, mark depth of return. Draw a straight line from return mark to nearest one-third marking at finished length in center.

2) Round upper corner into gentle curve; repeat for lower corner at return. Pin fabric layers together, and cut both layers as one. Center third is straight. Cut lining, using valance as pattern.

3) Place right side of lining and valance fabric together. Stitch ½" (1.3 cm) seam around valance, leaving upper edge open.

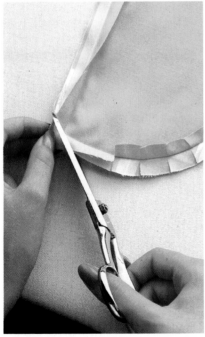

4) Press lining seam allowance toward lining. Clip curve. Diagonally trim corners.

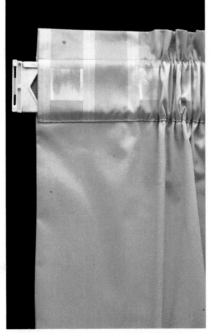

5) Turn right side out. Turn under and stitch rod pocket and heading. Insert curtain rod in pocket.

Unlined valance with ruffle. Stitch 1" (2.5 cm) double side hems on valance. Turn under and stitch rod pocket and heading. Make and attach ruffle as on pages 234 and 235.

Swags & Jabots

A classic *swag* is a draping of soft folds used as a top treatment with pleated or gathered side panels. The side panels of the treatment are the *jabots* or *cascades*.

Window width and personal preference determine the number of swags. Each swag should generally be no wider than 40" (102 cm). This size can be adapted to any window size by increasing or decreasing the overlap on adjoining swags. The length of a swag is usually from 15" to 20" (38 to 51 cm) at the longest point in the center. Shallower swags may be used on narrow windows.

The jabot length should be about one-third of the drapery or window length, or should fall to a point of interest, such as the sill or floor. Its shortest point should be lower than the center of the swag. Jabots are 9" to 11" (23 to 28 cm) wide. Pleated jabots are more formal than gathered jabots, which are less controlled. Instructions are given here for the pleated jabot, but cutting and sewing techniques are basically the same for a gathered jabot. To gather the jabot, zigzag over a cord and pull the cord up to the desired fullness.

For outside mounting, attach swags and jabots to a cornice or mounting board placed 4" (10 cm) above the molding if used alone, or about 4" (10 cm) above the drapery rod if they are used over draperies. The cornice return must be deep enough to clear the underdrapery. Jabot returns are the same width as the cornice or mounting board. In homes with beautiful moldings the swags may be mounted inside the window on a board that fits inside the frame, and there are no returns.

Make a test swag to use as a pattern for cutting the decorator fabric. Use muslin or an old sheet that will drape softly. The test swag provides an opportunity to experiment and determine the appearance you want. Do not hesitate to drape the muslin and pin it at different positions until you find the look you like.

For each jabot, you will need one width of decorator fabric and lining the length of the jabot plus 1" (2.5 cm). For each swag, you will need 1 yd. (.95 m) of decorator fabric and lining if draped tape measurement, left, is less than the fabric width; you will need 2 yd. (1.85 m) if draped measurement is more than the fabric width.

YOU WILL NEED

Muslin or an old sheet for test swag.

Decorator fabric and lining for swags and jabots.

Wide twill tape, width of the mounting board plus 2 times the return.

Mounting board or cornice; heavy-duty stapler.

How to Estimate the Size of a Swag

Drape a tape measure or string to simulate the planned shape of each swag. For double swags, drape two tape measures.

How to Cut Jabots and Swags

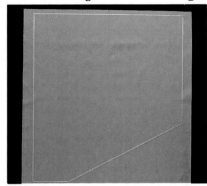

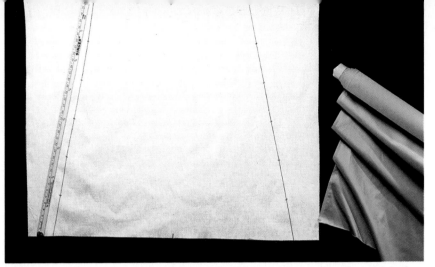

Jabots. Cut jabot 3 times finished width plus return and 1" (2.5 cm) seam allowance. On one side, mark shortest point plus 1" (2.5 cm). On the other side, mark longest point plus 1" (2.5 cm). From longest point, measure the width of return plus ½" (1.3 cm). Connect marks.

Swag. Cut muslin for the test swag 36" (91.5 cm) long. Cut the width the measurement from draped tape measure (left) plus 2" (5 cm) on each side for final adjustments. Mark width of window, centering marks at top of fabric. At lower edge, mark width from tape measure; connect the marks, forming diagonal guidelines. Divide each guideline equally into one more space than the number of folds; mark. For example, for five folds, divide into six spaces.

How to Make a Test Swag for Pattern

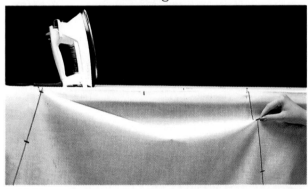

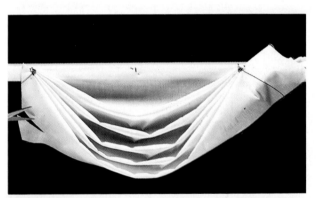

1) Fold muslin on first mark of diagonal line, and pull fold to the mark for upper corner; pin to ironing board. Continue pinning marked folds to corners, alternating sides and keeping upper edge straight.

2) Check the drape, and adjust pins and pleats as necessary. When folds are adjusted as desired, trim excess fabric 1" (2.5 cm) from outer edges and along the curved bottom edge about 3" (7.5 cm) from last fold.

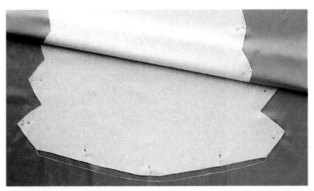

3) Unpin folds. Fold in half lengthwise to check that it is balanced and even; adjust cutting lines. Use as a pattern for cutting swag and lining. Add ½" (1.3 cm) seam allowances on upper and lower edges. This swag is not finished on ends and is mounted under jabot.

Alternative style. Fold muslin at first marks, and bring fold up to mounting board about 5" (12.5 cm) from ends. Drape smoothly, and continue folding, pulling each fold up and out slightly, toward end of board. The swag is finished at ends and can be mounted on top of or under jabot.

How to Sew a Swag

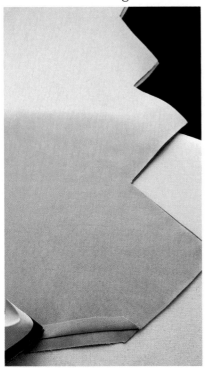

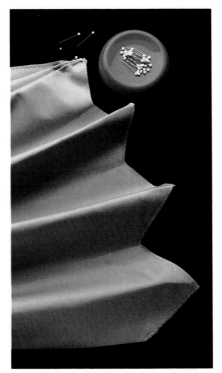

1) Pin lining to swag, right sides together, along lower curved edge. Stitch curved edge in ½" (1.3 cm) seam. Press lining seam allowance toward lining. Turn right side out; press stitched edge.

2) Pin swag front and lining together at remaining three sides. Overlock or zigzag raw edges together.

3) Pin pleats in place. The outside edge of each notch is the fold point.

4) Check drape of swag again by pinning swag to the side of ironing board or mounting board. Make minor adjustments as desired.

5) Stitch across all folds to hold pleats in place.

How to Sew Jabots

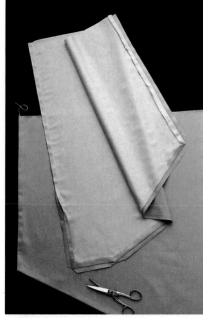

1) Place jabot lining and fabric, right sides together; stitch ½" (1.3 cm) seam on sides and bottom. Press lining seam allowance toward lining. Clip corners, and turn right side out. Press stitched edges. Stitch upper edges together in ½" (1.3 cm) seam. Zigzag or overlock raw edges.

2) Lay jabot, wrong side up, on large flat surface. On sides, fold under return and press in place. Turn jabot right side up.

3) Fold into evenly spaced pleats, starting on the outer edge; steam in position. Pleat other jabot in opposite direction. Check pleats by hanging jabot over edge of ironing board. Stitch ⅜" (1 cm) from upper edge to hold pleats in place.

How to Attach Swag and Jabots to a Mounting Board

1) Center swag on mounting board or cornice with edge of swag ½" (1.3 cm) from edge of board. Staple swag to board at 6" (15 cm) intervals.

2) Place top of one jabot at end of mounting board, with pressed fold at corner. Staple return in place. Position pleats on mounting board, overlapping swag. Fold under excess fabric at corner, and staple.

3) Cover fabric edges with wide twill tape. Staple tape along both edges, mitering at corners.

Padded Cornices

A cornice is a painted or fabric-covered wooden frame used as a tailored top treatment. When fabric-covered, the frame is padded with foam or bonded polyester to round the corners and give it a soft, upholstered look.

A cornice not only frames and finishes a window treatment by hiding the hardware, but also provides good insulation and energy-saving efficiency, because it encloses the top of the treatment and prevents cold air from escaping into the room.

Cornices are usually custom-built to fit the window. With simple carpentry skills you can build a cornice from plywood or pine boards. Any imperfections in the carpentry are covered with padding and fabric.

Measure the outside frame of the window after the drapery hardware is in place. The cornice should clear the curtain or drapery heading by 2" to 3" (5 to 7.5 cm), and it should extend at least 2" (5 cm) beyond the end of the drapery on each side. The measurements are the cornice *inside* measurements. Allow for the thickness of the wood when cutting.

The cornice should completely cover the drapery headings and hardware. Generally, apply the same guidelines for height as for any other top treatment. The cornice should be about one-fifth the height of the window treatment.

Use contrasting welting around the top and bottom edges to set the cornice apart when it is covered with the same fabric as the drapery.

When estimating fabric, railroad the fabric on a cornice to eliminate seams on plain fabrics. If the fabric cannot be railroaded because of a directional print, place the seams inconspicuously, never in the center. Prints should be centered or balanced.

✂ Cutting Directions

For face piece, cut decorator fabric 6" (15 cm) wider than front plus sides, and the height of cornice plus 3" (7.5 cm). Cut a 4" (10 cm) inner lining strip from decorator fabric, the same width as the face piece. Cut a strip of lining fabric the same width as the face piece and the same height as the cornice.

Cut a strip of batting or foam to cover the front and sides of the cornice.

Cover cording, pages 280 and 281, steps 1 to 3, to make welting slightly longer than the distance around the lower edge.

YOU WILL NEED

Decorator fabric and lining to cover cornice; optional coordinating or contrasting fabric for welting.

To build the cornice, ½" (1.3 cm) plywood for the front, top, and sides; carpenter's glue; sixpenny finishing nails.

To pad the cornice, 1" (2.5 cm) bonded polyester upholstery batting or ½" (1.3 cm) foam. If not available in local stores, you may be able to obtain through an upholsterer or upholstery supply.

5/32" cording slightly longer than the distance to be corded.

Cardboard upholsterer's stripping to cover lower edge and sides; heavy-duty stapler, ½" (1.3 cm) and ¼" (6 mm) staples; spray foam adhesive; angle irons for mounting.

How to Build a Cornice

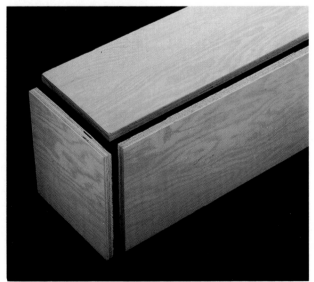

1) Measure and cut top to correspond to inside measurements for clearance. Cut front same width as top, and desired height. Cut sides same height as cornice and depth of top piece plus thickness of plywood.

2) Glue the top in place to front of board first. Remember which edges abut. Nail to secure. Then attach sides, first gluing in place to hold and then securing with nails.

How to Pad and Cover a Cornice

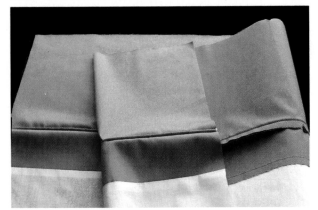

1) Stitch welting on right side of face piece in ½" (1.3 cm) seam, raw edges even. Sew welted edge to inner lining strip; sew free edge of inner strip to lining. Fold face piece in half to mark center at top and bottom.

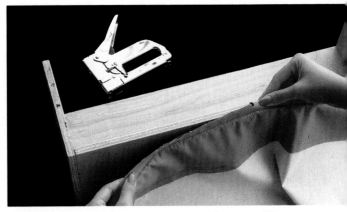

2) Mark center of cornice at top and bottom. Place *wrong* side of face fabric on outside of cornice, with welting seam on front edge of cornice; match center markings. Tack.

5) Fold lining to inside. Fold under raw edge, and staple at inside where top and face meet; at lower corners, miter fabric and staple close to corner. Tuck excess fabric into upper corners, and staple.

6) Rip excess welting seam back to end of cornice; trim welting to 1" (2.5 cm). Trim cord even with cornice edge. Staple lining to wall end of cornice; trim excess lining. Staple welting to wall end.

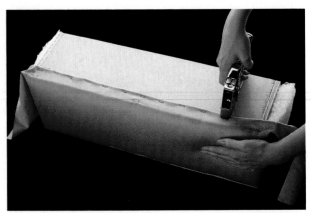

9) Tack at center and ends, removing slack. Do not stretch too tightly. Starting at center, turn under raw edge and staple to each end, placing staples 1½" (3.8 cm) apart, smoothing fabric as you go.

10) Pull fabric around corner to top back corner, removing slack; tack. Fold side fabric to back edge; staple. Trim excess fabric at back edge.

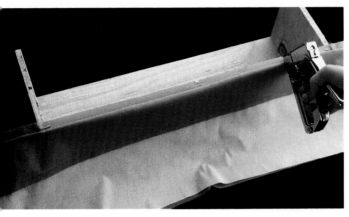

3) Pull seam taut to corners, and tack. Staple every 4" (10 cm) from center to ends. Flip lining back to check that welting is straight.

4) Place cardboard stripping tight against welting seam. Staple every 1" to 1½" (2.5 to 3.8 cm). Cut and overlap stripping at corners.

7) Turn cornice face up. Apply adhesive to front and sides. Place padding over glued surface, and stretch it slightly toward each end. Allow glue to set.

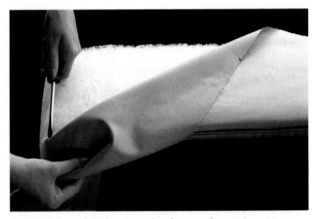

8) Fold face fabric over the front of cornice. Use a screwdriver to hold padding in place at corners. Gently smooth fabric toward top of cornice.

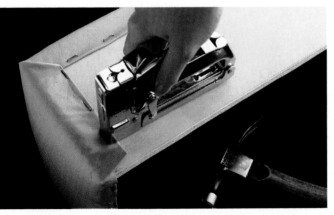

11) Fold fabric diagonally at corner to form a miter. Staple at corner and across ends. If fabric is bulky, tap staple with hammer. Repeat on both corners.

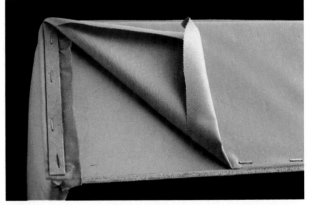

Welting at upper edge. Staple welting to sides and front, with seam at edge. On cornice front, place fabric over welting, with right sides together and raw edges even. Staple cardboard stripping at front and side edges as in step 4, above. Pull fabric to top of cornice, and fold under at sides and back; staple next to folds.

Pillows

Pillow styles range from simple to elaborate. Choice of technique affects your sewing time. Choose a simple knife-edge pillow, or invest more time in tailoring a box pillow complete with cording and a zipper.

1) Neckrolls are small round bolsters that are often trimmed with lace or ruffles. Sleeping bag pillows are the simplest neckroll bolsters to make. They are made with a drawstring closure at each end of a one-piece tube.

2) Shirred corded pillow is made by inserting gathered cording in the seam around the pillow. Cording is gathered using a technique, known as shirring, to gather the bias strip that covers the cord. Make cording in matching or contrasting fabric to add a decorative finish to a pillow.

3) Shirred box pillow uses shirring to gather both edges of the boxing strip. This makes the pillow softer than the traditional box pillow.

4) Flange pillow has a single or double, flat self-border, usually 2" (5 cm) wide, around a plump knife-edge pillow.

5) Mock box pillow is a variation of the knife-edge pillow, with shaped corners to add depth. Corners made using *gathered* style are tied inside the pillow.

6) Ruffled pillow features gathered lace or ruffles made in single or double layers. Pillow tops framed by ruffles in matching or contrasting fabric make attractive showcases for needlepoint, quilting, embroidery or candlewicking.

7) Box pillow has the added depth of a straight or shirred boxing strip. It can be soft for a scatter pillow, or firm for a chair cushion or floor pillow.

8) Mock box pillow can be made with *mitered* corners to create a tailored box shape.

9) Knife-edge pillow is the easiest pillow to make. It consists of two pieces of fabric sewn together, turned right side out and stuffed.

10) Corded pillow is a knife-edge pillow with matching or contrasting cording sewn in the seams. Use purchased cording or make your own. Or finish the pillow with a mock corded edge for a corded look without extra sewing time or fabric. Corded pillows are often called piped pillows.

To choose the right fabric for your pillow, consider how the pillow will be used and where it will be placed in your home. For a pillow that will receive hard wear, select a sturdy, firmly woven fabric that will retain its shape.

Pillows get their shape from forms or loose fillings. Depending on their washability, loose fillings may be stuffed directly into the pillow covering or encased in a separate liner for easy removal. For ease in laundering or dry cleaning, make a separate inner covering or liner for the stuffing, using lightweight muslin or lining fabric, or use purchased pillow forms. Make the liner as you would a knife-edge pillow (pages 278 and 279), fill it with stuffing, and machine-stitch it closed. Choose from several kinds of forms and fillings.

Standard polyester forms are square, round and rectangular for knife-edge pillows in sizes from 10" to 30" (25.5 to 76 cm). These forms are nonallergenic, washable, do not bunch, and may have muslin or polyester outer coverings. Choose muslin-covered forms for pillows with hook and loop tape closings. The loose muslin fibers do not catch on the rough side of the tape.

Polyurethane foam is available in sheets ½" to 5" (1.3 to 12.5 cm) thick for firm pillows and cushions. Some stores carry a high-density foam, 4" (10 cm) thick, for extra firm cushions. Since cutting the foam is difficult, ask the salesperson to cut a piece to the size of your pillow. If you must cut your own foam, use an electric or serrated knife with silicone lubricant sprayed on the blade. Polyurethane foam is also available shredded.

Polyester fiberfill is washable, nonallergenic filling for pillows or pillow liners. Fiberfill comes in loose-pack bags or pressed into batting sheets of varying densities. For a smooth pillow, sew an inner liner of batting, then stuff with loose fill. Soften the hard edges of polyurethane foam by wrapping the form with batting.

Kapok is vegetable fiber filling, favored by some decorators because of its softness. However, kapok is messy to work with and becomes matted with use.

Down is washed, quill-less feathers from the breasts of geese and ducks. Down makes the most luxurious pillows, but it is expensive and not readily available.

Knife-edge Pillow or Liner

Knife-edge pillows are plump in the center and flat around the edges. These simple pillows can be made in half an hour.

Use the knife-edge pillow directions to make removable pillow liners. Sew liners from muslin, sheeting, cotton sateen, or similar fabrics.

✂ Cutting Directions

Cut front and back 1" (2.5 cm) larger than finished pillow or liner. For hook and loop tape or zipper closure, add 1½" (3.8 cm) to back width; for overlap closure, add 5½" (14 cm).

YOU WILL NEED

Decorator fabric for pillow front and back.

Lining fabric for pillow liner, front, and back.

Pillow form or polyester fiberfill. Use 8 to 12 oz. (227 to 360 g) fiberfill for a 14" (35.5 cm) pillow, depending on desired firmness.

Zipper or other closure (optional) may be inserted (pages 290 to 293).

How to Make a Knife-edge Pillow or Liner

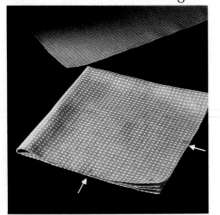

1) Fold front into fourths. Mark a point halfway between the corner and the fold on each open side. At corner, mark a point ½" (1.3 cm) from each raw edge.

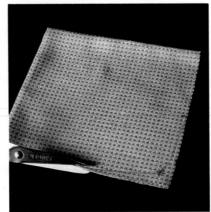

2) Trim from center mark to corner, gradually tapering from the edge to the ½" (1.3 cm) mark. Taper from ½" (1.3 cm) mark to center mark on opposite edge.

3) Unfold front and use it as a pattern for trimming back so that all corners are slightly rounded. This will eliminate dog-ears on the corners of the finished pillow.

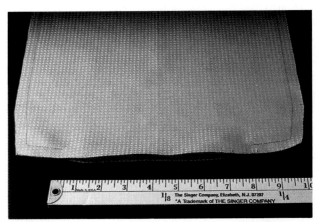

4) Pin front to back, right sides together. Stitch ½" (1.3 cm) seam, leaving opening on one side for turning and stuffing. Backstitch at the beginning and end of seam.

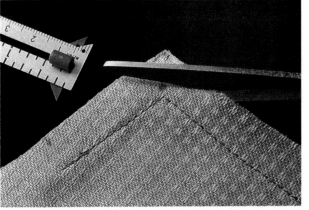

5) Trim corners diagonally, ⅛" (3 mm) from stitching. On pillows with curved edges or round corners, clip seam allowance to stitching at intervals along curves.

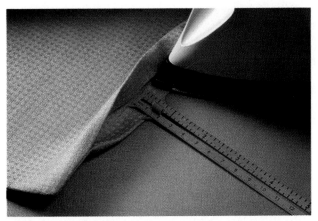

6) Turn pillow right side out, pulling out corners. Press the seams. Press under the seam allowances in the opening.

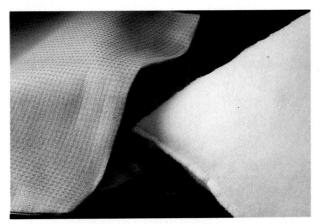

7a) Insert a purchased pillow form into the pillow, or stuff the pillow with polyester fiberfill as in step 7b, below. Use a removable form or liner in pillows that will be drycleaned or laundered.

7b) Stuff pillow or liner with polyester fiberfill, gently pulling pieces apart to fluff and separate fibers. Work filling into corners, using long, blunt tool such as a spoon handle.

8) Pin opening closed and edgestitch close to folded edge, backstitching at beginning and end of the stitching. Or slipstitch opening closed.

Corded Knife-edge Pillow

Cording adds stability to pillows and gives them a more tailored look. Cording is made by covering cord with bias strips.

✁ Cutting Directions

Cut pillow front and back 1" (2.5 cm) larger than finished pillow. For hook and loop tape or zipper closure, add 1½" (3.8 cm) to back width; for overlap closure, add 5½" (14 cm). Cut bias strips for cording as in step 1, below.

YOU WILL NEED

Decorator fabric for pillow front, back, and cording.

Cord (twisted white cotton or polyester cable), 3" (7.5 cm) longer than distance around pillow.

Pillow form or knife-edge liner.

Zipper or other closure (optional) may be inserted (pages 290 to 293).

How to Make a Corded Knife-edge Pillow

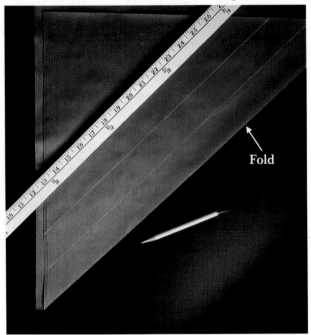

1) Cut bias strips. Determine bias grainline by folding fabric diagonally so selvage aligns with crosswise cut. For ¼" (6 mm) cord, mark and cut 1⅝" (4.2 cm) strips parallel to bias grainline. Cut wider strips for thicker cord.

2) Pin strips at right angles, right sides together, offset slightly **(a)**. Stitch ¼" (6 mm) seams **(b)**, and press open, making one continuous strip equal in length to perimeter of pillow plus 3" (7.5 cm). Trim seam allowances even with edges **(c)**.

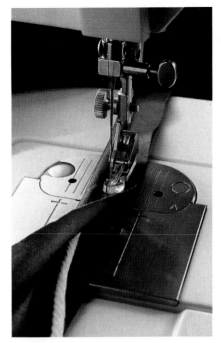

3) Center cord on wrong side of bias strip. Fold strip over cord, aligning raw edges. Using zipper foot on right side of needle, stitch close to cord, gently stretching bias to help cording lie smoothly around pillow.

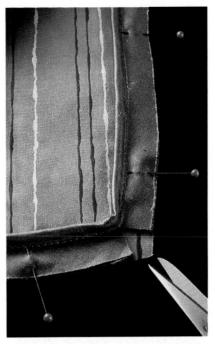

4) Pin the cording to the right side of the pillow front, with raw edges aligned. To ease corners, clip seam allowances to stitching at corners.

5) Stitch, crowding the cord; stop stitching 2" (5 cm) from the point where ends of cording will meet. Leave needle in fabric. Cut off one end of cording so it overlaps the other end by 1" (2.5 cm).

6) Take out 1" (2.5 cm) of stitching from each end of cording. Trim cord ends so they just meet.

7) Fold under ½" (1.3 cm) of overlapping bias strip. Lap it around the other end and finish stitching. Pin pillow front to back, right sides together.

8) Stitch inside stitching line, using zipper foot; crowd stitching against cord. Leave opening. Finish as for knife-edge pillow, page 279, steps 5 to 7b. Slipstitch opening closed.

Mock Box Pillow

Mock box pillows are variations of knife-edge pillows and can be made in three styles. Corners on gathered styles are tied inside the pillow. Mitered styles have a short seam across each corner to create a tailored box shape. Pleated styles have neat tucks at each corner. Pillows with gathers or pleats are sometimes called Turkish pillows.

✂ Cutting Directions

Knife-edge pillow form. Or, make a mock box pillow liner using the directions below.

Decorator fabric for pillow front and back.

Zipper or other closure (optional) may be inserted in center back (page 292).

How to Make a Mock Box Pillow with Mitered Corners

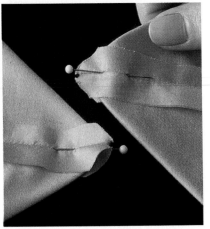

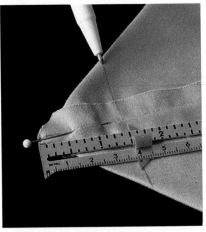

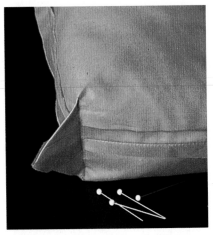

1) Stitch as directed on page 279, step 4. Press seams open. Separate front and back at corners. Center seams on each side of corner, on top of each other. Pin through seam.

2) Measure on side seam from corner to half the finished depth; for example, for pillow 3" (7.5 cm) deep, measure 1½" (3.8 cm) from corner. Draw a line perpendicular to the seam.

3) Stitch across corner of pillow on marked line; backstitch at beginning and end. Do not trim seam. Finish pillow as for knife-edge pillow, page 279, steps 6 to 7b. Slipstitch opening closed.

How to Make a Mock Box Pillow with Gathered Corners

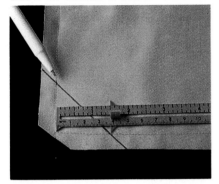

1) Stitch pillow front to pillow back as for knife-edge pillow, page 279, steps 4 and 5. Measure on each seamline from corner to finished pillow depth. Draw diagonal line across the corner.

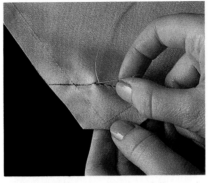

2) Hand-baste on diagonal line with topstitching and buttonhole twist or doubled thread. Pull up thread to gather.

3) Wrap thread several times around corner; secure with knot. Do not trim corner. Repeat for each corner. Finish as for knife-edge pillow, page 279, steps 6 to 7b. Slipstitch opening closed.

How to Make a Mock Box Pillow with Pleated Corners

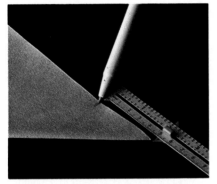

1) Fold corner in half diagonally. On raw edge, measure from the corner to half the finished pillow depth plus ½" (1.3 cm); for example, for pillow 3" (7.5 cm) deep, measure 2" (5 cm) from the corner.

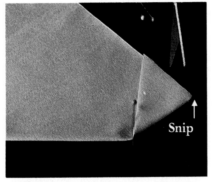

2) Mark measured point with ¼" (6 mm) snips through both seam allowances. Fold corner back at snips to form triangle. Mark fold with pin. Press triangle in place.

Snip

3) Spread corner flat, right side up. Fold fabric from snip to pin; bring fold to pressed center mark, forming pleat. Pin pleat in place. Repeat for other side.

4) Baste across pleat, ½" (1.3 cm) from raw edge, removing pins as you stitch. Trim triangle-shaped piece from corner. Repeat for each corner of front and back.

5) Pin front to back, right sides together, with front tucked into back to form a "basket." Match pleated corners precisely.

6) Stitch ½" (1.3 cm) seam, leaving opening on one side. Finish as for knife-edge pillow, page 279, steps 6 to 7b. Slipstitch opening closed.

Mock Corded Pillow

Mock corded pillows are corded *after* the pillow is assembled.

✂ Cutting Directions

Cut pillow front 1" (2.5 cm) larger than the finished pillow. Cut back the same length as front. For hook and loop tape or zipper closure, add 1½" (3.8 cm) to back width; for overlap closure, add 5½" (14 cm).

YOU WILL NEED

Decorator fabric for pillow front and back.

Hook and loop tape or zipper, 2" (5 cm) shorter than length of pillow.

Cord, ½" to 1" (1.3 to 2.5 cm), equal in length to distance around the pillow.

Pillow form or knife-edge liner.

How to Make a Mock Corded Pillow

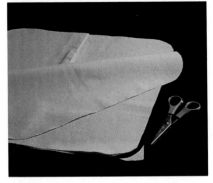

1) Trim corners of front and back into gentle curves. Insert hook and loop tape or other closure in center of pillow back (pages 291 and 292).

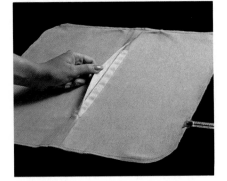

2) Pin front to back, right sides together. Stitch ¼" (6 mm) seam around entire pillow. Turn pillow right side out.

3) Pin cord inside pillow, as tightly as possible against seam. Ends of cord should just meet.

4) Stitch cord from right side, crowding stitching against cord, using zipper foot. Leave 3" (7.5 cm) opening where cord ends meet.

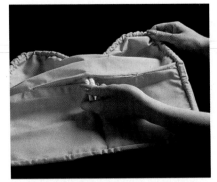

5) Pull out cord about 4" (10 cm) at each end to gather. Adjust gathers. Cut cord so ends just meet. Tack ends together.

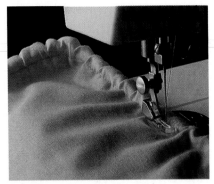

6) Topstitch opening closed, using zipper foot. Start and end stitching on previous stitching lines. Insert pillow form or liner.

284

Box Pillow

Box pillows can be used for cushions as well as for casual pillows. They are firm because of the boxing strip that is sewn between the pillow front and back.

✄ Cutting Directions

Cut pillow front and back 1" (2.5 cm) larger than finished pillow. Cut the boxing strip with length equal to distance around pillow plus 1" (2.5 cm) for seams, width equal to depth of pillow plus 1" (2.5 cm).

YOU WILL NEED

Decorator fabric for pillow front, back and boxing strip.

Polyurethane foam wrapped in batting. Or make a box pillow liner, using directions below.

How to Make a Box Pillow

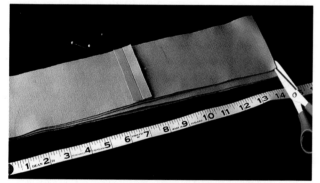

1) Stitch short ends of boxing strip, right sides together, to form continuous loop. Fold loop into fourths and mark each fold with ⅜" (1 cm) clip on both edges.

2) Pin boxing strip to pillow front, right sides together, raw edges even, matching clipped points on strip to pillow corners.

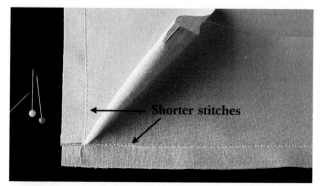

Shorter stitches

3) Stitch ½" (1.3 cm) seam, shortening stitches for 1" (2.5 cm) on each side of corner; take one or two stitches diagonally across each corner instead of sharp pivot.

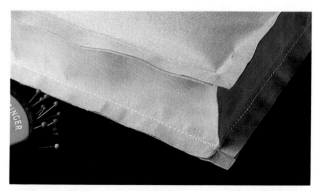

4) Pin boxing strip to pillow back, right sides together; match clips to corners. Stitch seam as in step 3, leaving one side open. Press seams, turning under seam allowances at opening. Insert form or liner; slipstitch opening closed.

Ruffled Pillow

Ruffles add interest to a pillow or enhance needlework pillows. Make ruffles from matching or contrasting fabric, or purchase lace or eyelet ruffling.

✄ Cutting Directions

Cut pillow front and back 1" (2.5 cm) larger than finished pillow. Cut ruffle strips twice the desired width plus 1" (2.5 cm) for seam, length two to three times the distance around pillow. Ruffles are usually about 3" (7.5 cm) wide.

YOU WILL NEED

Decorator fabric for pillow front and back and double ruffle.

Purchased ruffling (optional), equal in length to distance around pillow plus 1" (2.5 cm).

Cord (string, crochet cotton, or dental floss) for gathering.

Pillow Form or knife-edge liner.

How to Make a Ruffled Pillow

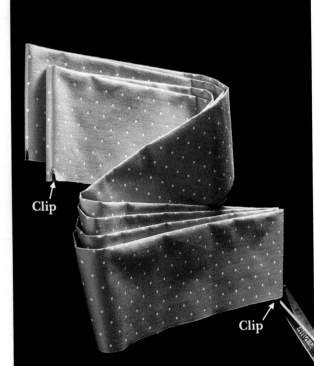

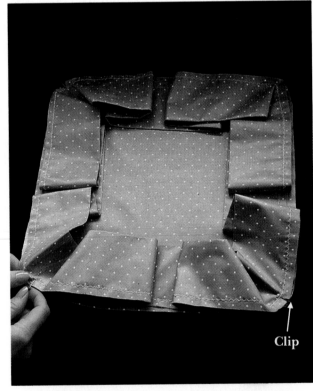

1) **Stitch** short ends of ruffle strip with ½" (1.3 cm) seam, right sides together, to form a loop. Fold strip in half lengthwise, wrong sides together; fold into fourths. Mark each fold with a ⅜" (1 cm) clip.

2) **Prepare** raw edge for gathering by zigzagging over a cord (page 234). For square pillows, match clips on ruffles to corners of pillow front, right sides together and raw edges even; for rectangular pillow, match clips to center of sides, right sides together and raw edges even. Pin.

3) Pull up the gathering cord until ruffle fits each side of the pillow front. Distribute gathers, allowing extra fullness at corners so ruffle will lie flat in finished pillow. Pin ruffle in place.

4) Machine-baste ruffle to pillow front, stitching just inside gathering row.

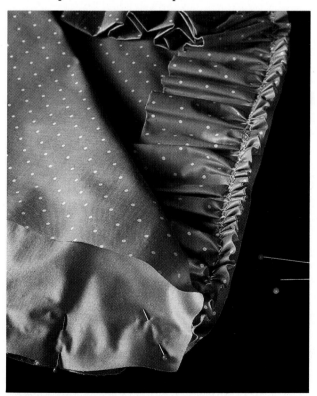

5) Pin pillow back to front, right sides together, with ruffle between pieces. Stitch ½" (1.3 cm) seam, leaving 8" (20.5 cm) opening on one side for turning.

6) Turn pillow right side out. Insert pillow form or knife-edge liner; slipstitch opening closed.

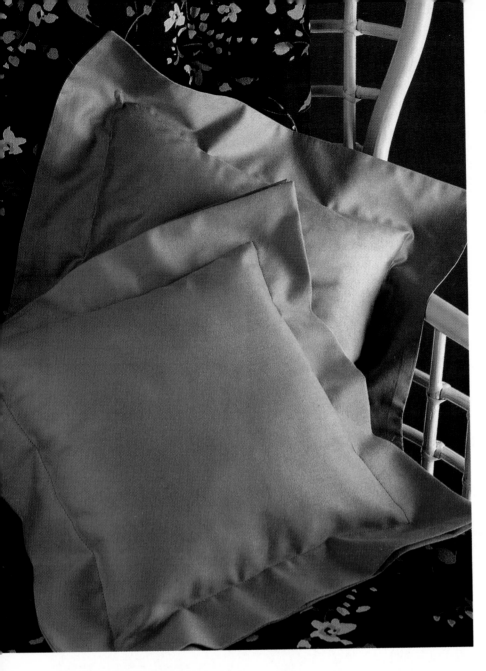

Flange Pillows

A *flange* is a flat border around a plump knife-edge pillow. Flanges may be single or double, and are usually about 2" (5 cm) wide. The double-flange pillow is made with a closure; the single-flange pillow is sewn closed.

✄ Cutting Directions

For single flange, cut pillow front and back 5" (12.5 cm) larger than stuffed inner area. This allows for 2" (5 cm) flange and ½" (1.3 cm) seam on each side.

For double flange, cut pillow front 9" (23 cm) larger than pillow form. This allows for a 2" (5 cm) flange and ½" (1.3 cm) seam on each side. For hook and loop tape or zipper closure, add 1½" (3.8 cm) to back width; for overlap closure, add 5½" (14 cm).

YOU WILL NEED

Decorator fabric for pillow front and back.

Polyester fiberfill for single-flange pillow, about 6 oz. (170 g) for 12" (30.5 cm) pillow.

Pillow form or knife-edge liner for double-flange pillow, to fit inner area.

Zipper or alternate closure for double-flange pillow, 2" (5 cm) shorter than length of stuffed inner area (pages 291 and 292).

How to Make a Single-Flange Pillow

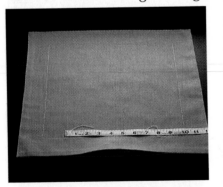

1) Pin pillow front to back, right sides together. Stitch ½" (1.3 cm) seam, leaving 8" (20.5 cm) opening. Turn right side out. Press. Topstitch 2" (5 cm) from edge, beginning and ending at opening.

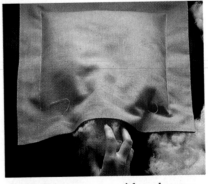

2) Stuff inner area with polyester fiberfill. Work filling into corners, using long blunt tool such as spoon handle. Do not stuff the flange.

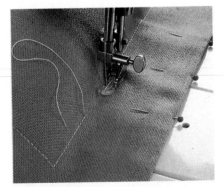

3) Topstitch inner area closed, using zipper foot, starting and ending at first stitching line. Slipstitch flange opening, or edgestitch around entire pillow.

How to Make a Double-Flange Pillow with Mitered Corners

1) Insert zipper (page 292), hook and loop tape, or snap tape (page 291) in pillow back.

2) Press under 2½" (6.5 cm) on each side of front and back. Place front and back together to make sure corners match; adjust pressed folds, if necessary.

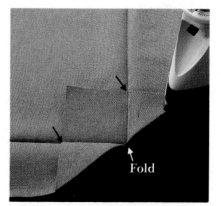

3) Open out corner. Fold corner diagonally so pressed folds match (arrows). Press diagonal fold.

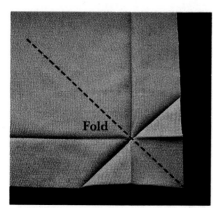

4) Open out corner. Fold through center of corner (dotted line), right sides together.

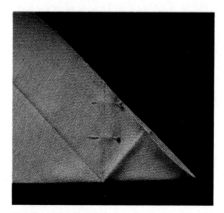

5) Pin on diagonal fold line, raw edges even. Stitch on fold line at right angle to corner fold.

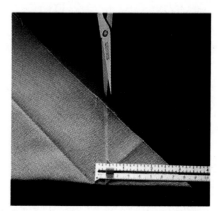

6) Trim seam to ⅜" (1 cm). Press seam open.

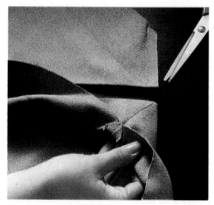

7) Turn corner right side out. Use point turner to get a sharp point. Press edges. Repeat with other corners, front and back.

8) Pin pillow front to back, wrong sides together, matching mitered corners carefully.

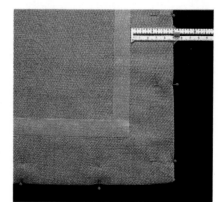

9) Measure 2" (5 cm) from edge for flange; mark stitching line with transparent tape. Topstitch through all thicknesses along edge of tape. Insert pillow form or liner.

Pillow Closures

A simple overlap closure is a technique for pillow shams (page 312) as well as an easy and inexpensive closure method for any pillow.

Snap tape and hook and loop tape are easy to handle and give closures a flat, smooth finish. Snap tape allows some give on closures and is suitable for pillows that are very soft. Because closure seam allowances are ¾" (2 cm) wide, use ⅝" (1.5 cm) tape.

Overlap closures are placed in the center back of a pillow. Zippers, hook and loop tape, or snap tape can be inserted in the center back or side seam. Except for pillows with overlap closures, cut pillows allowing for ¾" (2 cm) seam allowances on closure seam.

How to Sew an Overlap Closure

1) Cut pillow back 5½" (14 cm) wider than front to allow 3" (7.5 cm) overlap. Cut back in half, cutting *across* widened dimension.

2) Press under ¼" (6 mm), then 1" (2.5 cm) for double-fold hem on each center edge of pillow back. Edgestitch or blindstitch the hems in place.

3) Pin pillow front to back with raw edges even and hemmed edges overlapping in center. Stitch ½" (1.3 cm) seams. Turn right side out and insert pillow form or liner.

How to Sew a Side Seam Closure with Hook and Loop or Snap Tape

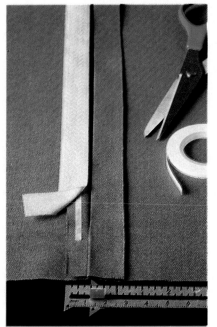

1) Prepare seam, page 293, steps 1 and 2. Cut tape 1" (2.5 cm) longer than opening. Trim one seam allowance to ½" (1.3 cm). Place hook side of tape along fold of trimmed seam allowance; ends extend ½" (1.3 cm) beyond opening. Secure with basting tape or pins.

2) Stitch hook side of tape close to edges on all four sides, stitching through pillow back and seam allowance. Stitches show on right side of pillow.

3) Stitch loop side of tape to wrong side of opposite seam allowance, overlapping tape ⅛" (3 mm) on seam allowance, and extending tape ½" (1.3 cm) beyond opening at each end.

4) Turn loop side of tape to right side of seam allowance and stitch to seam allowance on remaining three sides.

5) Place hook side of tape on loop side of tape. Pin pillow front to back along three sides, right sides together. Stitch ½" (1.3 cm) seams. Turn pillow right side out and insert pillow form or liner.

6) Snap tape. Apply as directed in steps 1 to 5 making sure balls and sockets are aligned for smooth closure. Use zipper foot to stitch close to snaps.

How to Insert a Centered Zipper in a Pillow Back

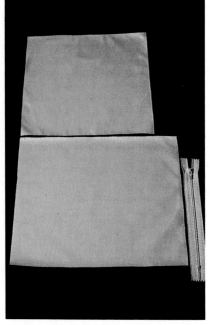

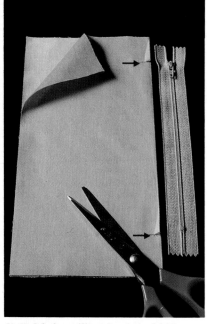

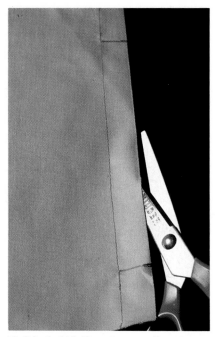

1) Cut pillow back 1½" (3.8 cm) wider than front to allow for a ¾" (2 cm) seam allowance at center back. Use zipper 2" (5 cm) shorter than length of finished pillow back.

2) Fold the pillow back in half lengthwise, right sides together. Press. Center zipper along fold. Snip into fold to mark ends of zipper coil (arrows).

3) Stitch ¾" (2 cm) seam from pillow edge to first snip; backstitch. Machine-baste to ½" (1.3 cm) past second snip. Shorten stitch length; backstitch. Stitch to edge. Cut on fold; press seam open.

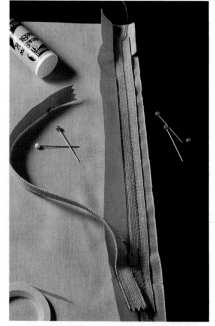

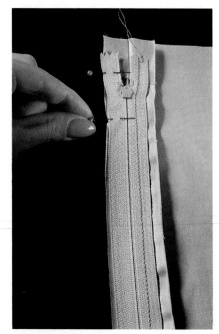

4) Open zipper and center it face down between snips with coil on seamline. Pin, or use glue stick or basting tape to hold right side of zipper tape on the right seam allowance. Machine-baste in place.

5) Close zipper, and pin or use glue stick or basting tape to hold the left side of tape to the left seam allowance. Machine-baste in place.

6) Spread pillow flat, right side up. Mark top and bottom of zipper coil with pins. Center ½" (1.3 cm) transparent tape over the seam; topstitch along edges of tape. Tie threads on wrong side of pillow; remove basting.

How to Insert a Lapped Zipper in a Pillow Seam

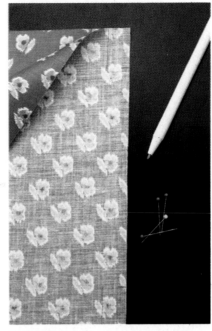

1) Use zipper 2" (5 cm) shorter than length of finished pillow. Pin pillow front to back along one side, right sides together. Position zipper along pinned seam, leaving equal distance at each edge. Mark ends of zipper coil on seam.

2) Stitch ¾" (2 cm) seam at each end of zipper opening; backstitch at marks. Press under ¾" (2 cm) seam allowances.

3) Open zipper. Place one side face down on seam allowance of pillow front, with zipper coil on seamline. Secure with pins, glue stick or basting tape. Using zipper foot, stitch tape to seam allowance only.

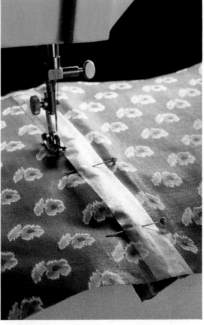

4) Close zipper. Spread pillow flat, right side up. Pin the zipper in place from right side, catching the zipper tape underneath.

5) Place ½" (1.3 cm) transparent tape along seamline as stitching guide. Starting at seamline, stitch across bottom of zipper. Pivot and continue stitching. At top of zipper, pivot and stitch to seamline. Pull threads to wrong side and tie.

6) Open zipper. Turn pillow wrong side out and pin front to back on remaining three sides. Stitch ½" (1.3 cm) seam. Turn pillow right side out, and insert pillow form or liner.

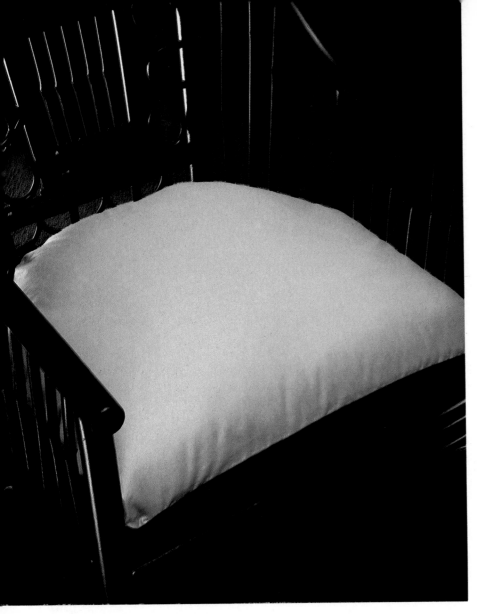

Cushions

A cushion is usually shaped to fit a chair or bench. It has a firm inner core, and is anchored to furniture with a tie or tab. Follow directions for any of the basic knife-edge or box pillows to make a cushion.

Because a cushion needs body, use a 1" (2.5 cm) thick piece of polyurethane wrapped with polyester batting to soften the edges, as a core for the cushion.

✂ Cutting Directions

For knife-edge cushion, cut front and back same size as area to be covered adding half the cushion depth and ½" (1.3 cm) for seams to each of the dimensions.

For box cushion, cut boxing strip desired width plus 1" (2.5 cm); cut front and back same size as area to be covered, adding 1" (2.5 cm) to each dimension for cushion fullness and ½" (1.3 cm) for seams.

How to Cut Fabric for Cushions

1) Measure length and width of area to be covered by cushion. For a square or rectangular cushion, use these dimensions to cut fabric. For a cushion with unusual shape, prepare a paper pattern.

2) Cut paper pattern in same shape as area to be covered. Mark the paper pattern to show where ties or tabs should be attached.

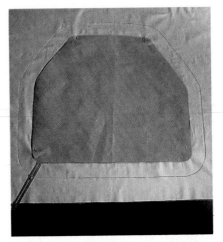

3) Use paper pattern to cut fabric for cushion, adding amount for depth and seams for cushion style. Transfer tie or tab markings to edge of right side of fabric.

Tufted Cushion

Add button tufting to chair or bench cushions to prevent filling from shifting inside the cover. Tufting is done after the cushion is finished. Tufted cushion covers are usually not removed, so zippers or other closures are not necessary.

Use covered flat buttons with a shank. Buttons for covering are available in kits, complete with a button front and back, and tools that simplify covering the button. Dampen the button fabric just before beginning. As the fabric dries around the button, it will shrink slightly to fit smoothly.

YOU WILL NEED

Long needle, with large eye.

Strong thread such as button and carpet thread or buttonhole twist.

Flat dressmaker buttons with shanks, two for each tuft.

How to Tuft a Cushion

1) Thread a long needle with extra-strong button and carpet thread or several strands of buttonhole twist. Thread strands through button shank; tie ends to shank with double knot.

2) Push needle through cushion, pulling button tight against pillow to create a "dimple." Clip thread near needle.

3) Thread second button on one strand of thread. Tie single knot with both strands and pull until button is tight against bottom of cushion. Wrap thread two or three times around button shank. Tie double knot. Trim threads.

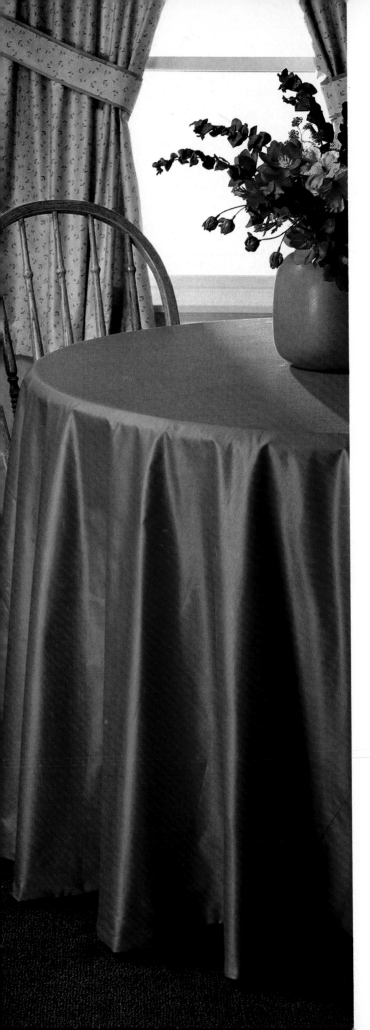

Table Coverings

Customized tabletop fashions are a simple way to change the look of a room without spending too much time or money. These easy projects make good home sewing sense for several reasons.

Home-sewn table fashions, unlike purchased ones, are not limited to a small selection of standard sizes. Design a tablecloth yourself, and scale it to the exact size and shape of your table. Choose from an abundant supply of fabric colors, patterns and textures to complement the decor of your room.

Because most tablecloths are wider than one fabric width, you must seam fabric widths together to make the tablecloth the width you need. Avoid a center seam by using a full fabric width in the center and stitching narrower side panels to it.

Use selvage edges in seams to eliminate seam finishing. If the selvage tends to pucker, clip it at regular intervals of 1" to 6" (2.5 to 15 cm). If selvages are not used in seams, finish with French or overedge seams. Use plain seams for reversible tablecloths.

Placemats, napkins and table runners give you an opportunity to experiment with finishing techniques you may be reluctant to try on larger projects.

Selecting Fabrics

When you design tabletop fashions, look for durable, stain-resistant fabrics that have been treated to repel soil and water. Permanent press fabrics offer easy care. Drape the fabric over your arm to see how it hangs.

For everyday use, lightweight cotton is appropriate; use a lightweight tablecloth with a table pad to protect fine wood tables. For an elegant look, use a sheer lace or eyelet tablecloth over a heavier cloth.

Small random prints are easier to work with than prints that may need matching. Avoid heavily napped fabrics or fabrics with difficult-to-match design motifs such as printed plaids or stripes, diagonals or one-way patterns.

Measuring the Table

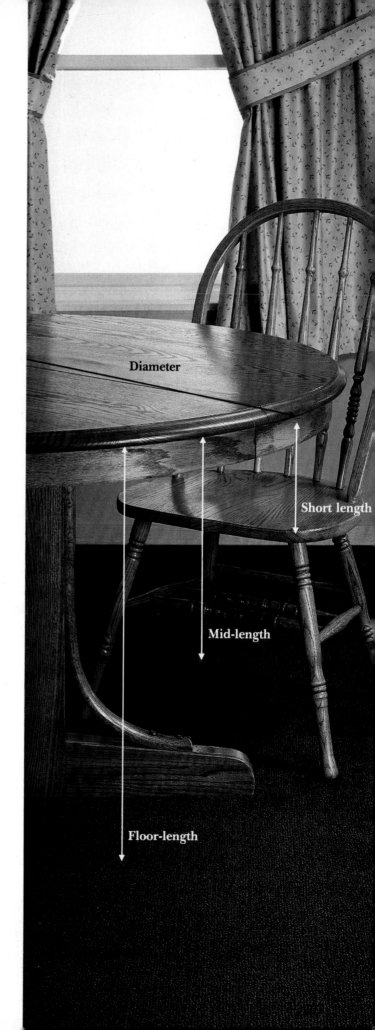

The length of the tablecloth from the edge of the table to the bottom of the cloth is the *drop*. Always include the drop length in your tablecloth measurements.

There are three common drop lengths: short, 10" to 12" (25.5 to 30.5 cm); mid-length, 16" to 24" (40.5 to 61 cm); and floor-length, 28" to 29" (71 to 73.5 cm). Short cloths end at about chair seat height and are good tablecloths for everyday use. Mid-length cloths are more formal. Elegant floor-length coverings are used for buffet and decorator tables.

Round tablecloth. Measure the diameter of the table, then determine the drop length of the cloth. The size of the tablecloth is the diameter of the table plus twice the drop length plus 1" (2.5 cm) for a narrow hem allowance. A narrow hem is the easiest way to finish the curved edge of a round tablecloth.

Square tablecloth. Measure the width of the tabletop; then determine the drop length of the cloth. Add twice the drop length plus 1" (2.5 cm) for a narrow hem allowance or 2½" (6.5 cm) for a wide hem allowance.

Rectangular tablecloth. Measure the length and width of the tabletop, then determine the drop length of the cloth. The size of the finished tablecloth is the width of the tabletop plus twice the drop length, and the length of the tabletop plus twice the drop length. Add 1" (2.5 cm) for a narrow hem or 2½" (6.5 cm) for a wide hem.

Oval tablecloth. Measure the length and width of the tabletop, then determine the drop length of the cloth. Join fabric widths as necessary to make a rectangular cloth the length of the tabletop plus twice the drop length, and the width of the tabletop plus twice the drop length; add 1" (2.5 cm) to each dimension for a narrow hem allowance. Put a narrow hem in an oval tablecloth because it is the simplest way to finish the curved edge. Because oval tables vary in shape, mark the finished size with the fabric on the table. Place weights on the table to hold fabric in place, then use a hem marker or cardboard gauge to mark the drop length evenly.

Diameter

Short length

Mid-length

Floor-length

Round Tablecloths

To determine the yardage for a tablecloth without a flounce, divide tablecloth diameter by fabric width less 1" (2.5 cm). Count fractions as one width. This is the number of widths. Then multiply number of widths by diameter and divide by 36" (100 cm) to find the total yards (meters).

For center of flounced-edge tablecloth, subtract two times the finished depth of the flounce from the finished length of the tablecloth. Determine yardage for center as for tablecloth above.

Determine the flounce length by multiplying diameter of center by 3½; double this figure. For number of strips, divide flounce length by fabric width. Then multiply number of strips by cut depth and divide by 36 for total yards (meters).

✄ Cutting Directions

For tablecloth without a flounce, cut center panel with length equal to tablecloth diameter plus hems. Add partial panels to form square.

For tablecloth with flounce, cut center panel with length equal to the diameter of center plus seam allowances. Add partial panels to form square. Cut strips for flounce the depth of flounce, plus hem and seam allowances and length as determined above.

How to Cut a Round Tablecloth

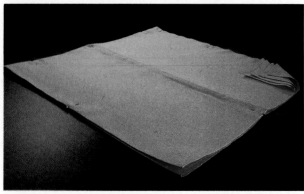

1) Join fabric panels, right sides together, with ½" (1.3 cm) seams to form square. Fold square into fourths. Pin layers together to prevent slipping.

2) Measure a string the length of the radius of the cloth. Tie one end of string around a marking pencil; pin other end at center folded corner of cloth. Mark outer edge of circle, using string and pencil as compass. Cut on marked line; remove pins.

How to Sew Narrow and Flounced Hems

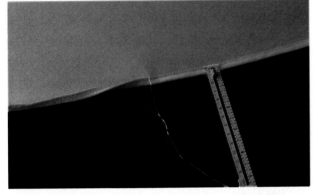

Narrow hem. Stitch around tablecloth ¼" (6 mm) from edge. Press under on stitching line. Press under ¼" (6 mm) again, easing fullness around curves. Edgestitch close to folded edge. Or, use narrow hemmer.

Flounced edge. Seam strips of flounce, right sides together, to form loop. Hem lower edge. Zigzag over cord to make ruffles (page 234). Attach flounce to tablecloth as for ruffled curtains (page 235).

How to Sew a Corded Hem

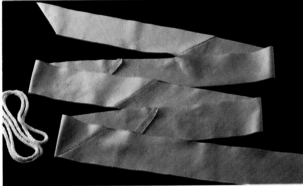

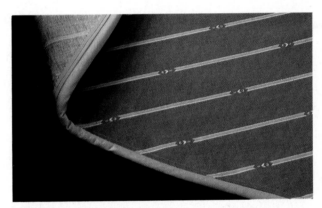

1) Multiply diameter of the tablecloth by 3½ to determine length of cording needed. Cut and join bias strips, right sides together, to cover cording (page 280).

2) Cover cording and attach to right side of cloth as for corded pillow, page 281, steps 3 to 7. Zigzag seam and press to back of tablecloth. Topstitch ¼" (6 mm) from cording seam.

How to Sew a Reversible Round Tablecloth

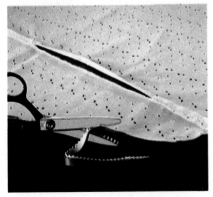

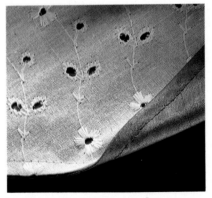

1) Join lining panels, leaving 12" (30.5 cm) opening in one seam for turning. Stitch the lining to the outer tablecloth, wrong sides together, ½" (1.3 cm) from edge. Trim seam or clip curves.

2) Turn tablecloth right side out by pulling outer fabric through opening in lining seam. Slipstitch opening closed.

3) Topstitch ¼" (6 mm) from edge. If lining is contrasting color, match upper thread to outer fabric, bobbin thread to lining.

Square & Rectangular Tablecloths

Make tablecloths the desired width by joining fabric widths as necessary, using full widths in the center and partial widths on the lengthwise edges. Straighten the crosswise ends of fabric (page 80) to square the corners. Use French or overedge seams, or use selvage edges to eliminate seam finishing.

Select the width and finish of the hem to complement the weight and texture of the fabric. Mitering is the neatest way to square corners because it covers raw edges and eliminates bulk.

Determine the amount of fabric needed for the tablecloth by dividing the total width of the tablecloth by the width of your fabric, less 1" (2.5 cm). Multiply this figure, which is the number of panels needed, by the total length of the tablecloth. Divide this number by 36" (100 cm) to get the total yards (meters) required.

Wide and Narrow Hems

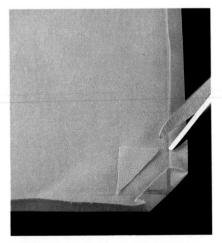

1) Wide hem. Press under ¼" to ½" (6 mm to 1.3 cm), then press under 1" or 2" (2.5 or 5 cm) hem on all sides.

2) Open out corner, leaving first fold turned under. Miter corners as for double-flange pillow, page 289, steps 3 to 7. Blindstitch or straight-stitch hem.

Narrow hem. Press under ½" (1.3 cm) on each side. Open corner; fold diagonally so pressed folds match. Press; trim corner. Fold raw edge under ¼" (6 mm). Fold again on first fold line; press. Stitch hem.

Quilted Table Covers

Quilting adds body to table coverings and provides additional protection for table surfaces. The thickness and slight puffiness of quilted table accessories also adds visual appeal. Use quilted fabrics for placemats, table runners and table mats. Finish edges with bias binding.

Prequilted fabrics are available, but quilting your own fabric provides the luxury of coordinating colors and prints, and the economy of making only the amount of quilted fabric needed for a project. The quilting guide foot with the attached guide bar makes the channel-quilting process easy. Lengthen the stitch length and loosen the pressure for even quilting. Begin by stitching the center quilting row, and work toward the sides.

Use polyester fleece or needle-punched batting for tabletop fashions. It will retain its shape and body when laundered.

How to Machine Quilt Fabric Using a Quilter Bar

1) Cut fabric, fleece and lining slightly larger than finished size of item. Place fleece between wrong sides of fabric and lining. Pin or baste all three layers together.

2) Mark first quilting line in center of fabric with yardstick and chalk pencil. (If not using quilter bar, mark every quilting row an equal distance apart.)

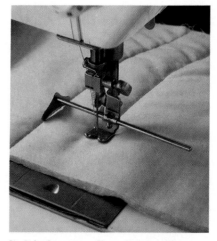

3) Stitch center line. Determine the distance to next quilting line. Adjust quilter bar to follow the previous row of stitching as you stitch the next row.

Placemats & Napkins

With timesaving fabrics and speedy sewing techniques, you can create a variety of placemats and napkins for special occasions and gifts. For casual dining, choose loosely woven fabric, such as linen or homespun, and fringe the edges. For a more formal look, choose fabric with a finer weave, and finish edges with a dense flatlock, zigzag, or decorative machine embroidery stitch and contrasting thread. Woven plaids and geometric designs are especially timesaving, because you can follow a design or woven line to eliminate marking.

Bias-bound edges are always appropriate on napkins and placemats, as are rolled or satin edges sewn on an overlock machine. When sewing bound, rolled, or satin edges, you can easily make placemats and napkins reversible by using two contrasting fabrics. The double layers not only give you two looks for the sewing time, but also provide extra absorbency. If desired, add a layer of lightweight polyester fleece for padding between the two fabric faces of a reversible placemat.

To save time when binding edges, cut a continuous bias strip long enough to finish several items; a 36" (91.5 cm) fabric square will yield a continuous bias strip about 17 yards (16.2 m) long and 2" (5 cm) wide. Fold under and press the raw edges of the strip quickly with a bias tape pressing aid.

How to Make a Continuous Bias Strip

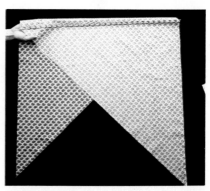

1) Mark each crosswise grain edge of a large fabric square with *one* pin. Mark each lengthwise grain edge with *two* pins.

2) Fold fabric in half diagonally on the true bias grain of fabric. Cut on fold line to divide square into two triangles.

3) Stitch lengthwise grain edges (double pins) in ¼" (6 mm) seam with right sides together. Allow points to extend ¼" (6 mm), so edges meet exactly on seamline. Press seam open.

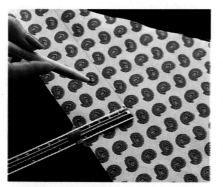

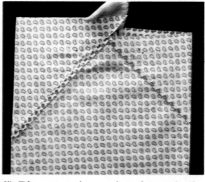

4) Mark cutting line for bias strip parallel to one slanted edge on right side of fabric. This edge is on true bias grain of fabric.

5) Pin crosswise grain edges (single pins) together with one edge extending beyond the other edge the marked width of the bias strip. This creates a slightly twisted tube. Stitch and press ¼" (6 mm) seam.

6) Cut fabric on marked line. As you cut, fold cut portion of strip over to use as a cutting guide. Continue folding strip back and cutting around tube to the end.

How to Use Bias Tape Maker

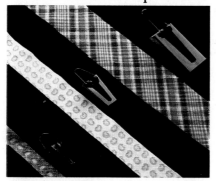

1) Cut bias strip according to size of tape maker. Cut strip scant 1" (2.5 cm) wide for ½" (1.3 cm) tape maker, 1⅜" (3.5 cm) wide for ¾" (2 cm) tape maker, 1⅞" (4.7 cm) wide for 1" (2.5 cm) tape maker, or scant 3¼" (8.2 cm) wide for 2" (5 cm) tape maker.

2) Trim one end of bias strip to a point. Thread point through channel at wide end of tape maker, bringing point out at narrow end. Insert pin in slot opening to pull point through. Pin point of strip to pressing surface.

3) Press folded bias strip as you pull tape maker the length of strip. Tape maker automatically folds raw edges to center of strip to create uniform bias tape quickly.

How to Apply Bias Binding to an Oval Placemat

1) Press bias tape in half to form double-fold bias binding. Press binding into curved shape to match shape of mat. To prevent puckering and remove slack, stretch binding slightly as you press.

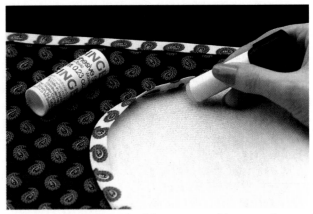

2) Baste placemat to backing, *wrong* sides together, with glue stick. Dab small dots of glue stick around edge of placemat on right side. Finger press one edge of binding into position. Baste other edge of binding to backing with glue stick.

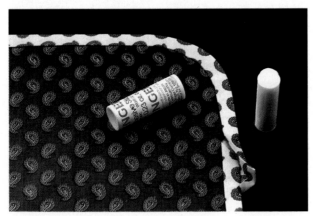

3) Join binding ends by opening fold and trimming across end. Fold cut edge under ¼" (6 mm). Lap over other end of binding, and baste lightly with glue stick.

4) Stitch along inner edge of binding with straight or zigzag stitches. The Even Feed™ foot may also be used to keep layers from shifting.

Shortcut Napkins or Placemats on an Overlock Machine

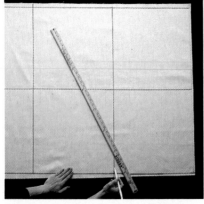

1) Mark cutting lines for finished size of napkins or placemats. You can make six 15" (38 cm) square napkins from 1 yard (.95 m) of 45" (115 cm) wide fabric.

2) Adjust overlock machine for narrow 3-thread stitch or rolled edge. Stitch on all lengthwise cutting lines. Then stitch on all crosswise cutting lines.

3) Apply liquid fray preventer to threads at each corner. After fray preventer dries, trim threads.

How to Make Fringed Placemats or Napkins

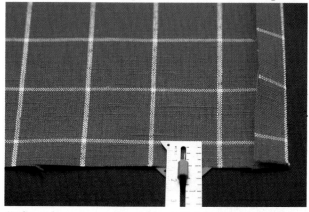

1) Cut placemat to the desired finished size. Mark a stitching line ½" (1.3 cm) from raw edges to indicate depth of fringe, or use a line from a check or plaid.

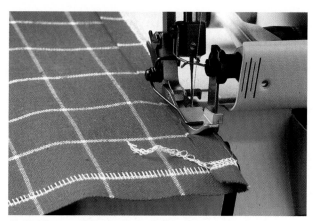

2) Fold one side on the marked line. Set overlock machine for flatlock stitch; sew along fold. Do not allow knives to cut into fold. Open fold to pull stitches flat. Flatlock remaining sides the same way.

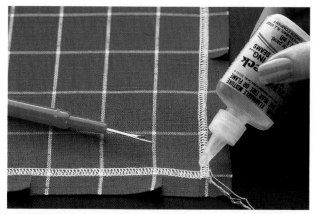

3) Seal stitches at each corner with drop of liquid fray preventer. Use seam ripper to remove stitches in fringe area. Cut up to stitches every 3" (7.5 cm). Remove threads to create fringe.

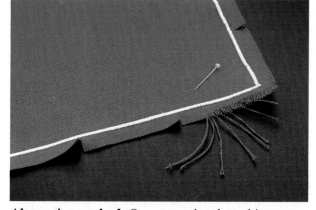

Alternative method. On conventional machine, use satin stitching or closely spaced zigzag stitches. Stitch on marked lines; pivot at corners. Cut up to stitches every 3" (7.5 cm). Remove threads to create fringe.

How to Make Reversible Napkins or Placemats

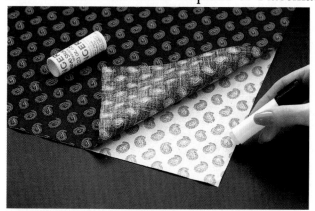

1) Cut napkin or placemat and contrasting backing the same size. Layer them, *wrong* sides together, so edges match. Use glue stick to hold layers together.

2) Adjust overlock machine for 3-thread stitch or rolled hem. On conventional machine, use satin stitching or overedge stitching. Stitch around all sides, handling the two layers as one.

Banded Placemats

Wide double banding creates reversible placemat.

✄ Cutting Directions

Determine size of finished mat and desired width of finished banding. Cut placemat center the size of finished mat minus two times the width of finished banding, plus ½" (1.3 cm). For each mat, cut two centers. Stitch centers, wrong sides together, a scant ¼" (6 mm) from raw edge.

Cut banding twice the finished width plus ½" (1.3 cm); length the distance around outer edge of *finished* mat plus ½" (1.3 cm). Use ¼" (6 mm) seams. Press under ¼" (6 mm) on lengthwise edges. Press in half lengthwise, wrong sides together.

How to Sew Banded Placemats with Mitered Corners

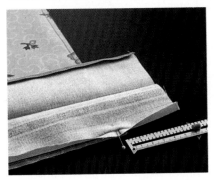

1) Mark beginning stitching point on band the width of finished band plus ¼" (6 mm). Place mark ¼" (6 mm) from corner of mat, raw edges even and right sides together.

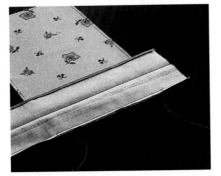

2) Mark and pin band at adjacent corner ¼" (6 mm) from edge. Pin between corners. Stitch on foldline from mark to mark; backstitch at ends to secure.

3) Fold band from mat diagonally. Mark out from corner stitching the width of finished band. Fold at mark, right sides together. Mark ¼" (6 mm) from corner of mat.

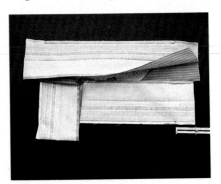

4) Repeat steps 2 and 3, above, for next two corners.

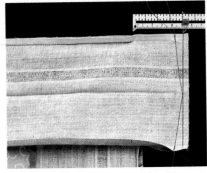

5) Measure width of finished band from stitching; mark. Mark and stitch as shown. Press seam open; trim. Fold band to reverse side, forming miters.

6) Fold band diagonally to miter corners on reverse side. Pin folded edge of band to stitching line. Slipstitch the mitered corners and edges of band in place.

Trimmed Placemats

Trimmed placemats have banding stitched to one side. Purchase finished trim or cut trim from fabric. The same method may also be used to stitch banding on square tablecloths (page 300).

✂ Cutting Directions

Cut the placemat 1" (2.5 cm) larger than desired finished size. Press ½" (1.3 cm) seam allowance to right side of placemat on all edges. Cut trimming long enough to go around edge of placemat, plus 1" (2.5 cm). You will need approximately 61" (155 cm) for each placemat. If making your own banding from fabric, allow ¼" (6 mm) on each side for finishing. Press under ¼" (6 mm) on long sides of banding.

How to Sew Placemats with Mitered Ribbon Trimming

1) Position short end of band ½" (1.3 cm) beyond edge of mat, aligning lengthwise edge of band with folded outer edge of the placemat; pin.

2) Fold trimming straight back at corner so fold is even with edge of mat. Fold trimming diagonally to form right angle; press and pin. Repeat at next two corners.

3) Fold end diagonally at first corner to form right angle; press. Remove pins. Baste on diagonal foldlines, using pins or glue stick.

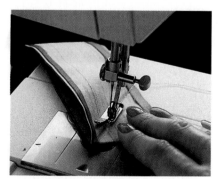

4) Stitch each corner of trim on diagonal foldline, stitching on wrong side and beginning at inner edge. Backstitch at beginning and end of seam to secure.

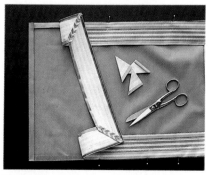

5) Adjust mat size or miters if necessary. Trim seam allowances of miters to ¼" (6 mm); press seams open. Press under seam allowance that extends at one corner.

6) Baste trim to mat, with outer edges even. Stitch outer edge, beginning at one side and pivoting at corners; backstitch. Stitch inner edge.

Six Ways to Make and Hem Napkins

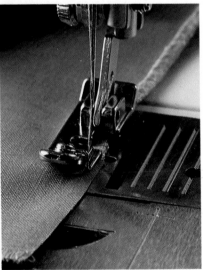

Satin stitch. Turn under ½" (1.3 cm) on all sides. Miter corners (page 300). Edgestitch along raw edge to use as guide. Use wide, closely spaced zigzag to stitch from right side over edgestitching.

Zigzag overedge. Trim loose threads from napkin edges. Stitch over raw edge, using wide, closely spaced zigzag. Use overedge foot or special-purpose foot to maintain zigzag width.

Decorative stitch. Press under ¼" (6 mm) and stitch. From right side, stitch with a decorative stitch, using straight stitching as the guideline. Blanket stitch (shown above) gives a hemstitched look.

Napkins

Coordinating napkins are the finishing touch to your tabletop fashions. Standard finished napkins are 14" or 17" (35.5 or 43 cm) square. Before cutting the fabric, square the ends, using a carpenter's square. For fringed napkins, square the ends by pulling a thread (page 80).

Napkin hems can be decorative. Experiment with some of the decorative stitches on your sewing machine. The hemming techniques shown here can also be used on tablecloths and placemats.

✄ Cutting Directions

Cut napkins 1" (2.5 cm) larger than finished size. One yard (meter) of 36" (91.5 cm) wide fabric yields four 17" (43 cm) napkins. A piece of fabric 45" (115 cm) square yields nine 14" (35.5 cm) napkins.

Narrow hem. Press under ¼" (6 mm) double-fold hem on opposite sides of all napkins. Edgestitch from one napkin to the next using continuous stitching. Repeat for remaining sides.

Double-fold hem. Turn under ¼" (6 mm) on all edges and press. Turn under another ¼" (6 mm). Miter corners as directed for narrow hem (page 300). Edgestitch close to folded edge.

Fringe. Cut napkins on a pulled thread to straighten edges. Stitch ½" (1.3 cm) from raw edges with short straight stitches or narrow, closely spaced zigzag. Pull out threads up to the stitching line.

Bed Coverings

Sewing for the bedroom is a good area to start, because these projects use easy-to-handle fabric and consist of seams and hems. Measure the bed with the blankets and sheets that are normally on the bed. Comforters, coverlets, and duvets reach 3" to 4" (7.5 to 10 cm) below the mattress on both sides and at the foot. For dust ruffle length, measure from the top of the box spring to the floor. These measurements give you the finished length.

Duvet Cover

To use the decorative border on a sheet, conceal the zippered opening under the border on the right side of the cover. Or add a decorative border to a plain sheet, using lace or ribbon trims.

✂ Cutting Directions

Measure the down or fiberfill duvet. For snug fit, make the finished duvet cover 2" (5 cm) shorter and 2" (5 cm) narrower than duvet measurements.

For back of cover, cut or tear a sheet 1" (2.5 cm) wider and 1" (2.5 cm) longer than finished size.

For front, cut or tear bordered sheet 1" (2.5 cm) wider than finished size; for bordered zipper flap, right, fold sheet in half lengthwise and mark a line 20" (51 cm) from edge of sheet; for zipper strip, mark second line 3" (7.5 cm) from first line. Cut on both lines. To determine the length to cut the

remaining front section, use chart at right. Line up sheet section with edge of table, and use a T-square to square lower edge.

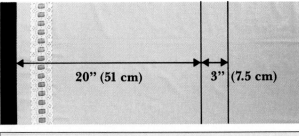

Cut Length of Duvet Cover Front	in. (cm)
1) Finished length of cover	
2) Bordered zipper flap, 20" (51 cm)	−
3) Width of border	+
4) 1" (2.5 cm) seam allowance	+
5) Front cut length	=

YOU WILL NEED

Flat sheets with decorative border.
Two zippers, 22" (56 cm) long.

How to a Sew a Duvet Cover from Sheets

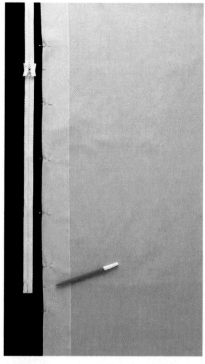

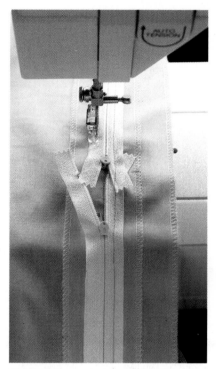

1) Zigzag or overedge raw edges of zipper strip and upper edge of front. Pin zipper strip to upper edge, right sides together. Mark zipper opening 22" (56 cm) in both directions from center.

2) Stitch 1"(2.5 cm) zipper seam, starting at one side. At zipper marking, backstitch, and then machine-baste across zipper opening; backstitch and continue to other edge. Press seam open.

3) Center open zippers face down on seam allowance, with teeth on basted seam and tab ends meeting in center. Using zipper foot, stitch on one side of teeth. Close zippers; stitch other side. Remove basting.

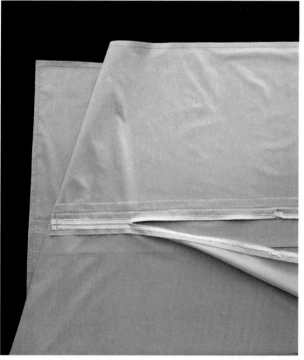

4) Pin decorative border section over zipper, right side up, with zipper seam 1" (2.5 cm) from inner edge of border. Stitch on edge of border through all layers. Open zippers.

5) Pin front to back, with right sides together and back side up. Stitch ½" (1.3 cm) from raw edge. To finish, serge or zigzag raw edges. Turn right side out; insert duvet.

Pillow Shams

Pillow shams can be plain, ruffled or trimmed with a flange or banding. A sham has an overlap, or flap pocket closure, on the back to make it easy to slip a pillow into it. The easiest sham to make is cut in one piece with the ends turned under and hemmed so that the overlap is part of the fold.

To add a ruffle or coordinating flange, cut the front, back and overlap pieces separately so that there will be a seam completely around the pillow. Seams on shams should be finished. Use French seams on one-piece shams and pillowcase shams; zigzag the seams on ruffled shams. Flanged shams have enclosed seams.

✂ Cutting Directions

For one-piece sham, cut fabric same width as pillow plus 1" (2.5 cm); length equal to two times the length of pillow plus 11" (28 cm).

For ruffled sham, cut front and back 1" (2.5 cm) larger than pillow. Cut overlap 10" (25.5 cm) wide, length equal to width of pillow plus 1" (2.5 cm). Cut ruffle two times desired width plus 1" (2.5 cm), and length equal to two times the distance around pillow, plus 1" (2.5 cm).

For flanged pillow sham, cut front 5" (12.5 cm) wider and 5" (12.5 cm) longer than pillow. Cut back 5" (12.5 cm) wider and 2" (5 cm) longer than pillow. Cut overlap 5" (12.5 cm) wider than pillow and 13" (33 cm) long. This allows for ½" (1.3 cm) seams and 2" (5 cm) flange. Cut banding or trimming desired width and long enough to go around entire pillow.

For ruffled pillowcase sham, cut fabric same width as pillow plus 1" (2.5 cm); length equal to two times the length of pillow plus 1" (2.5 cm). Cut ruffle two times desired width plus 1" (2.5 cm), and length four times width of pillow. Cut facing strip 3" (7.5 cm) wide; length equal to two times the width of pillow plus 1" (2.5 cm).

How to Sew a One-piece Sham

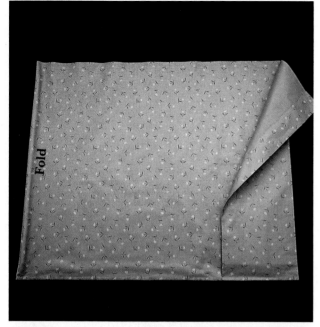

1) Stitch ½" (1.3 cm) double-fold hem at one short end. Turn under ½" (1.3 cm), then 2" (5 cm) at the other end; stitch. For overlap, press under 7½" (19.3 cm) on end with wider hem. Fold the sham crosswise, *wrong* sides together, so narrow hemmed edge is in pressed fold. Fold the overlap over the hemmed edge.

2) Stitch ¼" (6 mm) seam on two long sides. Trim seams to ⅛" (3 mm). Turn sham wrong side out. Press seam edges. Stitch ¼" (6 mm) from the edges for French seams. Turn the sham right side out. Insert the pillow.

How to Sew a Ruffled Sham

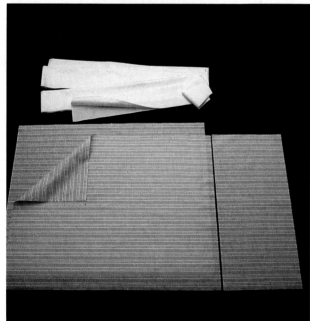

1) Stitch ½" (1.3 cm) double-fold hem on one short end of sham back. Turn under ½" (1.3 cm), then 2" (5 cm) hem on one long edge of overlap; stitch. Prepare and attach ruffle to right side of sham front, as for ruffled pillow, pages 286 and 287, steps 1 to 4.

2) Pin unfinished edge of overlap to one end of front, right sides together, with ruffle between two layers. Pin back to front, positioning back and overlap as shown. Stitch ½" (1.3 cm) seam around sham. Trim corners; finish seam allowances. Turn right side out and insert pillow.

How to Sew a Flanged Pillow Sham

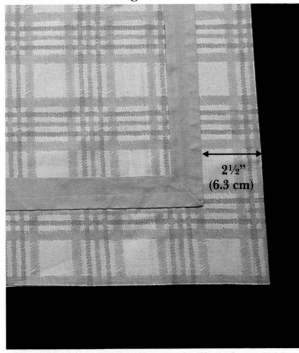

1) Position banding to front of pillow sham 2½" (6.5 cm) from edge. Miter corners, as for placemats with mitered ribbon trimming, page 307. Stitch *inner* edge of band only.

2) Make sham following instructions for ruffled sham (page 313) omitting ruffle; finish seams. Turn sham right side out and topstitch along outer edge of banding. Insert pillow.

How to Sew a Ruffled Pillowcase Sham

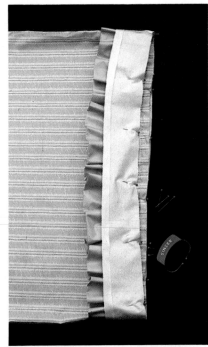

1) Fold sham crosswise, wrong sides together; stitch French seams (page 114). Prepare and attach the ruffle to right side of open end of sham, as directed, pages 286 and 287, steps 1 to 4.

2) Press under ½" (1.3 cm) on one long side of facing strip. Join short ends of strip. Pin right side of strip to right side of pillow sham with ruffle between two fabric layers. Stitch ½" (1.3 cm) seam.

3) Press seam toward pillow sham. Edgestitch or slipstitch along pressed fold of facing strip. (Facing strip is shown in contrasting color to make it more visible.)

Dust Ruffles & Bed Skirts

Dust ruffles and bed skirts are designed to hide the box spring and legs of a bed. They can be made to coordinate with a comforter or quilt. Gathered dust ruffles give a soft effect; pleated bed skirts are more tailored. Dust ruffles and bed skirts are gathered or pleated around only three sides of the bed.

Gathered dust ruffles can be made with either one or two layers of gathered fabric. When making a two-layered dust ruffle, gather the two layers as one piece. The type of fabric you choose determines the fullness of a gathered dust ruffle. Allow three times the fullness for lightweight fabrics; allow two to three times the fullness for mediumweight fabrics.

The directions that follow are for a gathered dust ruffle with split corners; the dust ruffle is attached to a fitted sheet. This open-cornered style, which is made in three sections, is suitable for a bed with a footboard. Dust ruffles may also be made in one continuous piece for beds without footboards.

Pleated bed skirts have deep pleats and they are made from medium to heavyweight fabrics. The directions that follow allow for a 6" (15 cm) pleat at each end corner and the center of each side. A 1" (2.5 cm) double-fold hem is used at the lower edge and sides of the skirt. The pleated bed skirt is for a bed without a footboard; the skirt is attached to a deck. The deck can be made from muslin or from broadcloth or a flat sheet in a color that matches the bed skirt.

✄ Cutting Directions

For gathered dust ruffle length, cut two pieces each the length of the box spring times the desired fullness, plus 4" (10 cm) for 1" (2.5 cm) double-fold side hems; cut one piece the width of the box spring times the desired fullness, plus 4" (10 cm) for 1" (2.5 cm) double-fold side hems. Dust ruffle depth is equal to distance from top of box spring to floor, plus 4" (10 cm).

For pleated bed skirt, cut deck 1" (2.5 cm) wider and 1" (2.5 cm) longer than box spring. Cut bed skirt on lengthwise grain of fabric. Cut two pieces the length of the box spring plus 18" (46 cm). Cut one piece the width of the box spring plus 18" (46 cm). Bed skirt depth equals distance from top of box spring to floor minus ¼" (6 mm) for clearance, plus 2½" (6.5 cm) for seam and hem.

YOU WILL NEED

Decorator fabric for dust ruffle or bed skirt.

Fitted sheet for deck of gathered dust ruffle.

Broadcloth, flat sheet or muslin for deck of pleated bed skirt.

315

How to Sew a Gathered Dust Ruffle with Open Corners

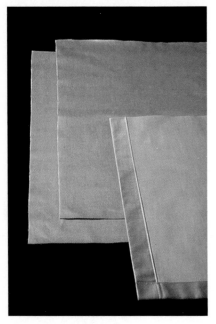

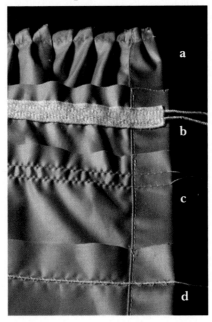

1) Stitch 1" (2.5 cm) double-fold hem along lower edges of the three dust ruffle pieces, then turn under and stitch 1" (2.5 cm) double-fold hem on both ends of each of the pieces.

2) Gather 1" (2.5 cm) from upper edge with ruffler attachment **(a)**, two-string shirring tape **(b)**, two rows of bastestitching **(c)**, or zigzag stitching over a cord **(d)**.

3) Place fitted sheet on box spring. On sheet, mark upper edge of box spring. Mark every 12" (30.5 cm) along this line. Mark upper edge of dust ruffle every 24" (61 cm) for double fullness, every 36" (91.5 cm) for triple fullness.

How to Sew a Pleated Bed Skirt

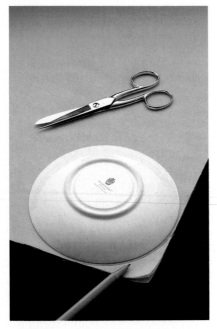

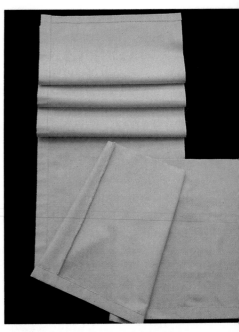

1) Fold deck in half lengthwise, then crosswise so corners are together. Using saucer as a guide, cut to curve corners gently.

2) Fold curved corners in half to determine centers; mark fold with ¼" (6 mm) clips. Also, mark center of each side with clip.

3) Stitch skirt pieces, right sides together, on narrow ends, with shorter piece in center. Stitch 1" (2.5 cm) double-fold hem on lower edge of skirt and on unstitched narrow ends of skirt pieces.

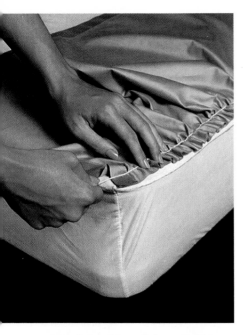

4) Pin right sides of dust ruffle pieces along three sides of sheet, raw edges on marked line and hems overlapping at corners. Match markings on dust ruffle pieces to markings on sheet. Pull up gathering cord to fit.

5) Remove sheet from box spring, keeping dust ruffle pinned in place. Stitch on gathering line, 1" (2.5 cm) from raw edge of dust ruffle.

6) Turn dust ruffle down over lower edge of sheet. If desired, topstitch ½" (1.3 cm) from seam, stitching through dust ruffle and sheet.

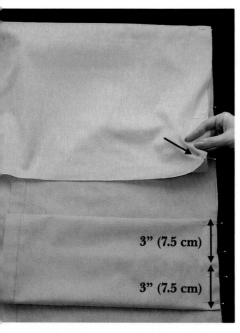

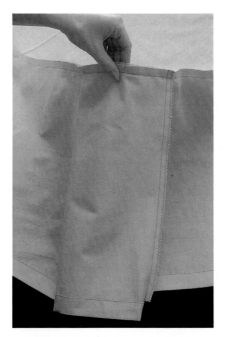

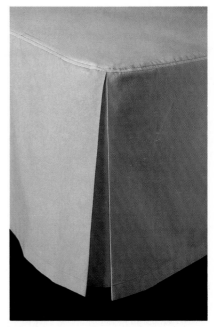

4) Pin skirt to deck, right sides together, with stitching of side hem at clip on one end of deck (arrow). Form 6" (15 cm) pleats at clips on sides and corners of deck. Seams will fall inside pleats.

5) Remove skirt and machine-baste pleats. Reposition skirt on deck. Pin, right sides together. Clip center of corner pleats. Stitch ½" (1.3 cm) seam.

6) Press seam allowance toward deck. Press ¼" (6 mm) double-fold hem at open end of deck; stitch hem. Topstitch the skirt seam allowance to deck. Press pleats.

Cy DeCosse Incorporated offers
sewing accessories to subscribers.
For information write:
  Sewing Accessories
  5900 Green Oak Drive
  Minnetonka, MN 55343